Two Post-Modern Plays

Jackets, In the Company of Men with **September**

'*Jackets* is a double-bill, exploring the machinations behind political martyrdom in eighteenth-century Japan and twentieth-century Europe. In the historical context the ethos is formal, with rigid castes, archaic codes of honour and noble death; in the modern urban riots the same structures still operate, but more subtly and more brutally. . . . an astonishingly powerful piece of political, polemical poetry.' *Robin Thornber, Guardian*

Part Two of *Jackets* was produced in the Studio Theatre, Leicester Haymarket in November 1989.

In the Company of Men provides a vivid and coruscating attack on the values encapsulated by boardroom power games, where the battle between successful tycoon Oldfield and his ambitious young son moves from skirmishing to violence.

Also contained in this volume is a short play commissioned by the World Wildlife Fund, performed in Canterbury Cathedral: *September* – about the death of Chico Mendes.

Edward Bond was born and educated in London. His plays include *The Pope's Wedding* (Royal Court Theatre, 1962), *Saved* (Royal Court, 1965), *Early Morning* (Royal Court, 1968), *Narrow Road to the Deep North* (Belgrade Theatre, Coventry, 1968; Royal Court, 1969), *Black Mass* (Sharpeville Commemoration Evening, Lyceum Theatre, 1970), *Passion* (CND Rally, Alexandra Palace, 1971), *Lear* (Royal Court, 1971), *The Sea* (Royal Court, 1973), *Bingo* (Northcott, Exeter, 1973; Royal Court, 1974), *The Fool* (Royal Court, 1975), *The Bundle* (RSC Warehouse, 1978), *The Woman* (National Theatre, 1978), *The Worlds* (New Half Moon Theatre, London, 1981), *Restoration* (Royal Court, 1981), *Summer* (National Theatre, 1982), *Derek* (RSC Youth Festival, The Other Place, Stratford-upon-Avon, 1982), *The Cat* (produced in Germany as *The English Cat* by the Stuttgart Opera, 1983), *Human Cannon* (published in 1985) and *The War Plays* (*Red Black and Ignorant, The Tin Can People and Great Peace*) which were staged as a trilogy by the RSC a[...]
Poems and Songs were pub[...]
1987. *Restoration* (Swan T[...]

by the same author

in Methuen's Modern Plays
A-A-AMERICA! & STONE
BINGO
THE BUNDLE
THE FOOL & WE COME TO THE RIVER
LEAR
NARROW ROAD TO THE DEEP NORTH
THE POPE'S WEDDING
RESTORATION & THE CAT
SAVED
THE SEA
SUMMER & FABLES
THE WOMAN
THE WORLDS

in Methuen's New Theatrescripts
DEREK AND CHORUSES FROM
AFTER THE ASSASSINATIONS
HUMAN CANNON
THE WAR PLAYS
Volume 1: Red, Black and Ignorant, The Tin Can People
Volume 2: Great Peace

in the Swan Theatre Plays series
RESTORATION

in the World Dramatists Series
PLAYS: ONE
(Saved, Early Morning, The Pope's Wedding)
PLAYS: TWO
(Lear, The Sea, Narrow Road to the Deep North,
Black Mass, Passion)
PLAYS: THREE
(Bingo, The Fool, The Woman)

Poetry
THEATRE POEMS AND SONGS
POEMS 1978–1985

Edward Bond

Two Post-Modern Plays

Jackets

In the Company of Men

with

September

METHUEN DRAMA

METHUEN MODERN PLAYS

This collection first published in Great Britain in 1990 by Methuen Drama, Michelin House, 81 Fulham Road, London SW3 6RB and distributed in the United States of America by HEB Inc., 70 Court Street, Portsmouth, New Hampshire 03801.

A CIP catalogue record for this book is available from The British Library.

ISBN 0-413-62650-4

Printed and bound in Great Britain by Cox & Wyman Ltd, Reading

The front cover illustration is taken from the *Jackets* poster designed by Andy White for the Haymarket Theatre, Leicester.

The photograph of Edward Bond on the back cover is copyright © Charles N. White.

Contents

Jackets

or

The Secret Hand

Jackets was premièred by the Department of Theatre Studies at Lancaster University on 24 January 1989, with the following cast:

Part One: The Village School

CHIYO	Margaret Eddershaw
TONAMI	Amanda Hadingue
KOTARO	Philip Coates
TYGO	Laurie Smith
GAULI	Adam Clayton
CHICO	Tim Meekings
FOOSHI	Richard Bousfield
GENZO	Chas Ambler
MATSUO	Charles Waples
HENBA	John Freeman
NCO	Ralph Ineson
THE MOTHER	Bernadette Hughes
VILLAGERS	Anne Baker
	Ceri Jones
	Robert Knowles
	Patrick Ladbury
	Jane Lindsay
	Nicky Sims
KAN SHU	Matthew Telfer

Part Two: The City

MRS LEWIS	Amanda Hadingue
MRS TEBHAM	Margaret Eddershaw
PHIL LEWIS	Charles Waples
BRIAN TEBHAM/THE OFFICER	John Freeman
THE PADRE	Chas Ambler
THE POLICEMAN	Ralph Ineson

Directed by Keith Sturgess
Composer and Musical Director Kim Baston

Part Two of *Jackets* opened at the Leicester Haymarket on 28 November 1989 with the following cast:

BRIAN TEBHAM	Tom Hudson
PHIL LEWIS	Ross Dunsmore
THE OFFICER	Tom Hudson
THE PADRE	William Whymper
THE POLICEMAN	Steve Ullathorne
MRS TEBHAM	Janette Legge
MRS LEWIS	Maureen Morris

Directed by Nick Philippou
Designed by Anthony Lamble
Lighting by Ian Moulds
Sound by Paul Bull
Music by David Sawer

Note

For this production Kan Shu was omitted from Section [C]. Instead, Brian came on and sat till the Padre came on. The Padre's words '– its the infantryman's best friend' were removed from their position in the printed text and placed after the Padre says 'Rifle, Tebham.' just before Brian leaves.

Note

The play is derived from 'The Village School' scene of *Sugawara* by Takeda Zumo. Part One is set in eighteenth-century Japan and Part Two is set in modern Europe.

The roles in Part One should be doubled with those in Part Two. Various doublings are possible, but in Part Two the roles of Brian and The Officer must be doubled.

Part One: The Village School
The New Pupil
The Show
Chiyo's Narration
The Identification
The Proclamation

Part Two: The City
[A] Mrs Lewis's Kitchen
[B] The Padre's Office
[C] The same – later
[D] The Street
[E] The Canal Path
[F] The Police Station
[G] Mrs Lewis's Kitchen

Songs

In the first production a chorus from the cast sang the songs in the following places in the text.

Children Sit Bowed at Your School Desks before the first scene.

D'You Think I'll Always Carry Your Load? in The Proclamation immediately after Kotaro's body is carried out and before Kan Shu asks 'What d'you want?'. While it is sung the Mother sits alone on stage. It is important that she does not take part in the song.

The Broken Cup immediately after Part 2, [A]. Alternatively it might be sung immediately after Part 2, [B]. While it is sung Brian might come on stage and sit in his chair. Kan Shu might follow him a little later. Both would then wait till the end of the song.

Two more songs were written for the production of the second part of *Jackets* at the Leicester Haymarket. In this production *Children Sit Bowed at Your School Desks* was not sung. The other songs were sung at the following places.

The Broken Cup between Sections [A] and [B], by all the performers except the actor playing Brian.

D'You Think I'll Always Carry Your Load? the first two verses between Section [B] and Section [C] and the last two verses in Section [C] after Brian leaves and before the Padre says 'Fool. Fool. Fool.', by the actor playing Phil.

The Song of Two Mothers between Sections [D] and [E], by the actresses playing Mrs Tebham and Mrs Lewis.

The Padre's Song between Sections [F] and [G], by the actor playing the Padre.

Songs for the First Part

Children Sit Bowed at Your School Desks

Children sit bowed at your school desks
The prisoner's safe in his cell
The rich man rides to his factory
The street traders haggle and sell
The tanks stand guard at the frontier
The sentries keep watch in the night
Children bow low at your schooldesks
And learn to read and write

Children add sums on your fingers
The judge is washing his hands
The soldiers are taught to pull triggers
The officers to roar commands
Are they trenches or graves they're digging?
And why have they cordoned the square?
Children bow low and write at your desks
When you look up the streets will be bare

Children stand straight to salute the flag
That flaps on the hangman's rope
Dont ask what your fathers are making
In the factory outside the town
There has to be food for the table
And a roof to cover your head
And doctors to call when the roof's blown down
And flowers for when you are dead

Children bend low and study
The world will go on its way
The rockets are aimed in their silos
So its safe to go out and play
And when the rockets are fired
And your city burns day and night
You'll be bent very low at the schooldesks
Where you learned to read and write

Children sit bowed and study
Let the world go on its way
Dont ask what your fathers are making
Its safe to go out and play
The wind whistles over the barbed wire
Your enemies live far away
They dont walk beside you as you go home
And watch over you all the day

D'You Think I'll Always Carry Your Load?

D'you think I'll always carry your load?
D'you think I'll always sweat and toil?
D'you think I'll give you my limbs and my blood?
Like the birds of the air! Like the beasts of the soil!

D'you think I'll always come when you call?
D'you think I'll always jump when you shout?
D'you think I'll always bow my neck?
Like a beast in a stall! With a ring in its snout!

D'you think I'll always fight in your wars?
D'you think I'll always give you my breath?
D'you think I'll always march to be shot?
Like the clowns in your court! Like the armies of death!

    The grass will grow on the fields of war
    Rust rot your rockets and radar discs
    Trees will stand where your watchtowers stood
    Your prisons and barracks vanish in fire
    I dont need your pity or fear your fists
    My anger will rise like the sun at dawn
    On the empty world where no one will mourn
    And only wind howl for your funeral pyre

Songs for the Second Part

The Broken Cup

A tear running down the side of a mountain
The heroes chained to the frozen peaks
A paper boat sailing in the whirlwind
Dead soldiers helmets thrown in a fountain
These are the questions! Who answers? Who speaks?

The lame man holds up the march
But marchers must rest
Let them rest while the lame man dances
His dance will cheer the marchers
Carry him on our backs
We'll manage!

The madwoman cant follow orders
Let her croon to the children
Her shouts will warn the enemy?
So would the children's crying
Let her croon – the kids will be quiet
We need her!

We found a dress in the ruins
Hung from a nail on a door
Don't borrow clothes from the dead
Let the curtain hang over the past
In these ruins we found a cup
Some things can only be drunk
From cups that are broken!

Trees that stand alone must bend in the storm
If a forest bent it'd uproot the earth
Collect bricks from the ruins
To build houses – or prisons for those who steal bricks
Decide!

We are strong
We came from the golden city
We fled from the promised land
We grow the harvest of plenty
In the parched fields of rubble and sand
We are brave – we are wise in measure – we are tough
People of the ruins who found the cup that was broken
Its enough!

The Song of Two Mothers

When you were young I told you
To wash your hands before you ate
I should have said sharpen your claws
And nourish the appetites of hate
So that you grow to flourish
In the city of the wolf
Where pity is the burden of the poor
And happiness is wealth

And when I sent you off to school
I should have hired a murderer
To teach you the tricks of his trade
And a butcher to teach you the rules of the game
And to stifle the voice of human shame
So that you grew to flourish
In the city of the wolf
Where pity is the burden of the poor
And happiness is wealth

And when you went into the world
I should have given you a pack
Of traitors to be your guide
And a knife to stick in the back
Of the comrades at your side
So that you came out on top
In the city of the wolf
Where pity is a liability
And happiness is wealth

And when I rocked you in your cradle
I should have hammered into your head
Be hard be hard as the nails
They'll knock in your coffin when you are dead
Instead I said child be gentle
And wash your hands and face
And sent you off to the lair
Where wolfs gnaw human bones
And I hear the human cry
In the groans of the market place
And in the traffic's roar I hear
Weeping and despair and fear
And Im so ignorant I try
To mend the holes in your shadow
And smooth the frowns of the sea
And wash the wounds of the sky

The Padre's Song

One hot summer day
Terrorists shot a soldier dead
He lay in the street
Leeking blood in his khaki
Like a baby messing its pants
They covered him with a clean white sheet
Nineteen and fit till he was hit
And got a hole in his head
His mouth's wide open – but he cant speak
So everyone else said what had to be said

The PM gasped animals
The opposition yelled scum
The colonel roared cowards
Only the dead man was dumb
TV presenters were outraged
Royalty was moved
A thug scrawled on a neighbourhood wall
Cut them up and feed them to pigs – hanging's too good for them
And the gutter press had a ball
And every cabinet minister swore
To give the last drop of the people's blood
And the army yelled more more more
Dont waste your life on the dole lads
Come and get your beret and gun
Have an army career in a hole lads
Funerals are fun

Business is good in the burying trade
The pound will rally round
The flowershops have got it made
Mechanical diggers dig the holes fast
And I've found my niche in life at last
Lowering lads in the ground
I keep clean white surplices ready to hand
The honour guard fire over the grave
And shit bricks – they could be down there – but look brave
And the bugle call sounds grand
There's nothing like a military funeral
To rouse the spirits of the land
Share prices will rise – but boom or bust
Go to your doom with a grin

Yours is to die and not ask why
We'll look after your next of kin
And give them money to ease their pains
And shovel earth on your remains
And pretend the earth is the sky
And at night as you lie and rot in your grave
In the ranks of the silent dead
The nation that said what had to be said
Pulls clean white sheets over its head
And goes to sleep in peace in bed
More more more
Get your beret and gun
Funerals are fun

Part One: The Village School

The New Pupil

A screen across the middle of the stage. Off, occasional shouts of schoolboys playing in the yard.

CHIYO *comes in.*

CHIYO (*calls*). Is the schoolmaster in please? (*Turns and calls off.*) Kotaro – quickly!

TONAMI *comes on from behind the screen.*

TONAMI. The schoolmaster's been called to town by the mayor.
CHIYO . When will he be back?
TONAMI. I dont know. Im his wife.
CHIYO (*calls off*). Kotaro – if the schoolmaster's wife sees you dont come when you're called she wont let him take you as a pupil.
TONAMI (*looking off*). Is he your son?
CHIYO. My husband's a cloth merchant. The war made people too poor to buy cloth. We have to travel far to make a living. It isnt good to take Kotaro with us. He should settle down so he can learn.
TONAMI (*calls*). Kotaro! – He looks a sensitive boy. Im sure my husband will take him.
CHIYO. We would be grateful. I have to go into town on business – may I leave Kotaro here and come back this evening to settle the fees?
TONAMI. Of course.
CHIYO. He's coming now you've called him.

KOTARO *comes on. He doesnt look at* CHIYO.

TONAMI. Good morning Kotaro.

KOTARO *bows to* TONAMI.

CHIYO. Say goodbye Kotaro. Behave so that we can be proud of you.

TONAMI. You may embrace your mother Kotaro. (KOTARO *doesnt move or look at* CHIYO.) Bring his change of clothes this evening.

CHIYO (*starts to go, then turns to look at* KOTARO). Goodbye.

KOTARO *doesnt look at her. She goes.*

TONAMI. Hands out. (KOTARO *holds out his hands.* TONAMI *looks at them.*) Palms. (KOTARO *turns over his hands.*) Good. Most of our pupils are farmers' sons. They have a hard life. You'll learn to survive. That'll help you when you're a merchant and times are so bad they bury people in their cot-blankets.

TONAMI *has rung a handbell. Four schoolboys come on:* TYGO, GAULI, FOOSHI *and* CHICO.

TONAMI. Quickly! Welcome our new pupil from the lowlands. Show him how polite mountain people are.

KOTARO *bows and the other boys giggle.*

TONAMI. Gauli – Chico: desks!

GAULI *and* CHICO *take the desks from a stack before the screen and set them out. The desks have flat tops and short legs: to write at them pupils squat on the ground.*

TONAMI. The schoolmaster set us a task. Fair copies of our alphabets. Fooshi: ink and paper.

Quickly and efficiently the village boys put out desks, ink and paper.

TONAMI. Kotaro's father is a merchant. Kotaro will be able to tell us all about the clothing trade. Kotaro will borrow the headboy's desk: *he's* working in the schoolmaster's study.

TYGO. Crawler.

TONAMI. What did you say Tygo? (*No response.*) Im glad to hear it. Gauli: desks straight please. (GAULI *straightens the line of desks.*) I want to see nice bold letters. Cheating wont help. Im going to get Kotaro's bedding roll and handbasin. Let's show the schoolmaster how well we work when he's away. I dont want to be ashamed when he comes back.

TONAMI goes out. The boys squat in a line: TYGO, CHICO, FOOSHI, GAULI *and* KOTARO. *They work in silence. Slowly* TYGO *pushes his desk till it shunts* CHICO'*s, then goes on pushing till all the desks are shunted together.* GAULI *giggles briefly and* FOOSHI *gives a short anxious whimper.*

TYGO. Our mountains are steep.

The line of desks reaches KOTARO'*s.* TYGO *pushes but* KOTARO *holds his desk still by pressing one hand flat down on the top. The line of desks stops.* KOTARO *goes on writing with his freehand.*

TYGO. Set stones on our fields stop the land slitherin in the river.

TYGO pushes harder. KOTARO *holds his desk down and goes on writing as before. His face is concentrated but without strain.* FOOSHI *jumps up and runs to help* TYGO *push.*

TYGO. Paths so steep they could set a door in 'em!

TYGO beckons CHICO *and* GAULI *to help him. They take up handholds along the edge of* TYGO'*s desk.*

TYGO. Hup!

The village boys push. KOTARO *writes as before: his desk doesnt move.*

TYGO (*strains. The other village boys stop pushing*). Clever little sod's nailed his desk down.

The village boys laugh at TYGO. *He sits on the floor facing away from his desk, levers his hands and feet against the floor and pushes with his back against his desk.*

TYGO. Hed enough of play-acting! – now I'll move him!

GAULI. Ont use nails – we'd've heard the hammerin.

TYGO. Hid somethin under the top!

FOOSHI (*looking under* KOTARO's *desk*). No he ont!

TYGO (*stops pushing*). Well thass a rum un! (*To the other village boys.*) Ont all gape! – that give him encouragement! (*Pushes again.*)

FOOSHI. He'll break the desks!

GAULI. Ont want no bother!

CHIYO. Not worth it!

TYGO (*stops pushing and walks round* KOTARO's *desk.* KOTARO *goes on writing*). Brought magnets into it somehow . . . thass how thass done!

Suddenly TYGO *dashes to his desk, throws himself on his back and pushes against his desk with his feet.* KOTARO *writes.*

FOOSHI. Stop it! Stop it! Stop it!

TYGO (*straining*). Push him through the wall an through the mountain!

CHICO. Goo it boy!

FOOSHI. He'll smash the desks!

TYGO. I'll push the mountain on top of him!

The line of desks breaks and all of them except KOTARO's *scatter – he goes on holding his down and writing as before.*

FOOSHI. Done it now boy! My leg's chip!

TYGO. I'll chip his head!

FOOSHI. Yoo know what a tarter she is: come through that door, point straight at it and say: chip leg!

TYGO. All right boy, you hev a bit of strength. Merchant buy cheap, sell dear: put our strength in their pocket. No wonder you're fit! See through yoor tricks boy, only I ont lettin on: suits me best you think Im ignorant. Tell you what though! – you come tradin round here I'll make dam sure people know all 'bout your tricks. Then we'll see who's smart!

KOTARO *writes as before.*

TYGO. Right! I give him fair warnin'! (*He pretends he's trying to get to* KOTARO *to attack him but the other boys are stopping him: he dodges about behind them, but really pushing them in front of him.*) Hold me back! Thass right boys! Save him from me!

CHICO. Git off!

TYGO (*pretending to struggle to pass the boys*). Stop me Gauli for the poor lad's sake! Devil now my rag's up! I'll turn him inside out! Rip his limbs off an stuff em in his pockets! Let me git at him!

GAULI. Bloody ass!

TYGO. I'll massacre him! Thank god there's a human wall between us!

FOOSHI *screams as* TYGO *pushes him.*

CHICO. Git off idiot!

TYGO (*pretending to calm down*). Thank God! – its pass! The power come over me!

FOOSHI. He damage my arm!

TYGO. There could've bin a massacre! Ont know me own strength! Pat a chap on the head an he goo through the ground! Thass a terrible talent for destruction! God bless you boys for savin the lad!

KOTARO *writes as before.*

FOOSHI. You massacre my desk – that'll be enough destruction for her!

GAULI (*to* FOOSHI). Look what he's up to boy.

FOOSHI *looks at* KOTARO's *script.*

CHICO. Whass he puttin down?

FOOSHI. Lor!

CHICO (*looks at* KOTARO's *script*). What is it . . .?

TYGO. Ont be fox by his squiggles. He'll say thass how they write where he come from! Tell a donkey it cant bray!

GAULI, FOOSHI *and* CHICO *look at* KOTARO's *script.* TYGO *stands apart.*

CHICO (*to* TYGO). He's writin proper words!

TYGO. Schoolmaster'll catch him out – he know every sort of writin there is!

GAULI. He's writin down what we say!

FOOSHI (*points to* TYGO). You said all merchants cheat! – now they ont trade with our dads an we'll starve!

TYGO. They'll trade! Ont miss a chance t' cheat!

FOOSHI (*scared*). Shut up you ass!

TYGO (*looks at* KOTARO's *script.* KOTARO *goes on writing*). She said write alphabet! – that's a whole dam book there boy! Tent right! This is a school – come here t' learn, not show off what yoo already know! Thass worse than cheatin!

GAULI. Now he'll write that down!

TYGO. 'I'm a bloody fool'! – write that boy! I'll give you plenty of dictation!

CHICO. Stop it Tygo!

FOOSHI. I ont said anythin! – Cant remember what I *hev* said, with all Tygo's rattle!

GAULI. We was only larkin!

CHICO. Give you a laugh help yoo settle down!

TYGO (*reaches towards script*). Whass that?

KOTARO *spits in* TYGO's *face. His expression doesnt change. He goes back to his writing.*

CHICO. He spit!

TYGO (*quiet, stunned*). No need for such depravity ol' chap! Are you sick?

CHICO (*quiet, explaining*). He's a gentleman. Thass how he learned t' hold his desk still an spit.

FOOSHI. Told him never t' push the desks! Ont my fault I cant read an write! Squiggles scare me – come out my hand like thass sick. Be even worse now he's broke my arm! (*Points to* KOTARO *as he writes.*) Look at that! Ont even got ink on his fingers! Writin so dam clear they'll hev t' read it! Yoo gone too far Tygo, you'll –

CHICO (*warning*). Desk!

The village boys frantically straighten the desks, squat and start to write. Silence. GENZO *comes in.*

VILLAGE BOYS. Mornin sir!

GENZO (*ignores the boys, calls*). Tonami!

GENZO *stands to one side deep in thought.*

FOOSHI (*whispers to* TYGO). Yoo hev the chip boy! See how yoo like it!

TYGO *and* FOOSHI *change desks.* TONAMI *comes in.*

TONAMI. Look how good they are!

GENZO (*to boys*). Home! School's over!

TONAMI. Not now they're working so –

GENZO. Out!

The village boys start to leave.

TONAMI. Desks – desks!

The village boys stack the desks at the screen, bob to GENZO *and hurry out.*

KOTARO (*to* TONAMI). May I be allowed to finish my –

TONAMI. Later.

KOTARO. The master will need an example of my work.

TONAMI (*moment's hesitation*). Take it over there. I dont want to hear you breathe.

KOTARO *takes his desk upstage, sits with his back to the others and writes.* GENZO *doesnt notice him.*

TONAMI. What's the matter?

GENZO (*low*). The message was a trap to get me into town. Henba was there! He's surrounded the town with his soldiers. He asked me four questions. 'Why does a general become a priest?' I didn't answer. 'Why does the priest hide on top of a mountain?' 'Why does he open a school for village idiots?' I started to say 'The wise man withdraws from the world when –' 'Tcha! – and why is his best pupil the son of the emperor my soldiers chopped to pieces and threw in the palace sewer?'

TONAMI. His spies were bound to find us even here.

GENZO. He ordered me to cut off the prince's head.

TONAMI. Ah no! What can we do?

GENZO. I came back through the pass. Rocks full of cracks as if they'd been thinking a thousand years and they dont even know where the path that runs at their feet is going!

TONAMI. Disguise him – smuggle him out through –

GENZO. Henba's soldiers are everywhere. By now he knows these mountains better than a snake with a glass belly. Even if we got the prince out how could he live? He knows how to order granneries to be built but he cant hold a beggar's bowl. He can send armies to die but he couldnt wash a scratch on his leg. He cant breathe without us!

TONAMI. He grew up in the hidden palace. Henba doesnt know what he looks like. Give him another head.

GENZO. Henba's as cunning as the thief who was hanged with the loot in his pockets! He's brought someone who'll identify the head with pleasure – Matsuo!

TONAMI. That traitor!

GENZO. He taught the prince archery. He stood so close to him he's adjusted the string over his face.

TONAMI. Children change! Matsuo hasnt seen him for a year!

GENZO. The prince belongs to the ruling class! That shows in his face! Where could we get a head like that? All we've got are peasants with as much breeding as cattle!

TONAMI. But dead? The face screwed up? Try! – or you'll spend the rest of your life –

GENZO. When the prince is dead we'll kill ourselves on his grave! You think I'd live after I'd killed him?

TONAMI. O god strike Matsuo blind!

GENZO. We asked god to give us victory!

TONAMI. Why are we talking of failing? Kill someone slowly – hack their throat – stamp their living screams in the dead flesh! Nothing's cruel or wrong if it saves the prince! This is the test! Kill one of this rabble! What gratitude do they show when we try to teach them to be human? I soil my hands on them like a washerwoman! We're entitled to their heads – we'll use them better than they can!

GENZO. If I peeled the skin from the prince's head in strips his class would still show: he takes care of his teeth. No matter what pain he dies with he'll look on the world with iron serenity. Does the sun set when you blow out your lamp – or one sort of fruit change into another sort because you bite it? The prince will die as he lived. If that isnt true we have no right to call ourselves leaders. Matsuo knows all this – even a *peasant* knows his dirt looks different when the sun shines on it! We need a boy who'd pass for ruling class – and where could we find him!

KOTARO *has stood. He bows to* TONAMI *and* GENZO.

KOTARO. Sir I hope I shall have the honour to call you master. M'am I have finished the calligraphic exercise.

GENZO. Who's this?

TONAMI. A new pupil. His mother left him. Kotaro you musnt interrupt –

GENZO. A pupil? To live in? Kotaro would you like to study

under me.

KOTARO. Yes sir.

GENZO. Then you shall. Go to the dormitory. Wait there.

KOTARO *bows and goes out behind the screen.*

GENZO. Who is he?

TONAMI. His family are merchants. His mother's coming this evening to –

GENZO. Late?

TONAMI. She didnt –

GENZO. Late enough! Too late! We'll give Henba his head!

TONAMI. We cant!

GENZO. *Merchant's* son? Why not! – monsters are born with two heads! Now a tradesman's fathered a gentleman! You begged the gods to blind Matsuo. The gods are wiser! They've sent us a head to deceive anyone!

TONAMI. But what if – !

GENZO. They say mountains creep forward. You dont notice till one day the path's changed direction or a wall of rock bars the old pass as if the stone floated there like mist! Matsuo hasnt seen the prince for a year – boys change fast! I'll creep up behind him – chop off his head with one stroke! He wont feel the wind of my sword on his cheek – it'll be blown away by his last breath! No disfigurement – a slight look of surprise – the eyebrows raised. Matsuo betrayed us because he thought our class was decadent. He'll take the raised eyebrows on the dead face as proof! O if he looked close he'd see the merchant's eyes narrowed to price up a customer – not a judge's piercing the accused! But he'll pass! *I* fell for him!

TONAMI. His mother will scream all over the mountain!

GENZO. Tell her he ran off because she'd abandoned him! We'll help her to search the – (*Stops.*) We cant, we cant!

TONAMI. Why not?

GENZO. Missing boy – screaming mother: the soldiers'll put two and two together. But the head's in our hands! If we let it go we're not fit to rule!

TONAMI. So the mother –

GENZO. Will be dealt with – if I must. All we live for, our culture, honour – one woman stand in the way of that? Not even a tradesman's wife! A whore! There *is* no husband to come prying! Its the war – an officer away from home. That boy's lucky! He was born above his rank – now he'll die above it: killed by an officer's sword! He came to learn. I'd've taught him to die for his country. Now he'll die before he's taught! Pass the exam without the study! Lucky lucky boy! Such abundance is extravagant! The gods are good to him! . . . Tonami, my officer's sword is under this priest's robe. If Matsuo sees we cheated I'll cut him down – and with luck Henba! – before I kill us both. – Its good we came here. If we'd crossed the frontier the foreigners would have sent the prince back to appease Henba. This village still has the old innocence. The houses and streets are built from stones gathered in the fields. In this bright light the crooked stream seems straight. Cattle and people born under one roof: the old die on one side of the wall, the cattle are slaughtered on the other. The sagas say the mountains give birth to dragons: in this squalor the prince will grow up to take back the riches of an empire.

The Show

TONAMI. Soldiers in the playground.

HENBA *and* MATSUO *come in.* MATSUO *carries a ritual cloth and headbox.*

HENBA. Is it done?

GENZO. I've finished the ritual ablutions.

HENBA. Get it over. He's seen my troops in the yard. Dont make him linger.

Off, villagers' voices.

VILLAGERS (*off*). Our boys! Please! Look their heads in the window!

HENBA (*calls*). What the hell –?

VILLAGERS (*off*). Schoolmaster! Gauli! Tygo! Yoo all right lads?

NCO *comes in.*

NCO. Villagers. Reckon one of their brats going to be killed.

HENBA (*looks at* GENZO). Its a trick! (*To* NCO.) Send one of the mob in. (*To* GENZO.) I'll sort those boys out inch by inch!

NCO *goes out.*

VILLAGERS (*off*). Our boys! Please!

NCO (*off*). Shut it! (VILLAGERS *murmur.*) One of you in there! – Lost your tongue now its your turn t' speak? Pick one of you out quick!

Slight pause. The MOTHER *comes in with the* NCO.

MOTHER (*uncertain who to speak to*). Sir – mister – villagers say one of our boys . . .? They on t' blame if they fail their lessons sir! Ont hev time t' study! Is it the grown-ups? Your war ont hardly reach us – we ont take sides. We're as harmless as our children. (*To* GENZO *and* TONAMI.) Never want their school!

VILLAGERS (*off*). Whass gooin on? (*Wail.*) Fooshi?

MOTHER (*calls to* VILLAGERS). Tellin 'em school ont right for young lads! (*To* GENZO.) Sit there all day till their limbs git distorted.

TONAMI. Be quiet!

MOTHER. We'll jist git our lads out your road. We'll tan 'em if they done wrong. Once I git my stick started I can win a race on a donkey thass bin dead three week!

GENZO. Must the prince die in the bellowing of a cattle market? You send him to the gods with a message of

disdain on his face to show them the misery and despair
you've brought to this country!

HENBA. Hush hush hush a few simple people looking for
their young – and you drag the gods into it!

VILLAGERS (*off*). Gauli we're here! Ont fret lads!

HENBA (*to* GENZO). Fetch their kids out. But dont try to
smuggle mine with them. Matsuo: dont be fooled be a few
rags and a smear of yardmuck. (*To* GENZO.) One at a
time. (*To* NCO, *indicating* GENZO *and* TONAMI.) Any
trick, run them through!

> TONAMI *and* GENZO *sit on one side of the stage.* GENZO's
> *hand is near the handle of the sword under his robe. The* NCO
> *stands behind them with a raised spear.* HENBA *sits alone.*
> MATSUO *sits with the ritual cloth and headbox by him on the*
> *floor.*

TONAMI (*calls*). Gauli.

> GAULI *steps from behind the screen.*

HENBA. Stop!

> GAULI *stops.*

MATSUO. He is not the emperor's son.

HENBA. Sure? Have his head if there's any doubt.

MOTHER. He's Gauli – Mr Looshi's boy!

HENBA. Shut up! (*To* MATSUO.) *Any* doubt!

GENZO (*disgust*). Doubt that pig's face? (*To* GAULI.) Grunt!
(GAULI *stares in incomprehension.*) Grunt boy! – show the
gentleman what's in front of him!

MOTHER. Grunt Gauli! Save yourself!

> GAULI *grunts.*

MOTHER. He grunted! Can he goo?

GENZO. The prince wouldnt grunt if your army marched
over his tongue.

HENBA. Fake priest, fake schoolmaster, fake *clown*: he

throws his voice! (*Stands close to* GAULI *and peers into his face.*) Grunt. (GAULI *backs away.*) He cant grunt!

GENZO. Your army took over the country like a corpse dressing itself up in living skin, and you cant tell the stink of a little gutter-rat . . .

MOTHER. Grunt Gauli! Doo a pig or they'll hev yoor head! (GAULI *squeals, half in imitation and half in fright.*) There! He squeal! Thass a proper pig sir! His family handle pork! (HENBA *walks away from* GAULI *in silence.*) Show the gentlemen how piglet goo when they git sight the old sow's dugs! (GAULI *squeals weakly.*) Help me boy! Ont my fault I hev t' ask such things! Gentlemen hev t' know so's they can run the country. (*To* HENBA.) Yoo heard 'un squeal sir. Poo he stink of pig! – gale ont blow it off 'un! Educated lad yoo're after ont even know pig squeal! Think they fly bout la-ing like a nightingale till they drop on his plate! (*To* GAULI.) Root boy! (*Calls to villagers.*) Gauli hev t' be a pig! Help him!

VILLAGERS (*off*). Pig? How they git a pig in there?

MOTHER (*calls*). No – Gauli hev t' be a pig!

VILLAGERS (*off*). What they want a pig for? Is they hungry woman?

MOTHER (*to* GAULI). On yoor knees boy! Show the gentlemen yoo ont too high an mighty t' be a pig! Root root root! (GAULI *falls to his knees.*) Im the farmer's wife! How doo pigs goo when she threw scraps 'fore 'em in the dut? (*Calls.*) Gauli hev t' be a pig t' save his neck!

VILLAGERS (*off*). Pig ont save their neck! (*They imitate pig sounds.*) Pig it for the gentlemen Gauli! They want a pig, yoo be a pig like a good chap! Gentlemen know best!

MOTHER (*shouts pig sounds to the villagers*). Help him! (*Pretends to scatter scraps.* GAULI *roots and makes pig sounds.*) Root root root! Yoo got it boy! (*Calls.*) We'll do it if we pull t'gether! (*Off, the villagers join in.*) There sir! – ont ask better proof'n that! Rest of pigs heard him they'd think he's their brother had singin lessons!

VILLAGERS *off, imitate a pig farm.*

MOTHER (*aside to herself*). My Tygo's in there! He'll come
out an play the fool! Then there'll be trouble! (*To*
GAULI.) Root lad! Keep rootin till the gentlemen say they
had enough!

MATSUO. He's not the emperor's son.

HENBA (*to* GAULI). Trot! Quick before I change my mind!

GAULI *runs off.*

VILLAGERS (*off*). My boy! Whass gooin on?

MOTHER (*aside to* TONAMI). Call my Tygo next missus.

TONAMI (*calls*). Fooshi!

MOTHER (*aside, to herself*). There! – she ont be advised when
I tell her for the best!

FOOSHI *creeps from behind the screen.*

HENBA. Stop!

FOOSHI *runs back behind the screen,* HENBA *goes behind it
and brings him out by the collar.* FOOSHI's *mouth opens and
shuts but no sound comes out.*

MOTHER. Thass Fooshi! Old Mr Goffre's boy. All right
Fooshi, Im here. Ont bother with him sir! Whole village
know he's a pig.

MATSUO. He's not the emperor's son.

Silence. FOOSHI's *mouth opens and shuts.*

MOTHER. Honk Fooshi!

FOOSHI *mouths silently.*

HENBA. Cant he do a pig?

MOTHER. He honk with the best of 'em sir. Trouble is he's
backward. Bag of nerves since his mother die. Cruel t'
drive his sort too far sir: they ont know the way back.
(*Calls to villagers.*) Fooshi cant git his pig out!

VILLAGERS (*off*). Want another pig? Well thass a rum un! Fooshi doo a pig or I'll larrup yer!

MOTHER (*to* HENBA). I swear t' god we're jist common muck from the bottom of the trash. Ont even best muck from the top. Ont fit t' contaminate your air! Let 'un goo.

HENBA (*suspicious*). See how she's set on saving this one . . .! A few rags and a foolish grin: fall for that?

MOTHER. Grunt Fooshi! Squeal! Honk! Root in the dut like the pigs! Yoo ont let me help yoo boy! (*Calls to* VILLAGERS.) Help him!

VILLAGERS (*off, imitating pig noises*). Fooshi be a pig when the gentlemen say! He doo a pig if yoo tell 'un t' shut up! Blast the boy why's he so stand-uppish? (VILLAGERS *imitate sheep*.) Ont want sheep! Want pig t'day!

MOTHER (*aside, to herself*). An I still hev t' handle my Tygo! He'll come out an say 'Im the prince!' Then all hell'll be let loose! (*Calls.*) Tygo yoo play me up when yoor turn come, there ont be enough of yoo left t' be a pig!

VILLAGER (*off*). Ont mind yoor lump of an ass missus – my Fooshi need help! Honk Fooshi! – yoo honk like a famish litter when yoo're asleep! (*The* VILLAGERS *make pig noises.*)

MOTHER (*beats* FOOSHI *with a cloth*). I'll pig yoo, git our lads kill! Pig! Pig! Pig!

FOOSHI *falls down in fright and gasps.*

MOTHER. There! Im gettin t' the pig in 'un now! (*Stamps feet.*) Thass the butcher – thass the butcher's knife flashin front the kitchen window – (FOOSHI *squeals in terror.*) – pig! – pig! – pig squeal now he smelt the butcher's apron! 'I'll hev the head off that pig! Singe that hide! Tie its guts for sausige!' (FOOSHI *squeals hysterically.*) There sir – thass prime pig! (*To* FOOSHI) 'Tip his blood in the black puddin bucket! Chuck his offal t' the dogs!' (*To* HENBA.) Now he's off yoo'll hev a job t' git him stop! Ont bin steady in the head since his mother die – an *she* ont normal!

HENBA. Chuck him out!

MOTHER *helps* FOOSHI *out – he squeals as he goes.*

VILLAGERS (*off*). Tie him down! Drop him in the pond – thass help afore! Howd steady boy!

HENBA (*shouting after* FOOSHI). Tell your father to lock you up in the sty! Not decent parading in front of the village!

MOTHER (*whispers to* TONAMI). Tygo!

TONAMI (*calls*). Chico!

MOTHER (*aside, to herself*). I despair of the woman!

CHICO *comes from behind the screen.*

HENBA. Stop!

CHICO *stops.*

MATSUO. He is not the emperor's son.

MOTHER. Chico – Chis' eldest.

HENBA. Family of pigs?

MOTHER (*thrown*). Hev yoo had enough pig sir? Shall he be a dog? Gentry find dog a useful animal sir. Chico'd make a good dog – allus larkin, full of spirits – hev us in heaps of an evenin! Chico doo how a dog beg! (CHICO *imitates a begging dog.*) There sir thass a perfect beggin dog! (Good dog Chico!) Proud jist watchin 'un! Prince ont know dogs beg. His dog eat off best plate an throw his scraps t' footmen!

HENBA. Seen better dogs in a cat home.

MOTHER. Yoo'll see the dog when I thrash 'un! (CHICO *howls. To* CHICO.) That racket's music t' my ears!

VILLAGERS (*off*). They got a pig that howl now? Wonders never cease! Do they want every sort of animal? (VILLAGERS *chorus farmyard imitations.*)

MOTHER (*calls*). Chico's doin dog!

VILLAGERS (*off*). Chico'll doo a crocodile if that helps the boss! (*They imitate dogs and farmyard animals.*)

MOTHER (*aside, to herself*). Thass gooin too well! My boy'll

spoil it! Stand there barefaced an say 'Im the prince'!
(*Calls.*) Im gooin t' whip Chico's dog!

HENBA Teach the hound to kennel!

VILLAGERS (*off*). She's makin a proper job! Dog ont
entitled t' ask for mercy!

MOTHER (*mimes pointing to a wall*). That ont a crack in the
plaster – thass my whip – (*Mimes taking down the whip
from the wall.*) – come yoo down off my wall, whip!
(CHICO *whines*.) His whine hev set my whip a'twitch!

HENBA. Scare him!

MOTHER. Wicked beast know what it deserve! Slink in its
corner! (*She mimes whipping* CHICO.) Switch! Switch!
Mouth droolin on the floor – drag body 'long behind it
like a floorcloth moppin up its spittle!

HENBA. Whip him mother!

MOTHER (*miming*). I'll whip him father! I'll flay the hide off
my hound! There! Whip so hard the skin jump off an run
down the lane – left the carcas stood there –

HENBA. Howling!

MOTHER. – till I whip it so it run off after its skin – the two
of 'em make a race of it, see which can jump in the ground
first!

HENBA (*laughing*). Whip him till his bones play dice! Look
at his legs! Lame him! (*Calls to the* VILLAGERS.) She's
lamed our dog! Walked in on its hind legs – crawl out on
its belly!

VILLAGERS (*off*). Us'll git the whippin gooin out here sir!
Allus ready t' lend a hand! Whip us-selve! Put on a good
show! Good dog! Smash! Smash! We're a-whippin sir!
(*Dog howls.*) Im a good dog sir! Whip me! Im smartin!
Make me howl!

HENBA (*calls to the* VILLAGERS). Harder! Make the walls
shake! The ground rattle!

HENBA *goes out.*

HENBA (*off*). Lame that skinny one – thrash him! (*Howls*

with laughter.) They're all lame! Lame dogs floggin each other! Whip yourselves dogs! Bite! Round and round! The dogs are whippin like the masters!

Off, the VILLAGERS *imitate dogs, masters and whips. Suddenly there's a big shout: in the village the real dogs have started to howl.*

HENBA (*off*). The dogs in the village! Howling!

Off, the VILLAGERS *roar with laughter. Onstage,* GENZO, TONAMI, MATSUO *and the* NCO *are motionless.*

MOTHER (*tentatively touches* CHICO – *she's unsure how the others will react*). Chico. (*Gently strokes his head.*) Good boy – help me an I'll git you out . . . (*The stroking changes to patting.*) . . . good dog . . .

HENBA *comes in.*

HENBA (*laughs*). The dogs in the village joined in!

VILLAGERS (*off*). I holla-ed louder'n Chico – I ought t' git his biscuit! Boot 'un woman! Make an ignorant dog if yoo show mercy! Quickest way t' spoil a good animal! Gratitude ont in a dog's nature – no more'n sense!

MOTHER (*to* CHICO). What doo a good dog doo when the whippin stop? (CHICO *slinks to* MOTHER *to lick her hand.*) Thass proof sir: he know dog through an through. Can he goo?

HENBA. Look dog – a rat!

MOTHER (*points*). Rat boy! (*Aside, to herself.*) God he's had the sense he was born with schooled out of him! (*Screeches like a rat.*) Git the rat boy!

CHICO *chases the rat.*

HENBA. Pounce dog!

MOTHER *screeches.* HENBA *runs round pointing at an imaginary rat running beside him.*

HENBA. Big fat plump rat! (*Points to* TONAMI.) After it –
up the lady's skirts!

> TONAMI *freezes as* CHICO *chases the rat round her. The*
> MOTHER *stays on one spot, screeches and illustrates the rat's
> movements.*

MOTHER. Im leapin in the air out a' reach the dog's jaws!

CHICO. Snap! Eeaarrgh!

MOTHER (*high screech*). Thass it sir – caught! Dog swep up
an took me out the air like a flyin graveyard full of teeth!
O his fangs is sharp! Honed an oiled on spittle an sweat!

HENBA. Worry the rat dog!

> CHICO *growls as he tears and worries the rat. Away from
> him, on another part of the stage, the* MOTHER *shakes as if
> she's being worried in the dog's mouth. She illustrates the rat's
> death and then the shaking of its limp body.*

MOTHER (*as the dead rat*). Done for sir! Dogs teeth rip the
bone. Bits stick out like a pin-cushion struck with a
hammer. Never git me t'gether again. (*Musical scale as
she ascends to heaven. Etherial voice.*) I'll hev a tale t' tell
the dead rats! Didnt I put up a rare show 'fore I die! Led
that dog such a dance its fleas ont know which end the
animal shit! Im dead but Im still pantin from the
agitations of livin!

VILLAGERS (*off*). Hev he kill the rat? Rats is ugly brutes!
Good guard dog keep the boss's store clean! Boss give dog
a whack for every rat droppin in the corn!

HENBA. Catch!

> HENBA *throws a piece of real biscuit to* CHICO. *He catches
> it, eats it and begs for more.*

MOTHER. Mongrels work up a terrible appetite for morsels.

HENBA. You've had your wages! (*He notices* GENZO,
TONAMI *and* MATSUO *staring icily at him. Calmly.*) Fossil
dogshit staring like the whites of a blindman's eyes. No

you didnt pass through the bowels of a dog: they're too human for you. – Late. (*To* CHICO.) Work hard. Scratch your fleas out in the neighbour's yard. Look after the old: you'll be old and mangey one day. Kennel!

CHICO *goes out.*

MOTHER. Now the calamity! Kep my boy last till the rest git off safe. He delight in bein reckless. Play the fool with the madman!

TONAMI (*calls*). Tygo!

TYGO *steps from behind the screen.*

MOTHER (*aside*). Now we'll hev it: 'Im the prince!'

HENBA. Stop!

TYGO *stops.*

HENBA. Who are you?

MOTHER *silently 'mouths' the words as* TYGO *speaks:*

TYGO. Im the prince!

HENBA. He's the prince. (*Pause.*) What do princes do?

TYGO *stares at* HENBA *a moment, then leans forward and spits at him.*

HENBA. The comic interlude. Poor lad you're not the prince. (*Turns away. Becomes quiet.*) You're two a penny. Cheer the army. Trumpets and laughter. Then dead soldiers poking out of the mud like tents stuck on horses' bones. Wind in the dead trumpeter's teeth. The sound he made when he was a novice. Broken cannons – like giants born dead. At night the mist in the mountains: a sea with upturned boats. I must go.

MOTHER. Ont taught him t' spit on gentry: his natural wickedness come out. (*Bows deeply.*) Ont harm a lunatic sir.

HENBA. Pig? Rat? Dog?

MOTHER (*lost*). He's anythin natural yoo choose sir. Rat –
dog? Or let him be your table.

HENBA. Table?

MOTHER. Your table when you come in from fightin. Full
of food. Ont say you're greedy! – celebration. Soldiers
pick the best from all your farms an shops an spread your
table. How else we show our gratitude? (*To* TYGO.) You
saw the table in the magistrate's parlour when they took
father in for stealin – an the priest's table when your sister
die. What yoo come home an show me?

TYGO (*rubs his stomach and groans*). Ee-er-ah.

MOTHER. There sir: poor man doin a table. Rich man see
table, mouth water: poor man, groan. Why? Table carry
food on its head – which is tantalisin t' the mouth – but
ont eat: so full table groan like empty stomach. There!
An they say the mountain groan cause it carry the sky –
if thass of interest. Be advised an let 'un goo. Easy pull
a chap up by the roots or shut the sty gate on 'un till the
butcher come: but might his god sit watchin on the roof?
– or squat up in a tree? Who's t' say? Be advised – an let
me take 'un out your road. (*No response. She calls.*) Tygo
did a table! (*No response.*) Gone – hidin their young in the
village. (*To* HENBA.) He'll do the fields when the wind's
famished: shake like the mountain with the gut ache. Or
the river in the drought: lie down like bones that grow
without the benefit of flesh.

She realises HENBA *isnt listening and stops. He looks up, goes
to* TYGO, *pulls his head down and boxes his ears.*

TYGO. Ouch that hurt!

HENBA. That'll teach you to scare your mother out of her
wits! Now hop it!

MOTHER *frantically signs to* TYGO *to go. He stands and rubs
his ears.*

TYGO. That truly hurt! Could've damaged my hearing! Ont

even spit t' hit!

MOTHER *pulls at* TYGO. *He goes.* HENBA *turns away.*
MOTHER *goes to him and holds out her open hand.*

MOTHER. Hope you liked our show sir . . .?

Her voice trails away politely. HENBA *looks through her and
points to the four desks by the screen.*

HENBA. Four. (*Points to* KOTARO'S *desk.*) A spare.
GENZO. The prince's.
HENBA. Finish it.

GENZO *goes to* MATSUO, *bows, takes the headbox and goes
out behind the screen. For a moment the* MOTHER *stands with
her open hand. Then she goes.*

Chiyo's Narration

CHIYO *comes on. Her scene happens in another place: the others
do not see her.*

CHIYO. When I left my son at the village school this morning
I lied. I ran along the road. I saw a vision. I thought the
tears in my eyes were a river in the sky. But I saw it was
this river on the ground.

Enemies heads are cut off. Common heads are thrown on
the victory pile but upper-class heads must be identified.
Matsuo betrayed his class. But he soon despised Henba
and his new allies. When they fight at his side – even
when their swords defend him – their sweat stinks worse
than the carnage of the wounded or the corruption of the
dead. And Henba doesnt trust him: when he looks at
Matsuo his eyes are like woodlice crawling along a crack
in a mirror. Today Matsuo must identify the prince's
head. Genzo wants to save him. Matsuo wants to help
Genzo. But Genzo can only get his hands on working-

class heads. He knows they'd never deceive Matsuo.
Matsuo cant tell him he'd pretend to be deceived. Genzo
would think its a trap. So Matsuo did the only thing he
could: he sent him Kotaro disguised as a merchant's son
– but Kotaro is his own son. He counts on Genzo using
Kotaro's head. Its his duty to use it just as it was
Matsuo's to send it. Their duty's clear – but they're
human and what will happen is as uncertain as the path
of pilgrims on the sea. Will Genzo kill Kotaro – or will he
kill the prince to save himself? Which head will he show
Matsuo? How will Matsuo react? With joy if the prince
is dead – or grief that his son's alive? With joy if the prince
is alive – or grief that his son's dead? With joy that his
son's dead – and joy that the prince is alive? Or joy that
the day is over – or grief that it ever began?

And me? When I go to the school you'll know more than
I do. Will I be a bereaved mother – or a wife shamed by
a husband who betrayed us all by weeping when he saw
his son's head – or even shouted the truth before Genzo
could kill him? Tonight will I weep with joy for a living
prince – or shout in triumph over my dead son? You who
know, pity those who must learn.

I walk under the willows. I tear at the branches. They
hang like empty strings giants tore from their parcels
and threw away – and ran off to play with the toys!
Children never play: they pretend – and stare at the
giants. Look! – willow branches! The air is full of
prayerwheels! If a bomb exploded and smashed the
prayerwheels – the flying pieces would spin faster! –
faster! – as if they prayed for those the blast was maiming
and killing! I tear at the willows! Let them pray for me
when I go back to the school!

CHIYO *goes out.*

The Identification

HENBA (*brooding*). 'Im the prince'. Who tells the truth? Liars. But they dont know it is the truth. When they open their mouth the oracle speaks.

GENZO comes from behind the screen. His robe and hands are spattered with blood. He carries the headbox. He puts it on the ground in front of MATSUO, then sits beside TONAMI with his hands close to the sword under his robe. The NCO still stands guard with his raised spear. MATSUO places the ritual cloth on his thigh. Staring straight before him he takes the lid from the box, lifts out the head and balances it on his left hand. Still without looking at the head he takes the ritual cloth in his right hand, wipes the face and puts the cloth on the ground. Then he holds the head before him and lowers his eyes to look at it.

MATSUO. The head of prince Kan Shu the emperor's son.
HENBA. Coin! (*Clicks fingers.*) These villages too high for war to reach – more ruined than towns put to the sword! Couldnt make a cripple's crutch from their huts. Thatch? – a corpse's eyelashes keep off more rain. He's dead but he'll go on bleeding other people's blood. His class are at home in the grave. Flourish in it. Chuck their earth over the living – we have to fight our way out like kids tearing open their mothers to be born. (*MATSUO gives him a coin.*) Too much. Brass. (*To GENZO.*) You can go. The school's shut. Try a church. (*The NCO lowers his spear. HENBA pockets the coin.*) When I tax people their grimy fingers cling to the coins – the dead teach them their grip. (*Takes another coin from MATSUO and glances at it as he drifts to the headbox.*) One head with a begging bowl for a mouth. (*Glances in the headbox. Shows the coin.*) Your father's head: take you a long time to suck that off. (*Drops coin into headbox.*) Dont say thanks. Im withdrawing his coinage. (*Turns to go.*) The village.

HENBA, MATSUO *and the* NCO *go out.*

GENZO. He was under the same roof as Kan Shu and walked away! – look at him marching to the gallows before they're built! – We must treat this body as –

TONAMI (*looking off*). The mother!

GENZO (*looking off*). Her? – Already?

TOÑAMI. O Genzo the gods are punishing us for killing her son and –

GENZO. Get rid of that!

> GENZO *gives* TONAMI *the headbox and she goes out behind the screen. He wipes his hands, covers his robe in a wrap and sits as if deep in thought.* CHIYO *comes in.*

CHIYO. The schoolmaster?

GENZO (*looks up*). Yes.

CHIYO. I left my son. The lady –

GENZO. I hope it went well?

CHIYO. – ? –

GENZO. Your business in town.

CHIYO. I finished early. (*Gestures off.*) I saw the gentlemen. I waited.

GENZO. You wish to pay your son's fees. We charge board and lodging and any –

CHIYO (*packet*). These sweets – I hope you dont think its wrong? – presents – ?

GENZO. A few small gifts do no harm.

CHIYO. May I give them to him.

GENZO. We wont disturb him. I'll make sure –

CHIYO. Yes – not disturb him – he couldnt say goodbye –

GENZO. He'll soon settle in to his new life. I'll make –

CHIYO. Neednt know Im here – just look through the – (*She goes towards the screen.*) – is this where –

GENZO. Please leave. Parents are not allowed in the –. Let me help you. (CHIYO *is staring at the screen with her back to* GENZO.) Dont try to see him. Thank you for the

sweets. I'll make sure he –
CHIYO (*calls*). Kotaro!

GENZO *takes out his sword and goes towards* CHIYO.

CHIYO (*calls*). Kotaro let me see you – let me see –

CHIYO *turns to see* GENZO. *He strikes. She dodges, screams and runs away.*

CHIYO. Help!

TONAMI *runs in from behind the screen.* GENZO *chases* CHIYO. *She picks up* KOTARO'S *desk, swings it at* GENZO, *then holds it in front of her as a shield.* GENZO *strikes. His sword hits the desk. One of* CHIYO'S *hands holding the desk is pinning* KOTARO'S *letter to the top. Instantly she knows the writing and lets go of the desk. It drops like a stone: she's left holding the paper in one hand. Instantly she automatically reads the first words.*

CHIYO (*reads*). 'Dearest mother you brought me here to die'!

GENZO *stops with his sword in his hand. He and* CHIYO *stare at each other. Then she reads on.*

CHIYO (*reads*). 'You and papa arranged it last night. Forgive me but your voices were so sad I listened at your door. It gave me great joy to learn that our prince still lived and even greater joy to learn that I would die for him. Perhaps you think I am too young to know what dying is? Your son has the courage to die since his parents have the courage to sacrifice him –'
GENZO. Who is this wonderful boy?
TONAMI. He wanted to finish the letter before Henba came!
CHIYO (*reads*). 'If only I were able to comfort papa when he holds my head. Alas this letter must come into papa's hands too late to lessen his pain at that moment.'
GENZO. Matsuo his father! Today we stood on the floor of a new shrine and didnt know it!

CHIYO (*reads*). 'Forgive your son for not bidding you farewell. I was afraid I would cry and leave you with unhappy memories. I bow to our dear earth before you and papa. When you die and come to the dark city of which we read, a small white figure will hurry from the shadow of the walls and run along the road with open arms – your son Kotaro.'

GENZO. Who are you?

TONAMI. Matsuo's wife.

GENZO. I report that your son's death was spotless.

CHIYO. Tell me! Forgive me – I need comfort now!

GENZO (*reporting formally*). I went to kill him from behind. There was no reason to let him know he was dying: it was not his concern. Commoners die as unknowingly as they live. Life and death arent trials for them. But he heard me and turned. He was waiting.

CHIYO. Thank you, thank you! Tell me! This is what I want to hear! Every detail!

GENZO. He stared at me – a look of respect. For one second I thought – crazily – 'He's studying my face to see what sort of schoolmaster I am – that's why he doesn't see the sword in my hand'. Astonished I looked to see if it was still there! Had I dropped it? No it was in my hand! I saw his face reflected in the blade – suddenly the reflection stretched as if it yelled in pain – distorted! I looked back at him: his face showed iron calm –

CHIYO. Thank you thank you! Tell me!

GENZO. The blade was swinging to his neck: that's why the image was distorted. His neck was reaching to the blade as if a hand was giving me his head!

CHIYO. And then! Tell me! Tell me! This is the moment!

GENZO. The image on the blade flew at the neck – cut into it – as if his spirit ate his living flesh –

CHIYO. Yes! Yes! Its come! His eyes look down inside the darkness in his neck – the head's lifting – a shaft of light –

GENZO. The image flew from the blade –

CHIYO. To paradise!

GENZO. – wiped off it by his blood!

CHIYO. No shout – groan – scream!

GENZO. He stands. Stock still.

CHIYO. O if I was there to kiss this hand as it killed him!

GENZO. His body rigid. Pumps the blood up through the neck –

> GENZO *opens his wrap to show his blood-stained robe.*

CHIYO (*clutching the robe*). Kotaro's blood!

GENZO. He falls to the floor! His blood falls down on him –

CHIYO (*clutching the robe*). I smell him! In his blood! His skin! His breath! My boy! Kotaro! Kotaro!

GENZO. – like dead rain searching for a living sea . . .

CHIYO. Thank you thank you! You are so kind! So kind to this poor mother! I bless the feet that took you to my son!

GENZO. Now I'll give you his body. (*Starts to go.*)

CHIYO. No – dont take his blood away – let me smell his hair – his clothes – his skin –

TONAMI. We'll let you have his body.

> GENZO *and* TONAMI *go behind the screen.* CHIYO *stares at the letter but doesnt read it.* MATSUO *comes in.* CHIYO *still stares at the letter.*

MATSUO (*points*). I sat there – the skin was dead – the scalp moved in my hand – like an animal burrowing – I was gentle, gentle – I must have pulled –

CHIYO. He wrote.

MATSUO. – his mouth fell open – slowly – as if he tried to speak –

CHIYO. Hush. Dont.

MATSUO. – the eyes were empty – but the mouth – puckered –

CHIYO (*half laughing, half angry*). Dont cry. They'll hear. Dont.

MATSUO (*crying*). – like a baby's – and spittle –

CHIYO (*cradles* MATSUO's *head*). No no.

MATSUO (*crying*). – ran down his chin – onto my hand –

CHIYO. You must be happy!

Two masks: CHIYO *laughing and* MATSUO *crying.*

MATSUO. – a red rim on my hand – as if a bucket had stood there – and spittle – bubbles –! Cruel!: all that's left of my human son! – as if a cleaning woman put her bucket there and slopped the water down the side!

CHIYO (*laughing*). He wrote to us! He knew he'd come to die!

MATSUO (*crying*). Knew? How?

CHIYO (*laughing*). He wrote 'be proud'!

MATSUO (*crying*). Wrote? Our clever boy?

CHIYO (*laughing*). Such a letter!

MATSUO (*crying*). Read. Read.

CHIYO (*laughing*). I know it by heart! A mother doesn't have to read that letter twice! Look! The writing! Not one blot – one mistake! Every word spelt right! Send that to the examiners! My son would pass their test!

MATSUO (*crying*). Read.

CHIYO *holds the letter at arm's length and recites without looking at it.* MATSUO *cries and stares unseeingly. From time to time his hand gropes towards the letter.*

CHIYO (*recites*). 'Dearest mother you brought me here to die. You and papa arranged it last night. Forgive me but your voices were so sad I listened at your door –'

MATSUO (*crying*). He said that?

CHIYO (*laughing*). And more! More! Be happy! (*Recites.*) 'It gave me great joy to learn that our prince still lived –'

MATSUO (*crying*). All in his letter!

CHIYO (*recites*). – 'and even greater joy to learn that I would die for him.'

MATSUO (*crying*). Joy! – to die for him! He said that!

CHIYO. Listen! Listen! (*Recites.*) 'Perhaps you think I am

too young to know what dying is' –

MATSUO (*crying*). No no! My son – he knew!

CHIYO (*recites*). 'Your son has the courage to die since his parents have the courage to sacrifice him'.

MATSUO (*crying*). Praises his parents! In his last letter! To spare them! He was older than his parents! Wiser than all the past!

CHIYO (*recites*). 'If only I were able to comfort papa when he holds my head.'

MATSUO (*crying*). Such a son!

CHIYO (*recites*). 'Alas this letter must come into papa's hands too late to lessen his pain at that moment.'

MATSUO. No! No! No more! Its making me live again! I thought I could be dead! I threw my skin over his head like a living shroud! His fingers are inside me! Scrabbling at me! A baby! Beating its rattle on the ground! Playing with bits of earth! Stones! My son is making me! Look – my father's face in the street before I'm born! My father gave birth to my son! I was missed! Missed out!

CHIYO. Listen! His letter! (*Recites.*) 'Forgive your son for not bidding you farewell' –

MATSUO. There's a beast called nothing! It ate me! No no! Who are you? Chiyo! My wife! I know you! Help me! Chiyo!

MATSUO *cries.*

CHIYO (*recites*). . . . 'I was afraid I would cry and leave you with unhappy memories –.'

Slowly the masks change. As CHIYO *recites she begins to weep and* MATSUO *to laugh.*

MATSUO. No no! (*Wipes his face.*) Cry? – he says cry to please you! Give you satisfaction! He knew how to speak to women not just men! No one must cry! The prince – what does he say about the prince? Give me the letter! (*He takes the letter from* CHIYO *and skims through it.*) Hu huh –. (*Laughs as he reads*.) 'Gave me great joy to learn that our prince still lived –'. Always prince – never self! Chiyo dont cry! (*Laughs and reads*.) 'I bow to our dear earth before you and papa –'! I forbid you to cry! You're shaming our son! Prince country parents sacrifice!! Always for others! Give! Give! Give! (*Reads*.) 'When you die and come to that dark city –'! Stop that! Bellowing like a she-cow by its dead calf! Joy! Joy! This letter is a National Monument! A sacred heritage! Look its creased already! (*Smooths letter. Reads*.) 'Even greater joy to learn that I would die for him'! (*Skims*.) Huh-huh! – 'A small white figure will hurry from the shadow –'. The bit that says he couldnt say farewell – he wrote that under your influence! I shouldnt have trusted him to you! You flaunted your despair in front of him like a whore touting for trade at her husband's funeral! Shut up! Is there no shame? He was young – one little flaw cant ruin this letter! It shows he was human! Child's flesh! Not stone! His monuments will be stone! The prince will hold his ashes!

CHIYO *weeps and stammers words from the letter to herself.*
MATSUO *turns away from her.*

MATSUO. Two heads. All that's left of the world. A foot apart. His and mine. Young and old. He tried to speak. A sound. No words. Whisper – use your last breath! Only a sound! – dumb circus animals pulling their chains when the storm's coming! In every hole: eyes nose ears neck – all the feet in a city – creeping – drunken cripples. His tears falling in his blood – I heard them! His tongue curling like a snail on a mountain of salt. (*Imitation*.) 'Aaeeghghii!' What did he try to say? (*To* CHIYO.) Stop it! – your drowning our son's last words in my head! Let me hear them! (*He stifles* CHIYO *with the ritual cloth*.) Damn you! Child hater! Murderess! You she-cattle market! (*Covers his ears*.) Forgive me Kotaro! Daddy will keep the sound in his head! Till he understands! Not let it die! What did you want to say? Tell me! Kotaro help me!

MATSUO *crawls to a corner and covers his ears.*

Its in my head! Eeaarrgh! Yeeargh! (*Pain and frustration together in one sound:*) *Eeiiaarrghgh*! No! No! Still! Control! Break it up! Remember syllables! Ee! Aa! Ee! Oo! Ahh!

CHIYO's *crying is now harsh and dry. Her words sound as if barked by a tired dog.*

CHIYO. The dirt in the gutters will get on my skirt. The brambles tear the stitches. Sparrows fight in the doorway. Flies go round my head – so close I can see the sun shine on the dust on their legs. But he'll never call me or pull my hand. Only his letter. When he wrote it – his arms – the mountains were rolled up on them like sleeves.

MATSUO. Iieeaarrgh . . .

GENZO *and* TONAMI *bring* KOTARO's *body from behind the screen.*

GENZO. Matsuo!

GENZO *and* TONAMI *set* KOTARO's *body on the ground.* CHIYO *and* TONAMI *kneel before it.*

GENZO. Father Matsuo it was my fortune to strike off your son's head. Now it is my honour to bring you his body. I report that his death was spotless.

MATSUO. Yes. Thank you.

GENZO. The gods put our old heroes in the sky. Now the sky over Japan is full of holy stars. Our new heroes are fires in the ground.

MATSUO. When I held his head he spoke.

GENZO. Spoke?

MATSUO. Eeaarrgh . . .

TONAMI (*to* MATSUO). I thought you made the sound.

GENZO. Errii . . .

MATSUO. If he could speak! The wind blows dead soldiers on their shields as if its rocking them in their cradles. There's no wind in this room – I cant even pretend he's speaking . . .

GENZO. I heard the sound. I thought it was the panic knocking on the inside of my skull – it was so clear. Eee-iii!

MATSUO (*bows to* KOTARO). Kotaro tell me! You are a wonder child!

MOTHER (*off*). Schoolmaster!

MATSUO. Eeaarrgh . . . (*Interprets*:) Emperor . . .? *Emperor*! Its not a sentence! A word! (*Distorted*.) Heeh-hher-herr! Proclaim the *emperor*! That's what he said!

GENZO. What?

MATSUO. The emperor's Kotaro's age! Kotaro was ready! Its wrong to hide him here! He'll die here! Proclaim him emperor and fight!

GENZO. Without an army!

MATSUO. With an oracle from the dead!

GENZO. Waste our last chance on –! No army? Led by a boy?

MATSUO. Fight or Kotaro's death is wasted!

GENZO. No! (*Tries to calm* MATSUO.) Our class isnt destroyed. But we need more than dead oracles. Matsuo there are years in front of us when we must be patient. Not act like toothless fanatics!

MATSUO. Now I know why I was a traitor! I understand everything at last! The gods sent me to Henba to learn from him! When he's beaten he fights! A great power comes out of nowhere and he's even stronger! And now he's won he *still* fights! He's raising a new army. Not from the military caste – from rabble!

GENZO. Good! Easier to cut down!

MATSUO. Give him time and he'll turn them into a modern

army! He doesn't need an elite. Just fodder! – human
mud to clog up the battlefields – cling to our wheels!

GENZO. He wont be ready to fight for years. The
administration's a stone round his neck. He needs civil
servants – tax collectors –

MATSUO. Fight him before he gets them! Say Kan Shu is
the emperor come back from the dead! Raise an army of
rumours! Recruit rabble that's too low for Henba! The
gods want chaos! That's how we'll beat Henba! An army
of skeletons armed with bones! The modern world! When
a city's destroyed the rats are let out in the ruins! Genzo
I long to live under a new emperor! Wash off Henba's
slime! The sun will lift me up from the bottom of the sea!
If we do our duty everything else will take its place.

The Proclamation

The MOTHER *comes in.*

MOTHER. Soldiers hev took our lads! Rid off on horse an
the lads gallop after on foot t' be soldiers!

GENZO (*to calm her*). Commoners cant be soldiers –

MOTHER. 'S all changed! Say our lads ont fight for bosses!
Foreigners come t' take our land – so they hev t' fight –
git a share of the loot! Ont true!

GENZO. Let these people mourn in peace.

MOTHER. World comes to its end t'day! Ont no respect t'
stay on your knees an let it pass! (*Goes to the other women.*)
If you're the mothers of kids . . .? (*She holds out her hand
in the gesture she used to* HENBA. *No response.*) Ont goo
empty handed. Cows roarin – old people cryin – dads
cursin! But no lads hollerin in the fields: whole world
seem empty! Why're you so hard? Where'll it end if the
common people fight your wars? Already one of the
chickens hev start t' mew!

CHIYO. Shut up you filthy hag! My son's talking to the gods

while they decide if he'll spend eternity in paradise – and you come and distract him! He's dead because we have to share the world with you animals! You smother us with your mountain of filth!

MOTHER (*wipes hands on the sides of her skirt*). Ont had time for a clean up.

TONAMI (*to* CHIYO). She cant understand. (*To* GENZO.) Get rid of her! She pollutes the dead! His corpse will go to heaven reeking of her breath!

CHIYO. How can she be so cruel!

KAN SHU (*off, behind the screen*). Be quiet! I am Kan Shu son of emperor Ry Shu. The earth shudders and the sky turns away from our enemy's cruelties and the restlessness of the poor. Now there is dissension among our followers. Today I assume the mandate of heaven and proclaim myself emperor.

GENZO, TONAMI *and* MATSUO *crouch before the screen. The* MOTHER *is left alone by the body. She hesitates, half bobs and then straightens.*

MOTHER (*to the screen, as she makes her open-hand gesture*). Mister . . .

KAN SHU (*off*). Genzo and Matsuo, defenders of the throne: drive the barbarian from the land!

MOTHER. Sir – the soldiers hev stole your schoolmates –

KAN SHU (*off*). Matsuo your son's death is amends for your treason. As a token of our grace we will send you Henba's head for identification.

MOTHER (*to herself*). No – waste of time t' ask. (*Looks at* KOTARO.) They kill you, my little ol' chap? Ont git no help here.

KAN SHU (*off*). Cremate your son in the playground. You may bring me his ashes.

MATSUO, GENZO,
CHIYO, TONAMI. } Emperor!

MOTHER *watches the others take out* KOTARO's *body.*

MATSUO. My son's cremated under the new emperor! His letter – we mustnt trouble people with the bits to his mother – take them out. They were put in by Henba's spies. 'Err! Corr! Ah!' There are more sounds in my hand! Write them down. Interpret his messages in times of disaster!

They take KOTARO *out. The* MOTHER *is left alone on stage.*

KAN SHU (*off*). What d'you want?

MOTHER. Git rested. Soon be out your way.

KAN SHU (*off*). The lady left some sweets. You will see them on the floor wrapped in a paper. Place them before the screen.

MOTHER (*to herself*). Ont see the lads no more. Threw their toys in the river an crossed the bridge. Thought mine had more sense! 'Stead he comes up with new rubbish! Say the army'll teach 'un t' do tricks! More likely how t' git blow t' bits! Then who'll pity him an his mates? Other mothers'll cuss us who bore 'em. Who'll pity them? Who'll pity us?

The MOTHER *puts the sweets by the corner of the screen and goes.*

Part Two: The City

[A] Mrs Lewis's Kitchen

A pile of loot on the floor. MRS LEWIS *and her friend* MRS TEBHAM *try on clothes.* MRS TEBHAM *is in a brown dress.* PHIL *watches and tinkers with a radio.*

TEBHAM (*brown dress*). Like this.

LEWIS. That's yours then. (*Hands her a bright formal dress.*) Get this on.

TEBHAM. I couldnt.

LEWIS. Try it.

TEBHAM (*getting out of the brown dress*). No – spend all the time worryin I was markin it.

LEWIS (*to* PHIL). You're not supposed t' look when ladies are changin.

TEBHAM. Too good t' wear round 'ere.

LEWIS. O dont make me cross. Try it before I change me mind.

PHIL. She's a free woman.

TEBHAM (*starts to put on bright dress*). Just t' keep 'er quiet.

LEWIS. I'll manage the buttons.

TEBHAM. I feel awkward.

LEWIS. Its your colour!

TEBHAM. Dont try t' force me when I've got it on, 'cause Im not takin it. (*Stands in dress.*) What d'you think? (*The others stare.*) Told you. Dont even fit.

LEWIS. Not if you stand like that! Look like a sack with a 'ole both ends. Stand straight woman!

TEBHAM (*straightens*). Its not suitable.

LEWIS. That colour gives you the eyes of a young girl!

PHIL *whistles.*

LEWIS. Dont she look a cracker! Right – that's yours!

TEBHAM. I'd never wear it.

LEWIS. Give a party! Pull all the fellas in that!

TEBHAM. I am tempted . . . If I keep it you must let me pay.

LEWIS. 'Ark at 'er!

TEBHAM. 'E's entitled t' somethin: 'e 'ad the risk.

LEWIS. What risk! (*to* PHIL.) You're not takin 'er money!

PHIL. I dont want 'er money!

LEWIS. Grabby little sod. (*Sorts clothes.*) The quality of this! Shouldn't be allowed! (*To* PHIL.) Oi stop oglin or wait out on the landin.

TEBHAM (*brown dress*). Let me stick with this. Least it'd get worn.

LEWIS. You're 'avin both so dont argue. (*Drops the brown dress on* MRS TEBHAM's *pile and hands her a coat.*) Try that. (*Sweater.*) O I love this! 'E's a good lad! Other lads'd come 'ome loaded with stuff for their own back – 'e thinks of his mum! (*She puts her arm round* PHIL's *neck.*)

PHIL. Get off!

LEWIS. Time we treated ourselves. Dont call this thievin. (MRS TEBHAM *starts to remove the bright dress.*) Leave that.

TEBHAM. Wont go with the coat.

LEWIS. You can slip the coat over for size.

TEBHAM (*puts on coat. To* PHIL). You be careful. They make films then pick out the faces.

LEWIS (*suddenly sharp, to* PHIL). You didn't see no one filmin?

PHIL. No.

LEWIS. Dont bring your troubles in 'ere! – Show Mrs T your jacket. And 'e got 'is radio.

PHIL *puts on jacket.*

TEBHAM (*coat*). I could wear this shoppin. (*Takes off coat and puts it on her pile.*) That dress worries me. It'd cost t' 'ave it turned up.

LEWIS. I'll turn it up. (*To* PHIL.) Pass me pins.

PHIL *hands* MRS LEWIS *a tin of pins. She kneels in front of*
MRS TEBHAM *to pin the hem.*

LEWIS (*pinning*). If we're goin round this smart we'll need
   proper shoes.
PHIL (*jacket*). Good?
TEBHAM. Nice. 'S'got a mark.
PHIL (*shrugs*). Drop of oil.
LEWIS (*pins in mouth*). I'll take it t' the cleaners. (*Hem.*) Too
   high – too low?
TEBHAM. Must need me 'ead testin.
PHIL. Take you disco'in in that!
TEBHAM. . . . See?: waste . . .

   Doorbell.

   Police.
LEWIS. Not 'ere! They couldnt pick 'im out the crowd!
PHIL (*going to door*). Not police.
LEWIS (*to* PHIL). Put this away. I'll see t' the door. Stay in
   there.

   They bundle the loot together.

   One of the flats pryin. Not safe t' draw your curtains,
   they take a fancy t' the pattern an nick 'em.

   PHIL *takes the loot out.* MRS LEWIS *opens the front door.*

   (*Off*). I dont believe it!

   MRS LEWIS *follows* BRIAN *in. He wears army uniform.*

TEBHAM. Brian! (*She embraces him.*)
BRIAN. Bin 'ome. Werent in – knew where t' find you! What
   you got on! Im on leave!
TEBHAM. How long? Why didnt you warn me?
BRIAN. Bin posted.
LEWIS. 'Ere?
BRIAN. Permanent.

LEWIS. What for?

PHIL comes in. He has taken off the jacket.

PHIL. Bri!

They exchange greetings.

LEWIS. 'E's posted 'ere!
PHIL. 'Ere?
BRIAN. The riots.
LEWIS. What riots! No riots 'less you lot come an start 'em!
Few kids let off steam and they send the bloody army?
My Phil was up there, so that's 'ow 'armless it was!
BRIAN (*to* MRS TEBHAM – *the bright dress*). That come from
there?
TEBHAM (*realises she's wearing the bright dress*). O. (*She starts
to take it off.*)
LEWIS. Yeh – that's what the army's for: not 'elp us – save
their shops! (*To* MRS TEBHAM.) Dont you dare take it
off!
TEBHAM. Pins catchin.
LEWIS. Looks a blasted sight better on you than some lanky
cow can afford their prices! Begrudges 'is own mother a
pretty dress!
BRIAN (*shrugs*). I never asked t' be posted!
LEWIS. Law forced the crowd up against the window – it
broke – they stampede – an the clothes are left all over
the road. 'E supposed t' stand an watch 'em trampled in
the glass? Wouldnt've bin there long if your crowd'd bin
around!
PHIL. Let 'im alone.
LEWIS (*folding the bright dress*). Suppose this means we dont
get our new shoes. (*To* PHIL.) Fetch 'er things. (*To* MRS
TEBHAM.) Leave your nice dress.

PHIL goes out.

LEWIS. You'd better 'ave some tea or somethin. Now you're

'ere. Its not lifted.

PHIL (*off*). Lay off!

LEWIS (*calls to* PHIL). Well! Im allowed t' pull 'is leg! 'Is uniform dont scare me. I knew 'im when 'e couldnt keep 'is nappies dry.

PHIL *comes back with a pile of clothes.*

BRIAN (*starts to go. To* MRS TEBHAM). Okay? – I only got a twelve hour pass.

TEBHAM. I thought you was stoppin!

BRIANB. Confined t' barracks 'cept on duty. Got the pass cause Im local. (*They stare at him. He shrugs.*) Uniform – provocation – walkin target . . .

PHIL. How many's the army sent?

BRIAN. Two regiments. Support – armour – all the gubbins.

PHIL. Bloody 'ell!

LEWIS. Makes us feel like the enemy!

BRIAN. It'll quieten down now we're 'ere.

TEBHAM. Better go.

BRIAN. Cheerio.

PHIL. See yer!

MRS TEBHAM *and* BRIAN *go.*

LEWIS. Left some of this at your girl's?

PHIL. Yeh.

LEWIS. Tell 'er not t' wear it in the street for a while.

They go.

[B] Padre's Office

PADRE *and* OFFICER.

PADRE. Sit you down. What's your problem?

OFFICER. For two month's I've been waiting for the rioters to act. So far they've only wounded twenty-nine of my men – though to be fair two of them had to be invalided out. Now at last a bit of luck!: a dead policeman.

PADRE. I read the lesson at the funeral.

OFFICER. I sold his killers the gun.

PADRE. Ah – a confession.

OFFICER. No I did it on orders.

PADRE. On orders!

OFFICER. The rioters will get guns. If they get them from us we'll know what they're armed with.

PADRE. But what am I to think at the next military funeral!

OFFICER. We must provoke them into using force before they're ready. Then fewer soldiers will die. The policeman's death is a help, but we need a dead soldier. Then we'd be allowed street searches, mass arrests, internment without trial, new weapons – the whole situation would improve. The men need a dead soldier too. Fighting people who speak your own language isnt easy. A dead soldier would do wonders for morale. The young men would go on the rampage. As it is, they sit and twiddle their thumbs – all for the lack of one dead soldier.

PADRE. God will call him in his good time.

OFFICER. God's good time is often a bad time for everyone else. The rioters are becoming organised. I've arranged to meet their representative to improve the gun-running. It'll be a hair-trigger confrontation. If one small thing goes wrong they'll panic and open fire – and there's the dead soldier. We agreed to wear a white tie to identify ourselves. Instead, it will be black! That's all it needs: they'll shoot!

PADRE. You'll make that sacrifice! My son we scorn modern youth! Yet you're making the supreme sacrifice as if the past had never left us! I struggled to keep the faith! Im not insulting the army, but barrack life isn't the place to –

OFFICER. Im doing this on my own initiative.

PADRE. My son we'll miss you – the men as well. And think! – only I shall know your secret! My funeral oration will be magnificent! No no I must forgo that pleasure – be calm, simple – 'another soldier has done his duty in the field'. One day I shall speak out! Till then – silence. You have your trial, I have mine. But I mustnt depress you: let's make arrangements for your funeral. The hymns in your honour! The flowers! – from the hothouses of the mighty to humble allotment greenhouses! Choose the hymns carefully! Many sound fine on an organ that are lost on a brass band. So often I've felt how let down the deceased would be if they heard them. Alas! the next of kin are left to bear that burden alone. I beg you not to spoil their occasion. Of course the choice is yours, but *Behold the Awful Dawning Breaks* has a fine counterme-lody on the tuba if the bandsman is up to it.

OFFICER. It will be televised.

PADRE. What a pity there is no widow! But you've left it too late to do anything about that. Dying warriors have been married from hospital beds, but we can hardly expect a young English bride to walk up the aisle to be greeted by a coffin – even in these days of novelty. Should she wear white or black? Should one play *The Dead March from Saul* or *Here Come the Bride*? One couldnt please both families. The organist would resign in a tantrum and they're impossible to replace. No no I cannot consider it. Besides dissensions at the wedding ceremony would not augur well for the future of a marriage already so heavily burdened in other respects. Of course your honeymoon would have been spent in paradise (and how many can say as much?) but you'd have been on your own. Well at least you can provide loving parents and the army will provide old comrades, a band, a salvo over the open grave –

OFFICER. I shall command the gun party.

PADRE. On a tape machine? I know of nothing against it but I shall need the bishop's ruling. We must avoid an exhumation. The methodists would fuss. The ecumenical movement affects us all in ways we have not forseen. Mankind is frail! Next of kin seem to regard exhumation as a mark of distinction. It brings out their one-upmanship. Let it take hold and they're digging up bodies all over the place. One could not venture out of one's door at night for fear of falling into a hole. The dead are risen and we're confined to our kitchens! Not that I want to deny your last wish – if such it be. A tape machine! Your last command might issue from the grave itself! Thousands of souls saved by –! But forgive me! – you've turned your back on the frivolities of this world –

OFFICER. Im not going to die.

PADRE. Not die? But you gave your word – to a padre!

OFFICER. I cant die. It would be dereliction of duty. The soldier's death will set the city ablaze. I cant desert my men when they need me most. I see civil war.

PADRE. But this is wonderful! Forgive me – when you spoke of sacrifice, I thought 'we have a right to expect sacrifice from an officer'! But now you tell me a common private, a man of the masses, the lowest of the low, vermin, scum, a squalid blemish on society's face – snatched from the gutter by the army, dressed in khaki, taught to say 'country' and 'duty' like a babe saying 'ma' and 'pa' – steps forth from the ranks and cries 'Take me! I claim my right to be this sacrifice!' Your example inspired this outcast. How else could the idea have got into his thick head?

OFFICER. A private's death does far more good than an officer's. Their mother's make better TV. An officer's lady cant be seen behind her veil.

PADRE. True! – it might be a sheet on a parrot cage. I've seen privates' mothers stagger up to the open grave as if its just gone closing time. Wives tearing their hair – you'd think they'd had to leave bingo when they only needed one number for a winning line. The whole nation benefits! But the deceased's mother mustnt know our secret! She could've sold it to the papers! She'd tear her hair out if she knew the money she was losing! We must deny her the consolation. She too must make her sacrifice. And the army will give her a medal to fondle. Those distinguished initials that look so moving after a private's name, as if a costermonger were selling caviar from a whelk stall. (*Announcing.*) Private – (*Stops.*) Who is he?

OFFICER. The rioters may know me from earlier dealings. It has to be someone who'll pass for me. Fortunately there's a Private Tebham.

PADRE. Tebham? (*Shrugs.*) He must be a christian to make this sacrifice.

OFFICER. He doesnt know.

PADRE. Not know he – ? (*Vaguely mimes shooting a starting pistol into the air.*)

OFFICER. No.

PADRE. But you've ruined it again!

OFFICER. Our soldiers are well trained but we cant expect too much. A man'll go into any danger as long as there's a sporting chance the bullets will go into his buddies and not him. Soldiers are gamblers. When a gambler's desperate he puts his shirt on an outsider: the difference is the soldier puts his skin.

PADRE. You promised me a sacrifice!

OFFICER. I promised you a body.

PADRE. Its not the same.

OFFICER. Millions are sacrificed in war and they dont know. God doesn't mind. I spare Tebham the great burden of *knowing*. I carry his cross for him.

PADRE. Im confused. Who am I to pray for at the funeral?

OFFICER. All of us.

PADRE. How can I? Tebham might be watching! I'd feel as if I was in an argument and using 'amen' as a debating point. You need a better leg to stand on by the open grave. Couldnt you drop him a hint?

OFFICER. He doesnt know why he was born in one street and I in another. Why I went to Harrow and he went to Puddle Row. What the government's up to. Or the stock exchange. In fact no one told him what he's been doing all his life. If you told him now he'd die of shock before he could get to the people who're going to kill him. *I* dont know what *I'm* doing. But I cant let that stop me. If I did there'd be chaos. Frankly I dont even know if its right to kill him. Its the best I can think of. But I'm not god. I might be wrong. Then the thing would drag on till many more are dead – and he'd be one of them. Its cruel to ask too much of people. Let them jump when I tell them and let me worry where they land.

PADRE. Why've you told me this?

OFFICER. I have a spiritual crisis padre: I need someone to know how clever I am. But I dont believe in god, so there's no one watching. You know the story of the emperor's new clothes. Well now the emperor's clothed and the mob's naked. They think they own the world but its still ours. If they found out they'd kill us. That's why we're stiff and cold: we pretend to be dead.

PADRE. Try the MO.

OFFICER. No padre. When you pretend to be dead, you die. I am the walking dead.

PADRE. Ah yes the MO couldnt cope.

OFFICER. Im a candle that shines because it burns at both ends.

PADRE. In the age of electricity?

OFFICER. I clean my teeth but I still think they're yellow. My buttons are polished. I get my tunics from Saville Row – but I put them on and feel like a tramp. The skin's flaking on my Sam Brown. I drag the world round on my heels like a ball of mud.

PADRE. Change your batman. Can I speak to – (*Forgets name.*) He's going to be sacrificed but doesnt know!

OFFICER. Tebham. I'll send him to you.

PADRE (*wheedles*). Couldnt he be crippled? Im good with penitents in wheelchairs. I'd sit with him for hours. Nothing would be too much trouble – provided he oiled the wheels.

OFFICER. No. Wheelchair heroes are a menace.

PADRE. Alas yes! If royalty arent bobbing up all the time they brood and end up writing pamphlets. Then the military police have to arrange an accident with the brakes.

The OFFICER *goes.*

[C] Same – Later

KAN SHU *comes in in Japanese Imperial regalia. He bows to the audience.*

KAN SHU. Emperor Kan Shu. The sweets were inferior.

BRIAN *comes on. No one in the scene is aware of* KAN SHU *– he is invisible.* BRIAN *slumps on a chair downstage, staring ahead with his rifle on the ground beside him.* KAN SHU *goes to* BRIAN, *picks up his rifle, walks to the side and releases the safety catch. The* PADRE *comes from his office.* KAN SHU *aims at* BRIAN. BRIAN *springs to attention.*

PADRE. Tebham?

BRIAN. Sir.

PADRE. Your company commander's spoken to you.

BRIAN. Sir.

PADRE. You'll undertake the mission?

BRIAN. Sir.

KAN SHU *shoots* BRIAN.

PADRE. Stand at ease.

BRIAN *stands at ease.* KAN SHU *goes to* BRIAN *and puts the rifle beside him on the floor.*

PADRE. You realise your danger? You stand face to face with an enemy who speaks your language and walks your streets but inhabits another world. He might be from Japan. Dont trust him.

BRIAN. Sir.

KAN SHU *goes out.*

PADRE (*turning*). My office is quieter. (BRIAN *starts to follow him.*) Rifle, Tebham – its the infantryman's best friend.

BRIAN *goes back for his rifle and follows the* PADRE *into his office.*

PADRE. Sit you down.

BRIAN *sits.*

PADRE. Tebham when did you last think of the fiery pit?

BRIAN. Dont know sir.

PADRE. Before you undertake this mission there are many things you should think of. D'you pray?

BRIAN. Sorry sir.

PADRE. Unwise Tebham. None of us knows when we're in need of prayer.

BRIAN. Dont worry about me sir: I can take care of myself.

PADRE. Dont boast Tebham. You're dealing with lunatics. They might have you shot.

BRIAN. They've got more sense sir. They want guns. Shoot squaddies anytime.

PADRE. Tebham – god lends each of us a soul to take care of and we owe it to him not to be too trusting. You dont make my task easy! Its all lager and ladies of the street! And when it comes to your funeral I know I've failed. Your pain is past – I still have to pray for your soul when I know the task is hopeless! Can you imagine the torment of that?: no. In one afternoon I endure all the suffering you're allowed to spread out over eternity! Tebham please pay attention.

BRIAN. Sir.

PADRE. Every night my prayers went unheard. Yet no cry of despair broke from my lips like a lonely sergeant-major shouting at an empty parade ground. Till last night! – when my prayers were answered!

BRIAN. Is everything all right sir? My mother – isnt –?

PADRE. Your mother?

BRIAN. Is she all right?

PADRE. Of course she's all right. As far as I know. I expect she's at Bingo or asleep. Isnt that how the mothers of this city pass their time? She didnt spend last night on her knees! Well she may have missed the jackpot! Last night I heard god speak! O not to me! Such are the ways of god! – to humble the mighty of rank by letting them hear him talk to a common uncouth private: you Tebham! Share god's bounty with me! I am a padre! Let me hear again the words god spoke to you.

BRIAN. What did he say sir?

PADRE. Didnt you hear?

BRIAN. No sir.

PADRE. Not one word?

BRIAN. Perhaps the radio was too loud.

PADRE (*aside*). I suppose its possible he forgot? (*Smacks his brow with his palm.*) Stupid! Stupid! You have no theological grounding so you heard after your *own* fashion! God sent a sign? The curtain fluttered in the window?

BRIAN. Dont have curtains in barracks.

PADRE. Well – a dream?

BRIAN. Had a few beers in the NAAFI. Dont dream when Im a bit . . .

PADRE. Then what am I to think? Has pride misled me again? (*Clasps hands prayerfully.*) O lord you ask much – sift my weakness through and through – and now – is it possible? – am I thy vessel? – to speak like the prophets of old? Yes! Yes! He speaks in my mouth! Arise! Gird up thy loins and go!

BRIAN. Shall I leave sir?

PADRE. Yes! You understand? Yes Tebham! Run fleetfoot to your Golgotha! – the bones will crack underfoot like pistol shots and make you feel at home. Leave! Go forth! Meet thy enemy! – and be shot!

BRIAN (*half rising*). Yes sir rightie-o will that be all sir?

PADRE. Yes! – that will do! – at any rate for the moment. Arise! Go forth! Be shot! (*Looks at* BRIAN.) You do understand what the lord wants Tebham? He sends you forth to be shot!

BRIAN. O dont worry about me sir: I can take care of myself.

PADRE. Dont keep saying I can take care of myself! God doesnt want you to take care of yourself! He wants you to be shot! How can I put it to you? The wheels turn – the great engine shudders – and you are caught up. Is that clearer?

BRIAN. Sorry sir – if I can do anythin t' oblige – only too willin t' –

PADRE. Tebham there is a plot to have you shot. Is *that* plain enough?

BRIAN. You're tryin t' tell me somethin sir.

PADRE. Dear god must I show you your dead body before you know your days are numbered?

BRIAN. You want me t' flog raffle tickets for Army Orphans?

PADRE. God in heaven! – beer and videos have addled his brain! To think the defence of this poor realm is entrusted to his hands! (*Pause.*) Of course when I say plot I dont mean plot. That's egging the pudding as your mother would say. (I see you're fond of your mother – at least we may credit you with filial piety however limited your grasp of military intelligence.) There is no plot. God doesnt want you to be shot. How shall I put it? *I* want you to be shot. No again I phrase it clumsily! I want you to *choose* to be shot! Got it! – I knew I would if I persevered.

BRIAN. Shot sir?

Slight pause.

PADRE. . . . (*Looks up.*) Forgive me Tebham: I was following my train of thought. Indulging an idle fancy. You spoke?

BRIAN. You want me to be shot sir?

PADRE. You sound surprised! Surely its clear why god sent me to you? He saw your weak grasp of the transcendental and sent me as his mouthpiece. Arise – go to your meeting – antagonize the enemy – (I believe a black tie is to be worn?) – and be shot! Great heavens Tebham our fathers died for us! – shall we refuse the torch? I give you salvation of the soul! Dress you in the raiment of sacrifice! – the white khaki of the lord! Go in the dignity of man! Say yes to the lord! Arise! Go forth! Be shot! With a bullet! – Is that clear Tebham? (*Points.*) In the head. (*Chest.*) Or here. (*Stomach.*) Or here. I leave the details of your martyrdom to you and your assailants.

BRIAN. Permission to leave sir.

PADRE. No!

BRIAN. You're not well.

PADRE. Yes yes its so easy: anything beyond the narrow limits of your little minds – and 'you're not well'! D'you think a padre doesnt know when god speaks? I could have you court-martialled for refusing god's command! O I've heard it all so often! A minor peccadillo with a rattle – the first insouciance of blossoming youth – and nanny said 'you're noo the well'! (She had a Scottish accent.) At school classmates I'd called chums turned on me and said 'you're not well'! Even in theological college when I found them puffing their poisonous gaspers in the gardener's shed and denounced them to the dean: 'you're not well'! (*Tries again.*) Is it that the idea is new to you? This chance may never come again. It hurts me to see you throw it away. Your funeral will be far more

impressive than a person in your station has a right to
expect. Can you seriously say your life is a more
attractive alternative? Year after weary year – no job,
dole, debts, a leaking roof, screaming kids, ageing and
falling apart in a vandalised city, in dread of nuclear
armageddon (fry up) – I shudder at what lies before you!
– when all the time you might be sleeping at peace in your
grave and I might be leading pilgrims to pray at its side.
Tebham Tebham how have we failed you? Surely no sane
man could hesitate when the choice is so clear? – Your
mother would get a pension. I hope that show of filial
devotion was not a flash in the pan!

BRIAN. Permission to go sir.

PADRE. Yes yes go! No! – sit! Could I have said something
– out of place? (*Realisation: claps head with hands*.) O fool!
Fool! Yes humble me with that pitiless gaze! I've
misjudged you! I said *take*! Take the medal – take the
pension – take the glory – wallow in your funeral! Take!
Take! Take! And your word is *give*! I see it all! (Thank
you lord for showing me the way!) Yes Tebham prostrate
yourself in the dust: *there* you are at home! You'd rather
be blown to human confetti than burden your comrades
with the labour of burying you! Give for others! For the
regiment – the country – for nothing!

BRIAN. You're mad.

PADRE. Ah. Mad. We've come to that. (*Reflects, then:*) No.
Mad is a good word – indeed a favourite of mine. But I
have no right to claim it. I am too lazy. I see your gaze
is the Gorgon's stare. Betrayed, again I stand alone.
(*Pause.*) Tebham in – I wont keep you much longer – my
zeal for your welfare my approach – lacked finesse. The
mot juste I think. Forgive me. How hard it is to don the
cloth in uniform! The sniggers. Jibes. O the officers are
no better. D'you smoke?

BRIAN. No.

PADRE (*takes out cigarettes and smokes*). I only do it to put the

men at ease. Sure? – they're Sobranie cocktails. Tebham
– I find it humiliating to ask – but this is a private chin-
wag – I'd be grateful if you didnt speak of this to anyone?
(*Exhales.*) Of course if you feel its your duty – (*Shrugs.*)
When d'you go on your mission?

BRIAN. T'morrow.

PADRE. Be silent till the day after tomorrow. Take a tip
from you spiritual adviser. You need time to reflect on
your future.

BRIAN. Yessir.

PADRE. O if you knew the crosses I bear. I – when I joined
the regiment I volunteered – you know how keen one is
when the ink's wet on one's commission – and perhaps
there was a touch of pride in it? – a wish to ingratiate? –
(are you sure you wont have a cigarette?) – I volunteered
to look after the mess wine money. The auditors couldnt
add it up. Dont even recall the sum. Of course I've lived
it down. Almost paid off the last few thous – (*Stops.*) A
weary life of scrimp and save. Couldnt even afford a hair
shirt – just a few cigarettes. I dont want that reopened.
Not that they'd take your word against an officer's.

BRIAN. Could you get me off route marches for six months
sir?

PADRE. If I had your assurance you'd be gainfully
employed. Perhaps you're learning French?

BRIAN. Sir.

PADRE. Useful as we're in NATO. (*Stands.*) Sorry to kick
you out. (A Gorgon is a figure in Greek mythology.) You
wont take it amiss if I pray for you.

BRIAN (*going*). Sir.

PADRE. Rifle, Tebham.

BRIAN *comes back, picks up his rifle and goes.* PADRE *sits
at desk. He beats his cap against the side of his shin and buries
his head in his arm.*

PADRE. Fool. Fool. Fool. You must control it! This absurd

obsession – crazy excess – this faith that drives you into –. It'll land you in trouble one day my lad. (*A great sob shakes him.*)

[D] Street

BRIAN *comes on in civvies. He takes a black tie from his pocket and looks round.*

BRIAN (*under his breath*). Jees.
PADRE (*off*). A word.
BRIAN. 'Op it sir.

PADRE *comes on.*

PADRE. Apropos our *tête-à-tête* –
BRIAN. You've got to go sir.
PADRE. – which was private –
BRIAN. Please sir.
PADRE. So if the military police are snooping round –
BRIAN. Sir you'll drop me in the shit!
PADRE. – they're run by the KGB. Dont say shit Tebham. We never know when we're going to meet our maker. What if that were were your last word? God wouldnt know whether it was your comment on this world or the next – neither would promise much for your future! (*Produces a paper.*) A paper! Of course I trust your word but you cant be too careful with the military police. Sign. (*Reads.*) 'I freely affirm that at no time has any officer of the corps of padres offered me a share in the mess wine money –'
BRIAN. Please sir!
PADRE. – 'or halfprice bibles donated for the eastern bloc –'
BRIAN. Piss off!
PADRE. I shall not stay to hear the cloth insulted. (*Goes. Stops.*) Your initials? It may be your last chance to do the good deed that will see you all right for the rest of eternity.

(*No response.*) Im not a prophet but I wouldnt be surprised if you came to a bad end.

PADRE *goes out.*

BRIAN. Hate ties. If I knew there was a tie in it I'd've said no.

BRIAN *puts on the tie.* PHIL *comes on behind him wearing a white tie and the looted jacket – his hand in one of the pockets.*

PHIL (*password*). Devonshire strawberries are very cheap for the month of –

BRIAN *turns to him.* PHIL *automatically pulls the gun from his pocket and aims: he shoots wide. They stare at each other.*

PHIL. You! Chriss!

PHIL *points the pistol at the black tie.* BRIAN *cowers and covers his head with his arms.*

BRIAN. Eeeaarrgh!
PHIL. Black tie! Black tie! Black tie!
BRIAN. They told me to wear a –
PHIL (*spinning round to search frantically*). Quick!
BRIAN. What?
PHIL. They 'eard the shot!

PHIL *tugs* BRIAN – *they run off together. The* PADRE *comes on wearing a white surplice and reading from the prayer book.*

PADRE (*reads*). 'Man that is born of woman hath but a short time to live and is full of misery. He cometh –' (*Stops.*) Someone's snaffled the body! (*Looks round.*) No blood? But I heard the –. O god its a miracle! At last! He's gone up to heaven! (*He is about to throw himself onto his knees – he notices a mark on the ground.*) What's this? Blood? No! No! (*Scrapes out the patch with his shoe.*) Not his blood! There was a miracle! That's been there for weeks! Blood all over the city! The sanitary department's a disgrace!

(*Realises.*) Ah its dogshit! – thank you Lord! – I saw him
go straight up to heaven – there was a blob of chewing
gum on his boot! My miracle! I'll get promoted! Be in
charge of the bishop's wine money!

The PADRE *goes out.*

[E] Canal Path

PHIL *and* BRIAN.

PHIL (*controlled*). Saw the black tie. Gun out. Squeeze – look
up – face: you. Couldnt stop the trigger – jerked wide.

BRIAN. Why d'you join that mob?

PHIL. I was in a store. Riot outside. Ground floor empty.
Tailor's dummy on the stairs. Evenin jacket. Tried it on!
Another dummy in the mirror: by the rails. Got a leather
jacket. Went over. Bent down. Not a dummy: bloke tryin
it on – shot in the stomach. I was in an evenin jacket
strippin a corpse an there's a war goin on in the street.
You cant live like that. *I'm* against lootin – not the lot
who own the stuff! You loot it an duck through the streets
dodgin the bullets – or slave your gut out every day till
yer can afford t' buy it an take it 'ome in the bus. What's
worse? – lootin from them or workin for them? Working
for them! – so they can loot us! That's the crime – an it
screws up all the rest! You're not 'ere t' stop us lootin –
you're 'ere because *we* want *our* lives.

BRIAN. Yeh – well. *I'll* 'ave a few things t' say when I get
back t' –

PHIL. You cant go back.

BRIAN. What?

PHIL. I dont know what they're up to but you're supposed
t' be dead. Worse now you know! They'll *ave* t' get you!

BRIAN. The bastards! Yeh! – sent me straight in! Not a
chance! I wouldn't go back if I could!

PHIL (*canal*). Fish live in that muck. Could've wore the evenin jacket fishin.

Pause. PHIL *takes a gun from his pocket.*

BRIAN (*turning away*). Dont Phil –

PHIL (*jerks gun to stop* BRIAN *turning*). 'Ave to – when you think it over.

BRIAN. No! Said I wont go back! Join you! Im trained! I can fight!

PHIL. 'He's okay – bloke next door – went t' school t'gether'. What's 'e been doin since? 'Joined the army – so okay they send 'im on special missions'.

BRIAN. Yeh – all right. So you dont know me. I go on the run.

PHIL. You know *me*! What if they pick you up? Dont 'even 'ave t' twist your balls anymore – give you a drug, plug a wire in your 'ead.

BRIAN. No!

PHIL. Or you're fed up bein on the run – want a meal or a hand-out – so you roll up t' the guard'ouse. Or you fancy yourself a hero with a medal –

BRIAN. No – its not like that! I joined the army t' get shot of this dump! Work – bit of dough, bit of life – before Im too clapped out t' use it!

PHIL. – or we blow your buddies up an you lose your rag (you're a good natured soul) – or you're stoned out of your mind and you want a fix – so you turn yourself in. Or you just miss the CO's smile. I dont know. Up to you. You know what's in your head. But we're not safe with you on the streets. Its not my neck. There's the others. We're organised now. I risk all that because we came from the same block? Never. – You got us into this mess. You think of a better way out.

BRIAN. You wont kill him. You'd've done it – not sat there! That's talk t' put it off.

PHIL. I dont do it for kicks.

BRIAN. I know when its real. Tell from the eyes. You dont even know 'ow t' use it! You missed once already!

PHIL. Im not trained t' make it easy. I dont go round in a uniform paid t' shoot mates. Dont gloat. When I look at you – I'd enjoy doin it! You're worse than that lot. They're looking after themselves – its their money, their jobs, their loot, their world – they own it! – its sense t' them! What're you lookin after? – your pig-ignorance – yes-sir-no-sir – the privilege of dressin up in their uniform an bootin your own people like a thug! Look·at you! You're not even a tailor's dummy! You *should* be shot! Like hosin shit off the street! Suppose there was no black tie? By now you'd be sellin me – my girl – people you dont even know! *You're not fit to live!* (*Collapses: he keeps gun aimed but lowers his head.*) Piss off.

BRIAN. Dont Phil – for chriss sake dont – its all right – *dont look like that* – you're not shoppin your mates. I've learned somethin. Jesus I must 'ave – 'avent I? I give you my word I wont –

PHIL. I dont want to know. I didnt mean all – that rubbish. (*Silence.*) I've got to go on the run.

BRIAN. Why?

PHIL. We cant be in the same city. Not safe.

BRIAN. I told you: I wont split on you even if they –

PHIL. Yeh you told me. An I told you what I thought of it. (*Slight pause.*) I go, then I dont 'ave t' worry. Blab or 'old your lip: 's no difference. Funny! – we grew up round 'ere – now as long as one of us is alive you stood a whole bloody army between us!

BRIAN. Up to you. What else can I do?

PHIL. There is somethin.

BRIAN. What?

PHIL. Give me this afternoon. We put you in a hood an drove you round in a van – then you got out – they must've trained you t' get out of tight corners – think of somethin. Dont go back till t'night. You can keep your word one afternoon: Im not asking you t' keep it your whole life.

BRIAN. What'll you do?

PHIL. Go home.

BRIAN. If you go on the run I'll look after your old lady as if she was me own.

PHIL. Okay? – till its dark. I can watch telly. Chat. Look out the window. Afterwards she'll know I came to say goodbye – didnt just run off. You know how she is.

BRIAN. You said if I went back they'd shoot me.

PHIL. Sell yourself. They mixed you up in somethin – go in deeper. That's your way out. Go back. You tell them you know they're killers: they know you'll graft for their money. Creates trust both sides. Roll in the shit. Im not just thinking of your own welfare. Its best if *you* do it, not one of their class. From time t' time you'll look in the mirror and puke – then you might pass some duff gen or send one of their trucks over a landmine. That's the best you can do for us now: roll in their shit.

BRIAN. Okay: shoot me.

PHIL. Leave it. Its not a game.

BRIAN. Shoot me!

PHIL. What d'you –! I made my decision! Get one of your mates t' shoot you! They're not so squeamish! Its true: if I was like them I wouldnt be sittin 'ere! Right now I 'ate you too much t' even touch your face, let alone lift my 'and t' shoot you . . .! Go away. Leave me alone. Piss off you bastard! You landed me in this! . . . You took me t' pieces. Now d'you want t' play with the bits? *Shove off*! (*Calms down.*) All right. Its okay. Im okay. You're okay. Just get yourself through this mess.

BRIAN. Shoot me. What else can we do? Why did you say all that! Sell myself? – t' that mob! – you dont know what sort of animals they keep! Shoot me! Your mates'll be safe! You'll be 'ere when the real fightin starts! Its your postin! – You put your life on the line: I can put mine! I said I'd join you. You wouldnt 'ave that. Joke of the year!

Sneered! All right: I can do this! Shoot me Phil! Its your job!

PHIL. No – no – no – we mustnt, dont let – they're twistin us round each other's necks like ropes! I'll go. The struggles goin on everywhere, I can join it wherever I am. You want t' do somethin, you'll find somethin. Let's stop now – Im going.

BRIAN. Shoot me! Please! Please!

PHIL. Why?

BRIAN. Shoot me!

PHIL. Why?

BRIAN. For five minutes! For tea with your mother! For a look out the window! Even I'm worth that! Now shoot me!

PHIL (*offering gun*). Shoot yourself: there's the gun. (*Puts gun on floor.*)

BRIAN. I cant. I've seen it. I know what happens. You do it. 'Elp me. Why must we drag it out? Why didn't you shoot me before? The gun was ready. It would've been easy then! I'd be dead! It would've done you good! – trained you for the fight! Kill me! You promised! Look I'll 'old the gun against my 'ead for you! You pull the trigger!

PHIL. Please – it dont matter – we can give ourselves time – learn t' think. (*Walks away.*) Wont it be like that – sometime – when we dont 'ave t' talk t' each other like this? (*Stops.*) We'll run for it t'gether – t' different cities –

BRIAN. No – its gone – I missed the chance – before I joined the khaki. I cant go back. We 'ave t' 'elp each other in a new way now. I cant leave this path alive.

PHIL. I said all that – I was scared – I didnt –

BRIAN. Dont lie! You see, its gone: they've taken it away! You're insulting yourself t' 'elp me! You said it so clearly! The truth for once! Dont lose your 'ead, dont spoil it! It was good t' listen to! – I cant risk stayin alive. Go back? – that mad'ouse?: they sent me out t' be shot! On the run?

– you stopped that too: I'd roll up t' the guard'ouse – pat on the back – CO's smile – take their cash – pissed out of me 'ead – open me mouth – spew up anythin they want – the sky's pink – the sun's black – an if you dont shoot me I'll name the lot – my mother – yours – my mates – anyone – not in five minutes – before they can start the clock! I'll see you dead! – an go down so deep and come to you under all the rest – they'll bury you under the lowest of the low – and shit on your grave – because you wasnt fit to live! – or fit to fight! – for anyone! – because you're sorry for your mate – you shared the streets with! . . . Now shoot!

PHIL. No.

BRIAN *dives for the gun, struggles with* PHIL *for it, gets it, walks away and turns to face* PHIL. *He holds the gun in front of his chest with the barrel pointing up at his own face.*

BRIAN. Look at me! This face! Look! One quiver? Where? Point? Cant! Not one! And Im afraid! – Now see what I can do when Im pushed! This is who I am! And dont forget it! Im their enemy!

He crouches over the gun and shoots himself in the stomach. Groans quietly, falls onto his back and rocks from side to side with his knees up. PHIL *goes towards him.*

PHIL. The bloody – I cant –. (*For a moment he tries to stop* BRIAN *rocking but cant.*) Look at – look – the size of the 'ole in 'is – you stupid sod!

PHIL *turns to go, stops, takes off his jacket and covers* BRIAN *with it. He goes out.*

BRIAN *stops rocking with his body angled to one side. Dead.*

[F] Police Station

MRS LEWIS *and* MRS TEBHAM *in street clothes. They talk quietly.*

LEWIS. Course its 'im! Why'd else they bring me 'ere? Never stays out all night and not say.

TEBHAM. What about 'is girl?

LEWIS. Goin round 'er's when the police came.

TEBHAM. Could be somethin entirely –

LEWIS. Then where was 'e all night – lyin bleedin in some gutter?

TEBHAM. Im not listening t' that rubbish.

LEWIS. Thank god I stopped 'im bringin that stuff in the 'ouse! Riskin my neck on that trash!

TEBHAM. You chucked it out?

LEWIS. Yes – found some burned 'ouse.

TEBHAM. They'll search the 'ole flats if they're suspicious.

LEWIS. You're all right?

TEBHAM (*nods*). In the park.

LEWIS. Could've caught 'im floggin it in the street.

TEBHAM. No – 'e said he never sold it for –

LEWIS. Cant believe anythin they tell you that age! – You could slip out an phone.

TEBHAM. Who?

LEWIS. Brian.

TEBHAM. Why?

LEWIS. 'E'll know where the fightin was – could've seen Phil.

TEBHAM. Fightin everywhere. 'Ow could 'e pick 'im out?

LEWIS. Try. (*Money.*) There's the money. Find a box in the street – not downstairs in the –

TEBHAM. It'd only put ideas in their 'eads if –

LEWIS. Go through the welfare. Say its compassionate.

TEBHAM. We 'ave t' wait.

LEWIS. At least try!

TEBHAM. Barracks wouldnt put me through.

LEWIS. You think 'e's dead.

TEBHAM. I told you I'm not listen t' that rubbish. We'll go round 'is girl's. She can say 'e spent the night there. If they find any –

A POLICEMAN *comes in with a white plastic bag.*

POLICEMAN. Sorry. Packed out there. Double time but we cant keep up. (*He takes the jacket from the white plastic bag and shows it to* MRS LEWIS.) Know this?

LEWIS. Im not sure.

POLICEMAN. You know if you've seen it. Distinctive article.

LEWIS (*looks at* MRS TEBHAM). All their stuff looks alike. Always buying. Too much money.

TEBHAM. Where d'you get it?

POLICEMAN. What's it matter if its not her's?

TEBHAM. Could jog 'er memory.

LEWIS. My lad's got a wardrobe full of jackets. 'E 'ad one similar.

POLICEMAN. 'S got your tab inside – cleaners.

TEBHAM. Why didnt you say? Worryin 'er if you know! (*To* MRS LEWIS.) It must be Phil's – if they got the cleaner's tab.

LEWIS. What's 'appened?

POLICEMAN. When did you last see 'im?

LEWIS. Yesterday lunchtime – I expect – I dont know. Where is 'e? What's 'e done?

POLICEMAN (*unfolds jacket to show blood stain*). A body was found last night by the canal.

LEWIS. 'E's dead.

POLICEMAN. Shot.

LEWIS. I knew it.

TEBHAM. Talk to 'er later. I'll take 'er –

POLICEMAN. She has to identify the body.

LEWIS. I said last night: 'Why did you let 'im out? If I 'ad 'im 'ere I'd 'old on to 'im. Both 'ands. All the time. Let people laugh! We could live like that'. 'Ear meself say it.

Tie a string to 'im like I did when 'e was a kid. Mothers
with kids in wheelchairs – *they* keep two 'ands on 'em –
they live like that. Why wasnt mine in a wheelchair?
That's not a mother bein selfish: 'e'd still be alive! – Cant
'e 'ave 'ad an accident? Be lyin in some hospital?

TEBHAM. Let me bring 'er back when she's –

POLICEMAN. Form says it has to be done now – so it can be
filled in. Best for her too.

LEWIS. The police shot 'im! What was 'e doin? – larkin
about – too full of life – so they shot 'im! It'll all come
out! I'll 'ave a proper enquiry!

POLICEMAN (*to* MRS TEBHAM). Keep an eye on her. (*Turns
to go.*) We'll see if she can recognise her son.

The POLICEMAN *goes.*

TEBHAM. Dont antagonise them.

LEWIS. Why not? 'E's dead! Im not lyin now! I want the
truth!

TEBHAM. You dont know 'e's dead.

LEWIS. 'E said! They found 'im on the –

TEBHAM. That could be a trick. They caught 'im liftin from
shops – put 'im in cell – got you down 'ere so's they
can search your place – they could string you along for
weeks –

LEWIS. Not dead? That's the sort of thing they do . . .! Trip
me up! That's why 'e stared at me! – not because I'm a
mother with a dead son, they seen plenty of *them*! 'E's
playin cat an' mouse! 'Is eyes – I can tell 'e knows Phil's
alive –

TEBHAM. We cant be sure –

LEWIS. No no you're right: 'e's alive! Thank god I got rid
of that stuff! They find anythin in yours, you didnt get it
from 'im. Fair's fair. You took your chance. Always was
'is fault: too generous. You can say you seen 'im in is
jacket, only nothin about the – (*Stops.*) But why's there
blood? (*Goes closer to the jacket but stops someway from it.*)

It looks like blood. It must be blood. 'Ave they dropped 'is jacket in someone else's blood then showed it to 'is mother? They couldnt be so cruel!

TEBHAM. They're cruel or they couldnt do the job.

LEWIS. Then he isnt dead?

TEBHAM. I dont know.

LEWIS. You said 'e isnt!

TEBHAM. I dont know! I dont know everything! I said 'e might not be!

LEWIS. Stop it! Stop it! I wont listen to you! (*She goes nearer to the jacket and crouches to stare at it.*) Its blood. Its nearly wet. I can smell the blood from 'ere? Why did you say 'e's alive – an now 'e 'as t' be dead! Who're you t' drag 'im in an out of 'is coffin? Tell me why there's blood on 'is jacket? God rot you woman! Why did you say 'e was alive? 'Ave I got t' be told 'e's dead twice!

TEBHAM. 'E lent 'is jacket to a friend?

LEWIS. Lent it? Lent it? 'Ark at 'er! No! I wont listen! She's a monster! – Lent it? Why should 'e lend it? Its 'is favourite jacket! What d'you know? What are you up to? You've got somethin 'idden! You're always 'angin round 'im! O dont think I'm jealous! I dont care what goes on – crawl into whose bed you like! – as long as they let 'im live!

TEBHAM. I dont know! 'E might be dead!

LEWIS. There! – she's at it again! Why're you doin this? They pay you? How many mothers you sold? You want us all dead? No no I shouldnt say such things. I dont know what t' do! . . . Lent. Lent. Shall I believe it? – or would I be a stupid woman? Why? Its the sort of thing 'e would do! Lend to anyone – always lendin – *give* it away the fool! – just cause it *is* 'is favourite jacket! – an it ends up on the back of someone who's not even grateful! Yes yes of course I believe it! That's not deceivin myself! Its starin me in the face an I didnt see it! A fine mother I turn out t' be! You'd think I *want* 'im dead! 'E lends 'is

jacket – doesnt say – an then there's all this fuss! When
did 'e last put it on? When did you see it last?

TEBHAM. I dont know.

TEBHAM. 'Asnt wore it for weeks! 'E give it away! I think
'e said! I know 'e said somethin! – Why cant I think?

TEBHAM. Wait an be quiet. You only 'urt yourself jumpin
t' conclusions. Dont do their job for them. Wait an be
ready t' fight for 'im – even if it comes t' the worst. That's
the only way we can 'elp ourselves. Let them play around
with their little surprises: when they've gone they've got
nothin. Then it'll be our turn. (*Shivers.*) But I 'ate their
places. You think the paint was alive before they spread
it on these walls. (*Pause.*) The jacket was stolen.

LEWIS. . . . O yes. Yes . . . (*Takes* MRS TEBHAM's *hands.*)
that's the best one of all. Thank you, thank you. Stolen.
By a complete stranger. Nothin t' do with us. My boy's
just the victim. 'S not 'is blood – not even 'is mates'.
You're so good t' me! Im sorry I said those things – silly
silly, didnt mean it – forgive me. I'll tell 'im 'ow good you
are. I let go of 'im, I wont let go of you. If you knew 'ow
it 'urts: but you wipe the blood off the knife even when
its in the wound.

TEBHAM. Not long now. Perhaps the lad'll belong t' some
other woman – goin on with 'er work and doesnt know
what she's got in front of 'er. I 'ope she forgives us when
she suffers. What else can we do?: I 'ope when 'er times
comes the pain's so sharp she cries out! – so she 'as t' see
why we were too weak to bear it an 'ad t' push it on to
someone else.

LEWIS. Let's go. We can walk in the streets. Keep goin for
days an still find places we've never been. We can be
'appy. Even the sun's out!

TEBHAM. You'd turn back at the corner. We 'ave t' know.
If its good news, you'd've wasted all that time runnin
away when you could've been sittin at 'ome with 'im.

LEWIS. Dont.

TEBHAM. And anyway they wouldnt let you out.

LEWIS. Suppose they mixed two jackets up? Someone's shot
– the police get it right for once – its a murderer– molests
little kids – strangles old people – anythin – the sort of
beast the police *would* run into – why should I feel sorry
for *is* mother? – she brought a monster in the world to
terrify us! – good riddance! That's 'ow the blood got into
it. Then Phil's brought in – drunk or brawlin – or 'e did
the murders an molested the kids – an Im the wicked
mother – I dont care as long as 'e's alive! Dont judge 'im!
– you're no better! Well. That's 'ow they got the two
jackets. Then they take them off an search the seams an
pockets – 'ow they do – an when they chuck 'em back
Phil's lands on the corpse. That's 'ow the blood got on it.
An accident! Phil didnt notice they give 'im the corpse's
jacket cause 'e's drunk or upset. There's bin a mix up!
Look what 'appens in maternity wards! *They* mix the
babies up! What's the difference between a baby an a
corpse? None! – I dont see it! The corpse cant say that's
my jacket – the kid cant say thats my mother! 'S'always
'appenin! Maternity wards! Prisons! Morgues!
Mad'ouses! Everywhere! There's no difference! They're
all their places! They mix 'em up!

TEBHAM (*tired*). Somethin like that.

LEWIS. What's the matter? Dont you believe me? You said
'e was alive – came out of the blue – I 'ad t' believe it! It
'urt me as much as when they said 'e was dead! Now I
tell you the truth – *prove* it – you see that sort of thing on
the news – an its too much bother! 'E's my only kid Mrs
Tebham . . .

TEBHAM. I know.

LEWIS. No. Yours is alive. Rides round in a tank. Mates t'
watch over 'im. Mine 'as t' run through the streets on 'is
own. You dont know. I stand 'ere – that little bit of floor
between us – an you might be in China. Even if 'e's dead
'e feels my pain. They can bury 'im – pile the earth on

top t' keep me from 'im – put the whole world between us if they like – and my pain would still get through and 'e'd feel it. Now I wish I knew for sure 'e's dead so I could give up 'ope an put 'im out 'is misery.

The POLICEMAN *wheels in a stretcher. On it the body lies under a white sheet. He stops the stretcher and puts on the handbrake: a slight squeak.*

POLICEMAN. We'll do this without fuss. (*To* MRS TEBHAM.) She wont react. Noisy one's crack up later. Get her home fast.

LEWIS. Im not lookin. (*To* POLICEMAN.) You got yourself in a mess: get yourself out of it. I 'avent done anythin! You cant keep me 'ere! . . . I cant look.

TEBHAM. I'll look for 'er.

POLICEMAN. The form says no: next-of-kin – in this case the mother. Please wait there. Its a serious offence to obstruct an identification.

TEBHAM (*to* MRS LEWIS). Im sorry, I cant 'elp you anymore.

LEWIS. Its all right: I 'ave t' do it.

POLICEMAN. Get it over so I can take him back to the quiet. No reason to parade him just because he's dead. In this job the dead are the only ones you respect: they dont try to cheat. They restore your faith in human nature. Stand there.

MRS LEWIS *stands at the head of the stretcher.*

POLICEMAN. I've taken hold of the sheet – I'll now lift it.

The POLICEMAN *lifts the sheet.* MRS LEWIS *sees the head but it stays hidden from* MRS TEBHAM.

LEWIS. It – it (*She looks at* MRS TEBHAM *and then points at the head.*) – it – its (*She bursts out laughing.*) – its not 'im! – not 'im! – not Phil! – not 'im! – not 'im!

TEBHAM. O – no? What did I say? Its wonderful! Thank

god! The wrong man! Mixed 'em up – or the jacket –
what's it matter? The relief! Im so glad!

LEWIS (*laughing*). Not – not – not like –

Still laughing MRS LEWIS *and* MRS TEBHAM *hug each
other. The* POLICEMAN *covers the head with the sheet.*

LEWIS. ⎱ Thank you! What you said! Couldnt believe it!
        'Elped so much!
TEBHAM. ⎰ Not 'im! Its marvellous! We'll 'ave a party! I
        wish I'd kept that dress!

MRS LEWIS *laughs and turns to face the body. She talks half
to it and half to the* POLICEMAN, *trying to control herself.*

LEWIS. Im sorry for the – I didnt mean to – no disrespect to
– (*She goes to the sheet and touches the covered foot.*) – sorry
– if you knew my son you'd understand my – your mother
would tell you 'ow I – so 'appy you're not mine! (*She
laughs and picks up a corner of the sheet to dab her eyes.*) The
relief – the relief – any mother would forgive the way –
the relief to know you're – (*She bursts into convulsive
laughter and stuffs the sheet into her mouth to stifle it.*) – sorry
– all this noise for – *it's someone else's!* (*Howls with
laughter.*) Eeeaarrghgh! Thank god thank god! (*Clutches
her stomach.*) The pain! 'Avent laughed so much since –!
My son's alive! 'E's 'ere – someplace – come back! Quick!
Pull meself t'gether! Go 'ome! 'E's waitin – (*Renewed
bursts of laughter.*) – tell me off: 'Where's me tea? Im
starvin!' – Pull meself t' –

TEBHAM. No laugh laugh I'd rather 'ear you laugh than
cry. Let the 'ole buildin know. New sound for some of
'em. Let 'em 'ear it in the drains. Give the cells a treat.

POLICEMAN. Glad Im not a bettin man. One comes in, not
a tear: next, clean out – whiter than the corpse – wouldnt
know who's identifying who if it wasnt for the tag. *This
one's* the cake-walk at the fun fair! (*Putting the jacket into
the white plastic bag. Nods at* MRS LEWIS.) There's our

good deed for today. (*To* MRS TEBHAM.) Take her home but she mustnt leave her notified address. Neighbours can do the shopping.

TEBHAM. That's as bad as lockin 'er up! Its not 'er son so why's she –

POLICEMAN. Let the desk know. You need an exit pass.

LEWIS. Give the little bleeder a piece of my mind when I see 'im. Pig! Pissed! – that's 'ow 'e got 'is jacket pinch! Little perisher upsettin me! Wish 'e was dead when I finish with 'im! (*To* MRS TEBHAM.) 'E say we can go?

TEBHAM. Yes.

The POLICEMAN *releases the stretcher brake: slight squeak.*

LEWIS. Dont worry me bein shut up there. Enough roamin chasin after 'im. 'E can stop in where I can keep an eye on 'im. 'Ave a few undertakin's before 'e sets foot outside that door again . . . (*She looks at* MRS TEBHAM.) Mrs Tebham – (*Looks round.*) – somethin's not right –

TEBHAM. What?

LEWIS (*gestures towards the stretcher*). I – its not – somethin in my 'ead –

The POLICEMAN *starts to wheel out the stretcher.*

POLICEMAN. Thanks for the co-operation.

LEWIS. – I – so relieved – it went – came out of me! – and – (*To* POLICEMAN.) No. (*To* MRS TEBHAM.) Tell 'im.

TEBHAM. What 'is it?

LEWIS (*sudden vehemence*). Tell 'im! Tell 'im! Stop 'im! If that's – (*Confused again.*) – its – my 'ead's full of –

MRS TEBHAM *glances at the* POLICEMAN *and he stops the stretcher.*

POLICEMAN (*quietly to* MRS TEBHAM). I've got other cases out there.

LEWIS. – faces – or –! Its not my son – but then – why do I know 'im? Seen 'im somewhere? Or was I – wrong an got

it –? Terrible! Tryin t' see 'im in my 'ead! 'Elp me! Its
wrong! I knew 'im! White – thing – plastic! Its my son! –
what 'e looks like when 'e's dead!

TEBHAM. No no there never was such a woman for scarin
herself! Come 'ome in the peace an quiet. Come back
t'morrow. No more fuss t'day. Let 'im take the poor lad
away.

The POLICEMAN *releases the stretcher handbrake: slight
squeak.*

POLICEMAN. Remember: exit pass.
LEWIS. Its my son!
TEBHAM. Its not!
LEWIS. Then why do I – know 'im? I didnt look properly! I
was too – me nails dug 'oles in me 'ands – I couldnt see!
Let me look! I must know!
TEBHAM. Poor woman, I'll never get 'er 'ome like that. (*To*
POLICEMAN.) She's said its not 'er son. Let me look t'
set 'er mind t' rest.
POLICEMAN. Nothing on the form against that.

The POLICEMAN *stops the stretcher and puts on the
handbreak: slight squeak.*

POLICEMAN (*sigh*). Drop of oil.

MRS TEBHAM *goes to the top of the stretcher as the*
POLICEMAN *is pulling back the sheet. She reaches it and
stares down at the head. Her face is blank. Silence.*

LEWIS. Why's she starin? She frightens me! Its my son!

MRS LEWIS *goes to the stretcher. She faces* MRS TEBHAM
*with her back to the audience. Slowly she doubles over in silent
laughter and – still completely silent and doubled – totters
away. She stops, bent double.*

LEWIS. Didnt recognise 'im! I was so relieved – I – (*She
whoops with laughter.*) – I didnt recognise 'im! (*She laughs*

and hobbles to MRS TEBHAM.) Sorry, sorry – I thought 'e was – told 'er 'e was –

She claws at MRS TEBHAM, *trying to turn her towards her to comfort her but laughter makes her too weak.* MRS TEBHAM *stands as before and stares blankly at the face.*

POLICEMAN. You recognise the deceased?

LEWIS (*pointing to* MRS TEBHAM). Its – its – (*She clutches at the sheet and buries her face in it.*) – its – (*She shrieks with laughter.*) – I told 'er – she stood there an I told 'er – I said it was a –!

She roars with laughter and as she hobbles away from the stretcher she holds the sheet against her face and drags it with her – the body is uncovered. MRS TEBHAM *stares down at the face.*

LEWIS (*clutching the sheet to her*). I looked at 'er an said – it wasnt mine – I said it was – (*She clutches her stomach and laughs.*) The pain! I said – I said – I said –. (*She sits on the ground roaring with laughter and drumming her heels.*) The pain! The pain! The pain! The pain!

She stuffs her hands into her mouth to stop the laughter. She covers herself with the sheet till she's completely shrouded. She rocks and her gentle laughter comes from under the sheet. MRS TEBHAM *glances across at her once, then looks back at the dead face: otherwise she doesnt move. Her blank expression doesnt change.*

LEWIS (*gently as she rocks under the sheet*). Nineteen years – sat at my table – days – days – washed 'is cuts – christmas toys – didnt know – no idea – swear it on this sheet – didnt see – said a stranger – and its– . . .

POLICEMAN (*to* MRS TEBHAM). Im keeping you in pending enquiries.

The POLICEMAN *releases the handbrake: slight squeak. He*

wheels out the stretcher. MRS TEBHAM *goes with him without looking back.* MRS LEWIS *takes off the sheet and sits with it crumbled in her lap and round her on the floor. She sighs once. She presses the side of her thumb against her teeth: one small jerk as if she's biting a thread. Then she calms herself by folding the sheet. She goes out with it.*

[G] Mrs Lewis's Kitchen

MRS LEWIS *and* MRS TEBHAM *both sit in chairs facing the audience.* MRS LEWIS *is upstage of* MRS TEBHAM *and* PHIL *stands beside her with a saucer and cup of tea. Near* MRS TEBHAM *there is a framed photo of* BRIAN.

TEBHAM. If I moved in she wont be on 'er own. You wouldnt be so tied down.

PHIL. 'Alf asleep. Struggled all 'er life. In the end you sleep on your feet.

TEBHAM. Only one rent.

PHIL. She liked company.

TEBHAM. That's settled then. Next door'll 'elp you shift my stuff along the landin. Then I neednt go in.

PHIL. You cant spend the rest of your life bein scared of the past.

TEBHAM. Brian's dead. If that didnt 'urt it wouldnt be worth goin on, would it? Going out?

PHIL. No.

TEBHAM. Go: we're all right.

PHIL (*blows on tea*). Gettin cooler.

TEBHAM. Dont treat 'er like a child.

LEWIS. Washed 'is face out of a medical bottle.

Doorbell.

TEBHAM. If its me, I went t' bed.

PHIL *gives the tea to* MRS LEWIS *and goes out. Slight pause.*

The OFFICER *comes in. Halfway through the* OFFICER'*s next speech* PHIL *slowly comes in and stands in the doorway to listen.*

OFFICER (*unsure who is* MRS TEBHAM, *to* LEWIS). Mrs Tebham . . . (*Turns to* TEBHAM.) I knew you'd be cross if the young man sent me away. No chance for a word at the funeral. Had to nurse the top brass. The padre was very moving. (*Slight pause.*) Brian was the best type of young soldier. Clean. Loyal. Carried his share of the burdens and enjoyed his share of the laughs. (*Looks around.*) We'll miss him. (*To* MRS TEBHAM.) I was a bit apprehensive about coming – me and Brian being alike. (*Picks up photo.*) Same hair – same eyes – same height though you cant tell from the head. (*Smiles and goes on looking at the photo.*) One christmas we swapped hats! – that sort of party! Tebham went round the barracks and was mistaken for me! (*Imitates* BRIAN.) 'They was throwin up salutes like a stop-watch goin backwards sir.' We're proud of our regimental christmases. Can I have this for my scrapbook?

TEBHAM (*snatches the photo from the* OFFICER). Who are you? What you come 'ere for? (*Without looking at the photo she wipes it on her sleeve.*)

OFFICER. I came to spend a moment with you today.

TEBHAM. You're nothing like him!

OFFICER. Different backgrounds. The mother's bound to see that.

TEBHAM. Come 'ere an pretend . . .!

OFFICER. I wont intrude. (*Preparing to go.*) The regimental almoners fund is available should any need arise.

LEWIS. Your tea!

OFFICER. Thank you I wont –

LEWIS. Must 'ave tea – its a funeral!

MRS LEWIS *stands, pours her tea into the saucer and hands it to the* OFFICER.

TEBHAM. 'Umour 'er.

OFFICER. Mouth *is* dry.

Before he can drink MRS LEWIS *fills the saucer to the brim and then lowers it in her hand. They stare at each other in silence.* MRS LEWIS *grins. Carefully the* OFFICER *raises the saucer to his lips. He drinks silently without spilling a drop.*

LEWIS. Clever little sod. (*She cackles shrilly and pokes him in the ribs.*) Cocky little bastard.

The OFFICER *finishes drinking and hands the empty saucer back to* MRS LEWIS.

OFFICER (*cold anger*). Brian died on duty. That's still something to be proud of. His death wont be wasted. Read the newspapers in the morning. You'll have a surprise.

PHIL. You give 'im a good send off sir.

OFFICER. That was our duty.

PHIL (*slowly coming into the room*). I went t' school with 'im sir.

OFFICER. Accept my condolences.

PHIL. Thank you sir that's much appreciated.

OFFICER. Tonight this city will be sealed off. The whole garrison deployed.

PHIL *carefully changes from slippers to street shoes.*

PHIL. 'E always said 'ow well organised you was sir.

OFFICER. Wish we had him with us tonight. Reinforcements dropped in from helicopters. That's a 'first use' against civilians.

PHIL. Landin on a city at night sir? – (*Sucks in breath through his teeth apprehensively.*) dont want no more Brians.

OFFICER (*reassuringly*). Its all in hand. Cordon the ring roads. Stop all civilian transport. As safe as anaesthetising a corpse. The code name's Fallen Warrior. My idea. The men cheered when they heard it. The heat's coming through the barracks walls. The city parks will be temporary holding pens – some of those we put in them wont hear the dawn chorus. I couldnt restrain Brian's chums if I wanted to. Tonight's the night. I hope you feel better about things Mrs Tebham. (*To* MRS LEWIS.) Your tea was excellent.

The OFFICER *goes.*

LEWIS. The dead are entitled to their tea. (*She starts to go back to her chair, then stops to explain vaguely.*) I always say – if they're dead – since I got it wrong . . . (*To* MRS TEBHAM.) You died too – but *you* came back. Now I'd let you lead me anywhere.

MRS LEWIS *sits in her chair.*

TEBHAM. You're goin out?

PHIL. Remembered somethin.

TEBHAM. Its dangerous if all 'e said 'is –

PHIL. I'll be all right.

TEBHAM. Be long?

PHIL. Try not. Dont wait up.

TEBHAM. Tell me –

PHIL (*calmly*). 'Ave t' 'urry.

TEBHAM. I may not see you again.

PHIL. Im only goin out t' –

TEBHAM. So was Brian. Who shot 'im?

PHIL. 'E was a soldier. Okay – is it better if 'e shoots someone t' take 'is place? Someone on the street t'night? You ask some 'ard questions. (*Goes to* MRS LEWIS.) Bit of luck Mrs T's movin in. (*No response.*)

TEBHAM. 'Ow did 'e get your jacket?

PHIL. She'll pull through. Only while you're 'ere we wont lie to each other. We dont 'ave to. (*Gesture to* MRS LEWIS.) Asleep. – 'E needed the jacket so I lent it. – 'Ave t' 'urry.

PHIL *goes out.* MRS TEBHAM *and* MRS LEWIS *sit facing the audience.*

In the Company of Men

Businessmen:
OLDFIELD *early sixties*
LEONARD OLDFIELD
HAMMOND *fifties*
DODDS *late forties*
WILBRAHAM *forties*

Servant:
BARTLEY *twenties*

Unit One: The Lounge of Oldfield's Town House
Unit Two: The same as Unit One
Unit Three: The same as Unit One
Unit Four: The Hall Lobby of Oldfield's Country House
Unit Five: The Ground Floor of a Derelict House
Unit Six: 'The Two Armchairs' – the same as Unit One
Unit Seven: Oldfield's Office
Unit Eight: The same as Unit Seven
Unit Nine: The Cellar of a Derelict House

The present time in London and Kent.

Unit One

Oldfield's House.

A room with two armchairs.

LEONARD *and* DODDS *standing.*

LEONARD. You neednt wait. I'll pass on your congratulations.

DODDS. He wont be long.

LEONARD. The television's caught him.

DODDS (*shakes his head*). He was on the earlier news. (*Slight
pause.*) I spoke to him on the phone. He told me to be here
at nine in the morning. He's going to give me his new
plans for the company. (*Slight pause.*) Did he say what
he'd've done if we'd been taken over?

LEONARD. He was sure he'd win.

DODDS. Is it all right if I change the subject? Wilbraham
came to see me. Its been a seesaw sort of day. Your father
was still fighting to keep his company – the last thing I
wanted to do was deal with Willy and his disasters.

LEONARD. Could he kill himself?

DODDS. Willy hasnt got the initiative. Leaves all the big
moves to others.

LEONARD. Why do people gamble like that?

DODDS. Because they cant solve their problems. It gives
them problems they dont have to solve – the decision's up
to fate. His company's run up debts of four millions. With
his reputation he cant get another loan. The debtors are
meeting tomorrow. They'll bankrupt him.

LEONARD (*half attention*). Im sorry he's in a mess.

DODDS. Its his father's fault. *He* learned to run a company

by founding one. He thought he could just die and hand
it to Willy on a plate.

LEONARD (*shrug*). He'll be free when its gone.

DODDS. With nothing to restrain him he'll go to the bottom.

LEONARD. *You* lend him money. He's your friend.

DODDS. You didnt think I was going to ask you to *lend* him
money? That *would* be throwing it down the drain.

LEONARD. You were working up to something.

DODDS. I was going to –

LEONARD. Tomorrow.

DODDS. The creditors meet in the morning. Let me tell you
the situation. His order book's patchy but the trade
outlook is good. He's got a modern factory – well
equipped – there's over-manning but some of the top
dressing's gone – rats leaving the sinking ship. If you go
in – cut the workforce – collect what's owing – went after
new orders – you could get the company back on its feet.
The potential's there but because of the debts it'll be
closed down.

LEONARD. How much?

DODDS. Half a million to hold off the debtors for a year.
But its not money that's important – the company needs
an input of energy and talent. Willy would pull himself
together if you were –

LEONARD (*shakes head*). Too many complications.

DODDS. Complications yes – but they can be *seen*: it isnt a
gamble. Your father's like a lot of intelligent men –
sometimes he's very stupid.

LEONARD. Stupid?

DODDS. You know you're being wasted. At your age time's
decisive. If you dont develop your potential over the next
year – even the next few months – you'll pay for it for the
rest of your life. Willy's creditors are moving in because
before long there wont be anything left to sell up. You
wont get another chance anywhere near as good. Its as
if someone had set up the ideal test to let you find out

what you can do – and at your age that means finding out who you are.

LEONARD. My father wouldnt allow it.

DODDS. Good heavens we mustnt tell him!

LEONARD. No?

DODDS. I've worked for him for thirty years and I've never wanted to leave. But I learned his faults long ago. He'd be breathing down your neck telling you all the right things to do. The company'd be a success – Willy would be saved – I'd've helped a friend – and you'd get nothing. It'd be a triumph and feel like the biggest ditch-job of all time.

LEONARD. You think I should go behind my father's back?

DODDS. He spits out the bait and chews the hook – he had to learn to do that. Well you learn more from your mistakes than someone else's success. Even if you fail it'd be money well spent. You can use your own money – or I'll raise a loan without your father knowing. If you succeed you'll be giving him more than money.

LEONARD. A lesson in cheating?

DODDS. Your father's trouble is he admires you too much. He wants you take over from him – its a passion: that makes him afraid of you. If you fail you'll get over it, you're young. But he's old so its *his* future at stake. You have to live out his ambitions. If you fail it means he dies a failure. He couldnt bear that after a lifetime of success. He's never going to let you take a risk. Sometime in the next year you'll have to go behind his back.

LEONARD. Give me a report on the company.

DODDS. I need something for the creditors tomorrow. Can I say you're seriously interested?

LEONARD. How many do you have to persuade?

DODDS. Five main suppliers.

LEONARD. This is my father's lucky day. You've left *my* chance till almost midnight.

DODDS. Willy was too ashamed to tell me about the

creditors before. He had a few drinks and turned up. You wont believe it but –

BARTLEY *comes in. He wears dark trousers, dark tie, white shirt and a servant's light-khaki house-jacket. He carries a glass of whisky on a tray.*

BARTLEY. Your father's in the hoose Mr Leonard.

LEONARD *takes the whisky from the tray.*

BARTLEY. Did you want anythin?
LEONARD. No.
BARTLEY. Mr Dodds?
DODDS. No thanks Bartley.

BARTLEY *goes out with the tray.*

DODDS. I was going to say Willy was like you once. His father was always going to give him his head, let him stand on his feet. By the time he died Willy was hooked on risk: gambling with fate instead of controlling it.
LEONARD (*curt amusement*). Have you noticed Bartley's wristwatch? The dial's a human face. My father tolerates his whims.
DODDS. *You* must decide.
LEONARD. That's like sentencing someone to death to encourage them to escape.
DODDS. If you were your father I'd be giving you the same advice.

OLDFIELD *comes in. He wears a city overcoat.*

DODDS. Congratulations sir.
OLDFIELD. Thank you. We did well today. Its turning into a stampede. When the stock exchange closed over sixty per cent of our shareholders had accepted my offer. Hammond will hold on to his ten per cent but we'll end up well into the eighties. Safe from take-over for all time.
DODDS. Have you heard from Hammond?

OLDFIELD. He'll send a line. Wont want to appear miffed.

LEONARD. I dont understand why he tried to take us. He could've got a better return on his capital somewhere else.

OLDFIELD. Was there anything in particular you wanted Dodds?

DODDS. Just to say thanks for seeing Hammond off so brilliantly. Its been a tense time. Our loyalty to you would've cost some of us our jobs.

OLDFIELD. Thank you. Hammond's patient – never moves without a purpose. And clever – doesnt even let his buttonholes know what buttons are for. (*Drink.*) Mine? (*He takes his whisky from* LEONARD *but doesnt drink it.*) O the shareholders didnt support me out of loyalty – never look for that! I put on a world-weary pose – gave the impression I was losing interest – that started rumours in the press – and it didnt cost me a lunch! They said I might withdraw my offer – and the shareholders panicked! – What dont you understand Leonard? D'you need a clairvoyant to tell you a bag of crisps is a bag of crisps? The prospects in the arms trade are good – its difficult to get in on our level – and Hammond was shopping: it was so clear I was even able to warn the accountants to prepare our defence in advance.

DODDS. Are you taking a rest?

OLDFIELD. No I feel as if I've got another leg – Im learning to walk again! We've beaten Hammond but we must be vigilant. An *internal* weakness: the wrong design compromise, a misreading of international relations – a *strategic* error of that magnitude could destroy us five years from now. When you make the guns you must be more alert than the soldiers who fire them. *They* need allies not enemies: *we* need enemies. We cant trust our allies, they're our commercial rivals – we cant trust our workers, they're like scavengers on the battlefield, they'd strip the dead – we cant trust our government, they use our rivals to beat us down – and then there's the

Hammonds and their fifth columns. We've got only one good reliable friend: our enemies. We build our life on trust in them, they're always at our side. That makes us lonely: but the ground under our feet is very solid.

DODDS. I must be off if Im to be fresh in the morning. Congratulations again sir.

OLDFIELD. Goodnight.

DODDS *goes.*

OLDFIELD. He hung on to congratulate me . . .!

LEONARD. I thought you'd gone on to celebrate.

OLDFIELD. No. You should've gone. You earned it.

LEONARD. I hardly saw you.

OLDFIELD. Yes it was a busy time. I can turn to Dodds and the accountants – but no one else. You're inexperienced but the fresh eye often sees what we miss.

LEONARD. Thank you.

OLDFIELD. O dear. Im tired and put it badly – (*Sighs.*) and you interpret me ironically.

LEONARD. No.

OLDFIELD. One day you'll know why I wish I'd had time to talk to you. When you're in my position most people tell you what they think will flatter you or flatter them. You have no reason not to tell me the truth. You have a valuable gift Leonard: you make people talk. But you dont always listen when they do.

LEONARD. If you end up with eighty per cent of the shares you as good as own the company. Will I get it when you die?

OLDFIELD. You get everything.

LEONARD. I want to go on the board.

OLDFIELD (*smells drink*). O no . . .!

LEONARD. There's no reason to wait.

OLDFIELD. Its too late to discuss this now. We wouldnt have time to finish.

LEONARD. It doesnt take long to say yes or no.

OLDFIELD. Dont be difficult. There are options – various ways of doing things. It needs to be – (*Stops.*) No I refuse to start. Its important, it deserves all my attention. Tomorrow afternoon after I've spoken to Dodds – and the accountants – Im seeing them after lunch. Then we'll shut ourselves away and –

LEONARD. Tomorrow you'll be busy.

OLDFIELD. Yes yes tomorrow's full. I wont mislead you. We'll set aside a definite time in the next few days and put it in the diary.

LEONARD. What's wrong with your drink?

OLDFIELD. My drink? – O my drink's unimportant. (*Puts the glass on the floor.*) Nothing wrong with it. Over the years I've built up a good board – they're all fighters – many of them are ex-service. Most of them have their sights on my chair. Now I own the company they wont get it. We must understand their disappointment. If I push you in over the top they'll resent it – rightly. Give you a hard time.

LEONARD. I'll learn to survive.

OLDFIELD. Survive? Why approach a great opportunity in such a grudging spirit? They want to be your friends.

LEONARD. Then there's no problem.

OLDFIELD. One cant even get a decent drink in this house.

LEONARD. Let me fix it for –

OLDFIELD. No no it doesnt matter. I can get by without my –

LEONARD. Its no trouble.

OLDFIELD (*weary*). Please Leonard – this fuss about a drink! Im not alcoholic. After the energy I spent today I'll sleep without a soporific. Did you *see* me on television?

LEONARD. You were very good.

OLDFIELD. I wondered since you didnt say. Was I good . . .? What were we talking about before you got agitated over my drink?

LEONARD. My place on the board.

OLDFIELD. In my opinion you're not ready for the board. If I put you on now they'll always associate you with weakness – I know men! – treat you as a spoiled pup on the grab. And as ninety per cent of the job is acting as transmitter between them – you can never be better than they're able or willing to make you. If they see you as weak, you become weak: *that's* the only basis on which they can deal with you. I've seen it so often. Men make their worst fears come true and call it fate but really its their own bad habits. If I was a foolish father I'd force you onto the board – teach you the hard way. That doesnt work. If you're thrown in at the deep end you break your neck on the ones who were thrown in before you. If I put you on the board you'd be an instant success! I have to think what you'll be when the honeymoon's over. You must learn patience. Its the hardest part for an able young man – it means taking a risk on yourself before you've proved its worth taking. Fortunately I have faith in you: I can wait.

LEONARD. If the board obstruct me I'll get rid of them.

OLDFIELD. What a reckless thing to say! I chose a board who could stand up to the leader – be their own men – and already you're sacking them for those very qualities! What sort of justice punishes people for being right? When I listen to you I feel I have to *protect* them from you! – that you'll never learn how to earn their respect!

BARTLEY *comes in.*

BARTLEY. Everything okay sir?

OLDFIELD. Yes thank you.

LEONARD. His drink isnt as –

OLDFIELD. O for heaven's sake! Why did I ever mention the drink!

BARTLEY. Is somethin nae right wi' the drink sir?

OLDFIELD. Its perfect. Exactly what I was looking forward to.

BARTLEY. That's all right then sir – I would'nae want t' think there was anythin wrong wi' it. Eh – ah understand congratulations are in order the night sir?

OLDFIELD. That's kind of you Bartley. I appreciate it. Yes its been a good day. I shant need you now. Go to bed.

BARTLEY. Is it the office in the mornin sir? Ah laid oot a suit.

OLDFIELD. Thank you.

BARTLEY (*stares at drink*). It'd be nae bother t' fix the drink sir. Was it the soda again? I cannae get the hang o' it.

OLDFIELD. No its fine. I shall drink it in a moment.

BARTLEY *goes out.*

OLDFIELD. How thoughtless of you to upset him in what way! You know he spills things. He'll be jittery all tomorrow. You might have spared me that. Harrassing servants is a sign of weakness of character. And I do not allow you to slight my board! You speak as if you were scrapping for a fight. Anyone can be tough with others: be tough with yourself. If you were ready for the board you'd be begging me to keep you off so you could enjoy your freedom a little longer. Other fathers would have to force their son on – but Im denied that pleasure.

LEONARD. I didnt say I wanted to get rid of them. I said I would if they tried to get rid of me.

OLDFIELD. Please dont tell me what I heard – I know the spirit of what you said. They offer you their friendship and you condemn them! This terrible impatience blinds you to every – (*Stops.*) Dont you see that if the job wasnt kept for you they'd be cutting each other's throats to get it? Some of the remarks reported to me – and I trust Dodds absolutely – make me despair of the havoc ambition causes even among comrades. You can come to them as the peacemaker.

LEONARD. Then there's no problem.

OLDFIELD. None – unless you make it. (*Picks up the drink*

and is about to drink it but smells it first.) . . . I wouldnt have believed it. (*Puts drink on floor again.*) I understand your frustration, but you must understand the responsibility I – I feel more than if you were my actual son. When I adopted you, in my eyes that was a contract. I honour my contracts. Natural fathers have rifts with their sons – we should be spared that. It should be our advantage.

LEONARD. Father I wont be put off. If Im to do your job I must have determination. But when I show it you say it makes me unfit for the job!

OLDFIELD. Precisely! Why is that a mystery? Learn to get what you want without grabbing – and without this shocking abuse of innocent people. Putting you on the Board – I looked forward so much to that. I meant 'pleasure' when I said it just now. But you've turned it into an ordeal. I feel like a blindman groping across a minefield. I cant do anything right for you. Get rid of your ambition – every scrap of pride – and start to think of the responsibilities you owe to others. Then I can be happy with you. I never had any ambition – it would have got in the way of my mission. The leader's life is service. There are no rewards – and it gets harder. If you dont know that in your bones then perhaps you should look round for a more comfortable future.

LEONARD. Is that what you want?

OLDFIELD. Dont be a child.

LEONARD. Then what do you want?

OLDFIELD. I told you! I'd hoped you'd begun to see! Or is this some new twist in your game? He served me neat whisky. Does he think I buy soda to clean the drains? Its impossible to make the most innocent remark without offending you Leonard. You fly off the handle and everyone feels guilty. You wont believe it, but I sit here asking myself if *I've* done wrong! Now you see why I asked to be spared this conversation . . . O god he's going to sulk! Its a father's duty to show his child his weaknesses so that he doesnt have to parade them in front of others. In your situation they could destroy you. Would you rather I lied? I've no intention of lowering the intellectual standards by which I live so that you can go on believing you're faultless – and that your talents will make running any company childs play! Im tired – this conversation must stop.

LEONARD. I cant win with you father.

OLDFIELD. Very smart. (*Silence.*) You certainly manoeuver yourself into a comfortable position: if you fail you blame me. That'll be next. I offer you everything and Im blamed because you cant take it: all I ask is a little patience. I dont want gratitude but – (*Stops.*) I shall never understand why you had to do this today! I thought for once I'd be allowed to come home to peace. (*Pause.*) Why should anyone expect gratitude? We work – and give others their livelihood and expect to have the skin flayed from the backs of our hands.

LEONARD. I dropped the subject five minutes ago.

OLDFIELD. I will not sit here and be tormented! The subject's dropped when I say – not when you want! You start a row and say drop it when you see how crude – and pushing your behaviour's been! You're intolerable! (*Slight pause.*) Dont try these tactics on the board. They wont handle you with kid gloves. (*Low, gruff.*) There are limits to what I'll accept. I tell you Leonard, if I didnt already have doubts this conversation would have given me them. Its a warning. I put you on the board – the first disagreement and you're squabbling with me in public! What's your scheme for handling the ministry when they welsh on a procurement? – order the unions out on a mass sulk?

LEONARD. Im sorry. Im sorry. Im wrong. It wasnt fair to ask you today when you're in a –

OLDFIELD. O? When Im in a what? (*No answer.*) Today's no different from yesterday or tomorrow. I can deal with

Hammond and that crowd without losing the ability to attend to my responsibilities. I could sit here till I'd settled the future of a hundred sons – if it was in their interest I did so. What you're doing is in no one's interest! Hammond wanted my property: you seem to want my peace of mind!

LEONARD (*slight pause*). Hammond wasnt such a push-over.

OLDFIELD. What did you say?

LEONARD. I said you sweated when the bankers took time over raising your second loan.

OLDFIELD. I see. You start off touting for your future and now you're holding an inquest on my past! Is there more? (*Silence.*) You may regret what you've said tonight. Your last remark – I hope it was your last – was not merely contemptible. I have to say this Leonard: you can be cruel. Its the worst vice.

LEONARD. Yes well the truth can be cruel.

OLDFIELD. Go on!

LEONARD. I told you: *I'd* stopped. But you – so I – (*Stops.*) O god. Please. Please. Its finished.

OLDFIELD. Six weeks fighting for your future and you treat me to this! Dodds and Bartley gave me their congratulations. You said 'Gimme-mine!'

LEONARD. Im not letting you blame me for this.

OLDFIELD *stands.*

OLDFIELD. Blame? You've a right to be heard with respect. We shouldnt end the day like this. When two people start talking about blame they're both in the wrong – that's my experience. Im always busy – on the move – it must seem as if I didnt care. Its really only when Im tired, isnt it? Im tired now. Hammond scared me. I wish you'd never have to deal with people like him. He thinks with his mouth open – *eats* everything. I try not to be impatient. When you're old, that's ugly. I shant change.

Its good we had this conversation, it forces me to say something essential to you. I dont have the rights of a proper father. You dont owe anyone that. If I cant be lived with – you mustnt deceive yourself: you should go. My money isnt worth it. You'd become corrupt. That would be the worst thing that could happen.

LEONARD. I shouldnt have asked. I knew the answer.

OLDFIELD. You should have gone out to celebrate what I'd won for you. Its not too late. If I was your age I'd have something to celebrate. (*Shrugs.*) I've burdened myself with my responsibilities for the rest of my life – I could've burdened Hammond with them. We'll make an appointment in the diary and sort this out. Goodnight.

LEONARD. Goodnight.

OLDFIELD *goes.* LEONARD *stands in silence.* BARTLEY *comes in quietly.*

BARTLEY. Could ah have a word Mr Leonard?

LEONARD. – ? –

BARTLEY. What the hell's goin' on? Ah cannae figure the half o' it. Mr Oldfield was in a shockin sweat the last weeks. The explanations in the press only make the whole thing more of a riddle.

LEONARD. Hammond tried to take over my father's company –

BARTLEY. Ay Hammond Hammond Hammond yous cannae get away from the name!

LEONARD. He tried to buy the shares. If the shareholders had sold him more than half he'd've controlled the company.

BARTLEY. Is that legal? A man can just buy up people's livelihoods like that?

LEONARD. My father offered them more money. Then Hammond offered more and so on. Today they sold my father over half –

BARTLEY. That means there'll be nae more Hammond the morrow?

LEONARD. Yes. The banks lent my father enough money to buy almost all the shares. We're now a private company.

BARTLEY. That must be an awful relief t' your father. It is t' *me*! I learned t' survive the hard way Mr Leonard – I have t' read between the lines before they're printed. If Mr Oldfield had lost he'd've nae worked for Hammond – and it'd've been doon the lavvy for me.

LEONARD. Im sure he'd –

BARTLEY. No no – ah rub along with Mr Oldfield. But ah'm dam sure he'd nae want me roond him all day when he's retired. An there's nae many gentlemen want a man with ma background – an most of *them* left the service with their own batman. We're nae nannies: the employer cannae increase his need! Ah'm nae talkin too much Mr Leonard?

LEONARD. My father doesnt need you tonight.

BARTLEY. Then there's the court martial. Mr Oldfield saw the unfairness o' that. But the prejudice is shockin! People think a court martial's roond one o' the last judgement. Telled them they gi' a wrong verdict an its blasphemy! – you're quarrelin' wi' god all mighty!

LEONARD. You'd get a reference.

BARTLEY. O nae doobt – a reference. Mr Oldfield'd gi' me that. He's one o' the best – as you ken yourself. In a manner o' speakin wor both his weans – he took wor both in. Have you never thought o' that? Oh ah'm nae sayin ah'm qualified t' stand side by side wi' yous – ah wouldnt go that far. You're sure ah'm nae talkin too much Mr Leonard? Yous said a wee crack wor in order. An then there's yon glass. Set like a trap for the dilatory servant. If ah took it in would ah m'bee disturb him? If he'd've wanted it he'd've took it or drank it afore he left. But if ah took it awae would he m'bee come lookin for it? An if ah leaves it it looks as if ah'm treatin the place as a midden. Would yous tell us wor ah'm expected t' do Mr

Leonard? (*No response.*) I would'nae want yous thinkin ah'm nae willin t' deal wi' the glass cause ah'm off duty. On or off never stop nae body givin me orders in this hoose!

LEONARD (*low, flat*). For chrissake.

LEONARD (*sudden malice*). Sorry t' land yous wi' the decision. Shall ah hang on or come back later . . .? (*Recovers.*) Och there's nae call for me t' adopt that tone. Yous must think ah'm a snotty-nosed little tear-arse. Im over-conscientious. (*Low.*) Scared t' shit ah'll lose my job, so ah do everythin perfect. (*Normal tone.*) I wor on my last roonds t' lock up afore ah switch on the alarm. Then ah saw your father's glass an had a slow panic. Best leave it where it is. Its doin nae harm.

BARTLEY *goes out.* LEONARD *sits in an armchair. He dozes – not in the comfortable position of a sleeper but as stiffly and awkwardly as a soldier shot and left in the street.*

Unit Two

The same.

Dawn. The electric light is on and the curtains are drawn. LEONARD *still sleeps in the armchair. His face is blank and his body is even more rigid and awkward, as if it had dried and contracted.*

DODDS *comes in. He has changed into a different business suit. He looks at* LEONARD *and draws the curtains.* LEONARD *wakes.*

DODDS. Morning. (*He switches off the lights.*) You slept here?

LEONARD (*wristwatch*). Is my father up?

DODDS (*shakes his head*). Im very early. You're all right?

LEONARD. Dropped off.

DODDS. Wilbraham's in my car.

LEONARD. You dont want me to see him now?

DODDS. Calm him down. If the creditors see him in this state they'll pull the plug.

LEONARD. I cant.

DODDS. Five minutes. I'll bring him up.

> DODDS *goes out.* LEONARD *curses under his breath. He straightens his clothes.* BARTLEY *comes in.*

BARTLEY. Mornin sir. I did'nae recollect you said anythin aboot an early breakfast . . .?

LEONARD. Coffee for three.

BARTLEY. D'you want anythin cooked? (LEONARD *shakes his head.*) Mr Leonard – last night –. When Mr Oldfield's tense he takes it oot on me – he pays so its his privilege. When it was settle ah had a little bevvy celebration – ah was that happy for yous. I would'nae want any little-bit indiscretion t' get on ma records or any o' that. You can rely on me Mr Leonard. So its no cooked breakfast then?

> DODDS *comes in with* WILBRAHAM.

DODDS (*introductions*). Leonard – Eric Wilbraham.

WILBRAHAM. Howdyoudo? Mr Oldfield its most decent of you to receive me at this hour.

BARTLEY. I'll serve coffee in ten minutes gentlemen. (*He turns to go.*)

WILBRAHAM. I say d'you think your man might kit me up with a shirt? Colin kindly bedded me down for the night but I've no fresh linen. In the daylight my shirt's a bit grubby.

BARTLEY. Nae bother sir.

> BARTLEY *goes out.*

WILBRAHAM. Awfully good of you.

LEONARD. Im sorry about your problems.

WILBRAHAM. I've been a fool. But the main thing is I know it. I've told Colin everything – opened the books – and I gave him permission to disclose everything to you. Im glad its come to this. I feel as if this morning I'll be driven to my funeral and afterwards I'll walk away and leave an empty casket.

LEONARD. I cant commit myself. Colin's preparing a report on your company. I look forward to reading it.

WILBRAHAM. Life is always worthwhile. The great offence is to deny that. Gamblers are used to coming home in the early morning when its daylight but the rest of the world's asleep. Drawn curtains, locked-up shops, a milk-bottle in front of a great office tower – the caretaker comes out and stoops to pick it up like some old crone – at least a thousand years old. You feel young – and your losses and drinking dont matter. The mornings are always beautiful, before the day soils itself and becomes shabby.

DODDS. Be positive eh Willy?

WILBRAHAM. That's how one must live. If you stand before a firing squad believe – absolutely – the army's about to mutiny or war will be declared and they'll be ordered to save ammunition. I inherited a company in profit – good prospects – good people – they hardly needed me – I had time on my hands – so I went on gambling. You wouldnt believe how much you lose! Not lose: it *vanishes* – as if you went to sit down in a chair and suddenly the room's gone – you're sitting in an empty field. You live in a world of illusions. But you dont want to hear this! – you dont gamble. I promise you you wont lose one penny of your investment. I *have* learned. Whatever I do now – right or wrong – is my responsibility. The past cant help me or harm me anymore. Perhaps this is what I've been striving for? I recall reading a magazine article ages ago which said that gamblers – O in some fearfully complicated way I didnt grasp! – wish to lose. That's the only way I can make my losses look like gains!

BARTLEY *comes in with a folded white shirt.*

BARTLEY. This'll fit the neck fine sir.

WILBRAHAM. How kind. To lend me a shirt.

WILBRAHAM *takes off his jacket, tie and shirt.* BARTLEY *puts the jacket on an armchair, unfolds the clean shirt, holds it up by the outer tips of the shoulders and waits.*

WILBRAHAM. So – you'll back me.

LEONARD (*to* DODDS). Will Mr Wilbraham's creditors leave the bankruptcy petition on the table for a week?

DODDS (*reassuring*). I'll phone round before the meeting.

WILBRAHAM. They'll jump at the offer. If they shut me down they'll be lucky to get 10p in the pound. Your father's name will carry the day. (*To* BARTLEY.) Thank you. Of course Colin explained that your father knows nothing about this. All the same. If things go wrong again – he'd be bound to bail us out. What better security could they want?

LEONARD. Im not interested in merely lending money.

WILBRAHAM. No. Colin spoke of that. Its to be as you wish. I'll put you on the board.

LEONARD. I want –

WILBRAHAM. I welcome your contribution. Fresh eye of youth – that's not a cliché, it means money.

LEONARD. I want to be managing director.

WILBRAHAM. O. (*To* BARTLEY.) It *does* fit.

BARTLEY. Yessir.

WILBRAHAM (*to* LEONARD). Colin hadnt spoken of that.

LEONARD. *If* his report removes my considerable doubt.

WILBRAHAM. My people – there's been a misunderstanding – they wouldnt accept a new MD. The position isnt offered. I've hidden nothing – it would be pointless to try to do so. Our situation is desperate. But I've learned my lesson – forgive me if I repeat myself but I must assume I wasnt clear – and now Colin has arranged this last chance for me. I cant throw it away – it would be worse than a gamble.

LEONARD. Im not interested in less.

WILBRAHAM. I must think. (*Cuff links.*) I've spoken to my colleagues of – our rescue plan – they gave me their support – heart warming – I no longer had a right to it. If I go back to them with – say I've put them in the hands of –. (*Controls himself.*) Let me just say I couldnt carry my board.

LEONARD. Carry's the word! Chuck them out! They helped you to get in this mess –

WILBRAHAM. No no you mustnt say that! If I'd heeded their advice –

LEONARD. – and now I've got to get you out of it! If they want their jobs they'd better earn my confidence sharp!

DODDS. All this –

WILBRAHAM. You cant treat them like that! Some of them were my father's friends – they've served the company for years. I couldnt face them, knowing what I've heard. The offer of a seat remains open, of course – but I cant put them in a position where I wasnt able to protect them. (*Pause.*) I've fooled myself. I thought for once I hadnt! Colin – its your fault – you brought me here under a misapprehension –

DODDS. What nonsense! We havent time to thrash out these details now. Leonard wont be silly and jeopardise his position before he's read my report.

WILBRAHAM. Suppose you were MD. The company wont be easy to save. We know the competition – the wrinkles – you'll need our help. I wouldnt have the heart to offer it if I'd been humiliated.

LEONARD. Chairman-MD. Full personal control. Or no money. No one deserves charity – in my experience they drink it or gamble it.

BARTLEY *goes out with* WILBRAHAM'S *jacket.*

WILBRAHAM. You want to take my company from me.

LEONARD. Stay on the board – if you think you can contribute.

WILBRAHAM. For how long – and under what sufferance?

LEONARD (*conciliatory*). Suppose I put money in and the company fails? If you're not chairman you've got an excuse, you say it failed because I –

WILBRAHAM. A highly paid messenger! – not even highly paid!

LEONARD. Anyway the board'll be glad to be shot of you – if they're not too geriatric to notice you've gone!

WILBRAHAM. Im in trouble. I may lose my livelihood. But Im not a pauper. Dont push me. Im not speaking from pride. This is my last chance. I know Im ready for it. Im chastened and sober. Otherwise I wouldnt have come here – it would've been wrong. Colin will bear me out if your own judgement cant tell you. You can still make good money out of me. – You silly man! I know what Im doin, *you're* the one who's in confusion. You'd burden yourself with the daily running of my piddling company when you've got the Oldfield giant to absorb you? Anyone would think you were in a trap you show such confusion!

BARTLEY *comes in with* WILBRAHAM's *jacket, giving it the final flick with a clothes brush.*

BARTLEY. I'll put your dirty shirt in a carrier Mr Wilbraham.

WILBRAHAM. Thank you.

BARTLEY *helps* WILBRAHAM *into his jacket and then goes out with the brush and the dirty shirt.*

WILBRAHAM (*to* LEONARD – *the shirt*). Thank you. I'll have it returned.

DODDS. This is absurd! Leonard must state his interest to the meeting. That doesnt commit anyone. It gives you a week of discussions without costing a penny.

LEONARD. I want his agreement on paper before the meeting.

WILBRAHAM. No. I'd sooner dig up my father and pawn his graveclothes. I've been a bloody fool. But when I got up from the gambling table and left appalling losses behind me – my affairs in ruins – I could look the others in the face. It was my money I'd lost. Im sorry I cant put it any better. There are some things – they get talked about so often because they're so important – and then anything we say about them is a cliché. That's the only way we can tell the truth. Listen: if we cant hear the clichés as if they were the truth told to us for the first time – then I think we'd all be dead. Last night I was like a condemned man in a cell. But I looked forward to the morning. I'd found a purpose. The drink, stupid night time sweats, the illiterate gossip in the press (their style is far worse than the imbecilities they're describing – not even honest clichés: frigid banalities) all that was in the past. The last ten years ripped from the calender. And now Im asked to put my inheritance and my expectations in the hands of a boy who – grabs so brashly that he crushes everything he touches! I wont do it. I'd be gambling in a week. I'd rather face my creditors Dodds, they want my money (*Turns to* LEONARD.) – I dont know what you want – it lies beyond my experience, and that's been shady and desperate enough. I see it in your face – your features are like your prison number.

DODDS. Willy Leonard's right: no one can trust you after all the –

WILBRAHAM. You cant know! You havent been in my situation! (*To* LEONARD.) You dont teach dogs to walk on their hindlegs by cutting off their front ones! – they die of your cruelty.

LEONARD. Perhaps this report will show your company's prospects are good. Brilliant! But they're out of your reach. You cant get them without me!

DODDS. Willy dont be unreasonable. Let Leonard –

WILBRAHAM. Shut up! (*Pause.*) Shut up! (*To* LEONARD.) Send this employee from the room! 'Thrash out the details'? If I were suicidal – Im not – you'd both have murder on your hands! (*To* LEONARD.) So cocky! So sure! You dont know what you're doing or even who you're talking to. I could stab you in the back through a three foot wall. I should give in to you and destroy you. It'd almost be worth it to see the surprise on your face! And you wouldnt even have the fun of gambling (*Bitterly.*) or the comfort of walking home in the morning – just the despair.

DODDS (*wristwatch*). We're getting nowhere.

LEONARD. Run him to his creditors. He can tell them he's a reformed rake – signed the pledge – a born again christian – discovered monetarism! It'd almost be worth going to see! A revivalist meeting!

WILBRAHAM. Im so bored with you. I feel like a scientist watching mice when he's forgotten what experiment he's doing. When you ask so much you can only take it from yourself.

LEONARD. I dont want you to give me anything but your enmity! Not the chair – I can *take* that! But when its mine be my enemy! Trick me. Cheat me. Swindle me. Promise me. Please. Enmity! Enmity! Enmity and hate! I'll thrive on the worst you can do! The more stones you throw at me the more I can bury you with! Dont tell me you cant hate? I couldnt stand the let down! If I took all you've got and you didnt hate me – I'd be robbed! All I ask of you is *honesty*: hate me and say it! I'll help you – give you every reason to hate me. Im a gambling machine designed so you cant win: you never have a chance – that's what the machine's *for*! But you must go on gambling. That's our situation. Now do something.

WILBRAHAM (*cries*). I dont know why Im crying. 'S not appropriate. 'S what fathers do: whip their child and cry.

– Why are we so sordid?

LEONARD (*flat*). You'll spoil the shirt.

WILBRAHAM. We're bastards but we dont deserve to live like this. No – (*Sniff.*) not a spoiled shirt. I put on a show. (*Sniff.*) Bloody fool – crying over you doesnt help you. If I could make your mistakes and let you stand by and watch, I would. When it was over you'd pay me far more for what you'd seen than what you'll pay me now. The degradation wouldnt hurt me, Im hardened to it. Yesterday I was at the bottom. Last night was a consolation. Now its the bottom again. What next? What d'you want from me? (*Hand on* LEONARD's *shoulder.*) I hope you have all the luck – the big successes. (*Sniff.*) Come to me if things go wrong, I'll help. Looking down at a gambling table's like looking down at a map of the world: its surrounded by a ring of ghosts. (*To* DODDS.) Scribble his bit of paper.

BARTLEY *comes in with a carrier bag.*

BARTLEY. Your shirt's in the carrier Mr Wilbraham.

LEONARD. I wont be at the meeting.

WILBRAHAM (*to* BARTLEY). Thank you for your help.

BARTLEY. Let me put it in the car for you sir.

LEONARD (*to* DODDS). They'll accept your verbal assurance.

BARTLEY (*to* WILBRAHAM). Coffee's in the mornin room sir. 'Long the passage – ah left the door open. Its sunnier in there.

WILBRAHAM *goes out.*

LEONARD. He's drunk. There arent any overnight conversions – you cant escape from yourself.

DODDS. He's not drunk.

LEONARD. Only because the facts have caught up with him. All *that* was pride and guilt. When the pressures off he'll be back to his bottles and wheels. Glad to be rid of his responsibilities – probably realise it before he gets to the coffee.

LEONARD *and* DODDS *go out.* BARTLEY *picks up the glass left the night before. It is full. He drinks it and goes out with the empty glass.*

Unit Three

The same.

A few weeks later.

LEONARD *and* DODDS. LEONARD *has a file of papers.*

LEONARD (*evenly*). It could never have worked. Start ruthless or pay later. The meeting was vital – a full board – the accountants. Plans for expanding after recovery. He sat in a haze of whisky fumes pushing a piece of paper up and down with one finger. Terrified to pick it up – it'd shake.

DODDS. He warned you.

LEONARD. Im not taking stick for him. (*Mutters.*) He'll booze when he's a skeleton – use his bones for straws.

DODDS. What?

LEONARD. Gambling's *his* problem, his booze is the company's.

DODDS. Indeed.

LEONARD. If he had any guts he'd make a clean break – start something new – open a gambling hell. Follows me round like dogshit on my shoe.

DODDS. Nasty.

LEONARD. The whole company know he's a failure. Surely he suffers under that? Well the board's agreed: he's out. I can turn the company round in a year – we've even had some luck: the orders are better than you forecast – but not if I carry passengers. Anyway for the first time in my life Im happy. Why should I let him spoil it? Get him in. (DODDS *starts to go.*) He hasnt been drinking? Cant stand him like that.

DODDS. No.

LEONARD. Take him out to Annabel's if they still have him. The company's farewell gesture. Let him off-load his bile on you.

DODDS *goes out.* LEONARD *goes to an armchair, sits, opens the file and immediately begins to study the papers in it. The door opens and a large man in a brown suit comes in.* LEONARD *reads for a few more seconds – not long enough to be impolite – shuts the file and stares at it for a few more seconds before looking up.*

LEONARD. Mr Hammond – ? (*Stops.*) My father's not – was he expecting you? (*Silence.*) He's in the country. (*Slight suggestion of intrigue.*) You knew.

HAMMOND. Morning. We'll get this straight out in the open.

LEONARD. Wait . . .! (*Rapid think.*) All right – I'll talk to you and we – (*Stops.*) Im in the middle of – I'll put it off and –

HAMMOND. No need. You're not keeping Willy waiting – I sent him packing.

LEONARD. Who let you in? You've come to hurt me.

HAMMOND (*puzzled*). Hurt? I dont know about such things.

LEONARD (*moves towards door*). I want a witness to this conversation.

HAMMOND. That's the last thing you want. I dont believe you've even guessed? As managing director of Wilbraham Engineering you owe me four million three hundred odd pounds. Overdue. I want immediate payment.

LEONARD. I've got a debtors' waiver for one year.

HAMMOND. No.

LEONARD. Yes. You werent on the list.

HAMMOND. Not when you checked. Dodds gave you five names. Between then and the date of the waiver I bought the debts. The waiver says 'debts outstanding' – nothing more. For the sake of form you do owe the five a few thousand each. Your bit of paper doesnt cover my four millions.

LEONARD. Why was the paper worded like that?

HAMMOND. I told Dodds to word it like that.

LEONARD. And not serve you notice of the creditor meeting.

HAMMOND. That would've been Willy's slip. Seen worse. Busy time – company upheaval. Mistakes happen in the best run companies – and he's known to drink.

LEONARD. Any lawyer would rip through that in his sleep.

HAMMOND. Let sleeping lawyers lie, they do less harm. I knew Willy's dad – the evil bugger. Sorry for the lad. When his firm got in a bad way I bought the debts. Give my old friend's son a breathing space. Then I find he's been took-over, kicked out the chair – now kicked out the company (I read his dismissal notice on the desk on my way in.) – by a young pop-up artist who doesnt give a monkey's who he hurts! We're not safe. That young tear-away's pants need taking down for the sake of decent public life.

LEONARD. What did you pay Dodds? Or did he do it out of the malice of a pure heart? This is to hurt my father.

HAMMOND. Hurt? I dont have time or inclination to go round doing hurt. Listen: I dont have to present my bill, now or ever. I reckon you might get this company back in profit. You started right – kicked Willy out – but any sane man'd rid himself of that louse. Suppose you fail? Trade slump – labour trouble – reorganisation snarl-ups – a whole host of things! – not to mention your own mistakes: you trusted Dodds. I wouldnt have. I dont trust *myself* – and I dont know half what Im up to! Dont *you* trust me neither. We'll put it on a business basis. I'll bail you out and see you through any rough patches – you'll

get all the resources of my organisation behind you –
money – insider gen –

LEONARD (*candid*). I have to ask you to explain Mr
Hammond. Are you threatening me or offering me
something?

HAMMOND. I own twelve percent of Oldfield's equity. When
time takes its toll and you inherit, you top me up to fifty-
one per cent: controlling interest. Your father's getting
on and lately he's been under a strain. Dodds has put it
all down nicely on a bit of paper. I checked it, its safe to
sign – no catch: it says what it says.

LEONARD. I'll pay you off. Borrow from my father.

HAMMOND. Dont haggle if you cant offer something with
a bit of relish. Would I go to all this bother if you could
wriggle off the hook so easy?

LEONARD. The other creditors had faith in me! I'll give you
a good return on capital! All I ask is – (*He stops.*)

HAMMOND (*after a short pause*). I wish there was another
way. (*Slight pause.*) You cant even try borrowing behind
my back – Hong Kong or somewhere – they'd want your
balls and they'd be mine by then: the first sign of messing
and I'll stick my bill where your father sees it. And if that
didnt scare the Willies out of you you'd've gone to him at
the start – when Dodds came to you with his evil little
plan. I'd've gone to him. So would Dodds. So would
Tom, Dick and Harry. You're the only person in the
world who couldnt. And its got worse! The first move you
made on your own you put his whole company at risk!
Dear o dear. If he saw the cock-up you're in – just try
lifting a corner so he can peep – he'll cut you off. He'd
never forget. O he'll fill your pockets – but his company'd
vanish out of sight like Mont Blanc going down the plug
hole. So would all the other loot I dont know about –
(*Taps his chest.*) the treasure store up within. The whole
world really. That's what you're scared of losing – not
the company or the money. The little no-man's land

between father and son. That's where it all turns. That's what handed you over to me. Dodds was right. Strange. I can see it in your face. It'd be a different world if we went round with our boots on our heads – as we would if we had the sense. We walk on our feet but drag our face through the dirt. Its painful to see you lad. There's one certain thing left in your young life: you wont get your hands on a spanner from your father's works unless it comes through me. They say he's a right bully. I'll make amends. Controlling share – not the lot. Leave you your proper incentive. And if you're hoping I'll die before your father, that wont help – apart from the incidental pleasure it'd give you. My shares go to my assigns. (*Calls.*) Dodds! – you dont mind me being free? Im taking the risk out of your future. Me behind you, you cant fail. When your company's a success, come out in the open – partly: bounce about in front of your father – rattle his bones.

DODDS *comes in.* LEONARD *ignores him.*

HAMMOND. We've been building paper castles.

LEONARD (*half-musing, half aloud*). No no that's not the problem. My father's slow because he doesnt want his company wrecked. Its every father's problem: hand on because they die. If its an athlete – runner – jumper – he gives up early and trains the young. Then he's happy. Business men are in their prime when they're old. That's why there's distress. Not hate and treachery – that's for friends. In families – there's distress *because* they're loyal. He'll take his share of blame. Its wrong to judge him.

HAMMOND (*to* DODDS). You comment.

DODDS. Your father came to me as company secretary and raised his doubts about you officially. When you help to arm the nation you have obligations.

HAMMOND. Be inventive! Expand! All sorts is possible! When you sign my paper I'll sell you my shares in

Oldfields – for a price. Then you give them to your dad as a present. Say you talked me into it. How's that! He's not to know I'd just be putting money in my own piggy bank! The things you've got to learn! Take Respectability Dodds – a perfect specimen of the devious and corrupt. Or Willy – the Inexplicable. No one needs to stand alone in this world: we can share each other's enemies. Just remember whose back your knife's in. If I push you too hard you run to dad and get disinherited: then you disinherit *me* at a stroke! Not every lad's in a position to disinherit a man old enough to be his father. I'll have to be a good boy! When I bind you to me, Im the rope: if I bind too hard, I break. Our friendship's based on betrayal. Not many friendships have such a solid base my son – that's usually reserved for love affairs.

LEONARD. Go to hell. You havent thought of everything.

HAMMOND. I have, I have! I bet you Wilbraham Engineering I have! Cheer up! It looks like collapse and its the rocket taking off. Dont judge by the common man's standards. If a strangler got his hands round my neck I'd crush his wrists with my chin. I would. I wouldnt let him tear hisself away. Hold him eyeball to eyeball and let him plead while his fingers dribbled down my shirt. I succeed because I enjoy my enemies: but I dont let them enjoy me – Im not an ecumenisist!

LEONARD. I cheat my father every day till he dies?

HAMMOND. Well you made a nice start when you went behind his back to Willy and it'll come easier with practice.

LEONARD. If I get a chance to hurt you I shant hesitate.

HAMMOND. I wouldnt want you to. You'll be my trainee by then. Its only the humbug I cant stomach. (*Pats* LEONARD's *back.*) We'll do.

LEONARD. I wont sign.

HAMMOND. I'll give you a couple of days for the sake of

your dignity. I enjoyed meeting you – helping a young lad by putting opportunity in his way. But you're not the only iron in the fire. (*To* DODDS.) I'll expect the paper by Monday. (*Starts to go.*) You were a sitting duck and as you were sitting on the roof of an armaments factory it seemed wrong not to take a shot.

HAMMOND *goes out.*

DODDS. We'll go to your father's shoot. It'll look suspicious if we both dropped out.

LEONARD. What's the first thing I'll do when I get the company?

DODDS. By then we'll know so much about each other we'll both have to keep to heel. Hammond's a bad friend but a worse enemy. If you want anything to use on your father, I can let you into the –

LEONARD *has walked out.* DODDS's *voice doesnt rise or trail way but stops abruptly in mid-sentence. He goes out.*

Unit Four

OLDFIELD's *Country House*

The Hall Lobby.

Apart from BARTLEY *everyone in the scene wears shooting clothes.*

BARTLEY *comes in carrying the Oldfield AS42 Rifle and a case of magazines and rounds. He wears a dark suit with a fawn windcheater over the suit jacket, and calf-length wellingtons. He sets the AS42 down on its dipod and puts the case next to it. He starts to shell rounds from their packets.* WILBRAHAM *comes in.*

BARTLEY. Like spring oot there the mornin sir.

WILBRAHAM. Good morning. Is this where we assemble?

BARTLEY. The hoose party ay. Day guests oot on the drive.
Yous can join them if yous wish sir.

WILBRAHAM. I'll hang on. Somewhat nippy. (*Looks at the
AS42.*) . . . Good lor . . .!

BARTLEY. Ay sir – new Oldfield AS42. Nae a prototype –
first factory run. Mr Oldfield's takin it oot the day. He
allus takes a new –

WILBRAHAM. You couldnt find me a drink?

BARTLEY. Ay sir. Can ah offer you ma flask? (*Takes out his
pocket flask.*) Mr Oldfield does'nae like liquor drunk
before the shoot. (*Fills flask cap.*) Has t' act canny in his
line o' trade. Accident here – the peaceniks'd put it doon
t' the hand o' god. When you're desperate you bring god
in t' anythin. I carry a wee drop for the gentlemen's
emergencies. (*Hands cap to* WILBRAHAM.) There you go
sir.

WILBRAHAM. Obliged to you.

BARTLEY. Not at all.

WILBRAHAM (*drinks*). I had intended not to drink before
lunch. This nip in the air . . .

BARTLEY. Och it'd be suicide t' go oot in that damp wi' oot
a liquid breakfast. Could yous manage another sir? I'd
advise it t' dilute the first.

WILBRAHAM *holds out the cap.*

BARTLEY (*pouring*). Mr Oldfield does'nae let me join the
beaters. But ah flit aboot. Ah keep *this* top up.

WILBRAHAM *drinks. He holds the empty cap in his hand.*
BARTLEY *poises the lip of the flask over it and looks
questioningly at* WILBRAHAM.

WILBRAHAM. No no please. (*Hands cap back to* BARTLEY.)
I mustnt.

BARTLEY *takes the cap and screws it back on the flask.*

BARTLEY. It'll come t' nae harm if wor leave it t' mature a
while longer.

BARTLEY. I was up at six.

BARTLEY. Is that right sir?

WILBRAHAM. I intended to take a brisk walk. Then I
thought: ridiculous – let the poor bloody birds spend their
last morning in peace.

BARTLEY. O ay sir?

WILBRAHAM. I sat in the armchair and looked at the trees.

BARTLEY. Much more sensible sir. You'll get plenty brisk
walks the day.

WILBRAHAM. Yes.

BARTLEY (*pocketing flask*). I dont know if you'd agree with
me sir but there's a fine view o' the trees oot your room.
Panoramic.

WILBRAHAM. Bird song always makes the world seem
empty. I played in a woods when I was a boy. My aunt
owned one in the country.

BARTLEY. Tell me the lad wor's nae at haim in a wood.

WILBRAHAM (*quietly*). How bloody stupid it all is . . . I wish
I didnt have to go out. Im not at all in a fit state to kill
things. I could say I was indisposed – stay in? (*Shakes
head dismissively.*) I'd drink. (*Looks at AS42.*) How
barbarous . . .

BARTLEY (*offering a small tin box*). Would you take a
peppermint sir?

WILBRAHAM. No thank you.

BARTLEY. T' keep the kelt oot.

LEONARD *comes in. He stops in the doorway, looking at the
AS42, sees* WILBRAHAM *and turns to go.*

WILBRAHAM. Dont go.

LEONARD (*going*). Im looking for my father.

WILBRAHAM. I must have a word.

LEONARD *stops*.

WILBRAHAM. Im most grateful.

BARTLEY. I'll tell Mr Oldfield you're lookin for him Mr Leonard.

BARTLEY *goes out*.

WILBRAHAM. I've been trying to speak to you since I got here.

LEONARD. You have nothing to –

WILBRAHAM. Im absolute scum. You cant possibly forgive the harm I've done you. I destroyed myself and now Im used to harm others. Odd isnt it? I've nothing against you. Dodds came to me with his filthy proposal. He poses as my friend. Men like him are vermin. I wouldnt be his friend if he were my one salvation on the day of judgement. What could I do? Im not in control of my performance. Before I met you I prayed (of course I dont believe in god, my gambling losses cured me of that: he's just a nervous tic left over from school chapel) 'O god let him be a crook, a bastard – and let my innocence shine out'. Then I'd be exonerated in the eyes of the mythical bystander in books on ethics: he'd see *Im* the victim. I was only doing to you what you'd spend your life doing to others – my one fault was to punish you before you'd had time to commit the crime: but surely in the eyes of heaven that's almost a virtue? And there you were: innocent. Its cruel to be that innocent! I was so ashamed. I had one hope: he'll see Im scum. Surely he wont trust me? O god he's so innocent he does! I reek of deceit – fraud – dishonesty – filth! Even he must see it! Find me out! Get on my scent! Run me down! Expose me! Help me you fool! I chatted on about early morning walks and milk bottles – I was as bogus as I dared – extravagant under the circumstances – remember Dodds was watching. You were too greedy to notice what you were eating.

Yum yum you lapped the poison up and asked for seconds! Make me chairman! You were like a victim pointing out the places to stick the knife in. I was to blame – I led you on. That was my crime: I let you make me your victim. I couldnt believe the confusion you were in. This man is more evil than I am, I thought: yet he's innocent. Dont you think the world's in great danger when such things can happen? When corruption's so deep it comes from innocence, everything's contaminated by innocence! We can never get away from it! And I connive. Always I let it happen. Yet I long to do good! Im such scum! Such scum! Such scum! How can you stay and listen to me Mr Oldfield?

LEONARD. Why're you here?

WILBRAHAM. Hammond sticking me under your nose. What can you expect from a man who always wears brown? He'd wear a brown dinner jacket if he could get a decent tailor to make him one. Im the stench of failure – if you dont sign his paper you're supposed to end up like me. Last night I was reformed – again. I put a bottle of Laffite under the bed. I even got up at six to torment myself by sitting with it. Its still unopened. Then I came down and scrounged a guzzle from that gillie. I had to chat him up. How the homespun philosophy comes to one's lips! I invented an aunt who owned a wood. Always stay down-wind of a servant – they turn nasty. He offered me peppermint: how low I've fallen! Scum! I told you I didnt deceive you from malice? There was no pleasure in it. You seemed a long way off. It was like god shooting at cardboard cut-out men for target practice. Thank you for hearing my confession while Im fairly sober. This evening I'll get drunk and buttonhole you. You'll have to listen to the most fearful sentimental garbage. I do apologise. D'you know why a drunk buttonholes the sober? He tries to force his own self-love onto them by making them tell him he's wonderful – it might even

sound true coming from someone sober. But they tell him
he's a drunken swine – and bring him face to face with
his own self-hate. Then the anger swells up. – My
confession didnt interest you?

LEONARD. No.

WILBRAHAM. A mistake. Adding to another's torment
doesnt lighten our own. (*Shrugs.*) Why should you accept
the apology of a scum?

LEONARD. Sell up what's left and go.

WILBRAHAM. Too late. I gamble any money I get hands
on. If I was wounded I'd sell my bandages to bet on the
2.30 though I'd bleed to death before they came under
starters orders. I told you you were my last chance. You
did right to squash me – a civic duty – but its a pity you
had to damage yourself so badly to do it. Im scum beyond
redemption. Not even a ruin: a waste lot where the
builders dumped their things to rot. Even now when I
apologise Im a puppet doing Hammond's dirty work: I
exhibit my admonitory vileness. Would it help you to call
me scum?

LEONARD. No.

WILBRAHAM. You may should you wish. To relieve your
feelings. I shant take offence. (*No response.*) We're
civilized men who've found this small way to help each
other. Relieve yourself on me. Please. Say scum. Scum.
Its a useful word – not easily confused except with skunk.
Almost an anagram of muck – and mucus. (*Silence.*) You
make people talk but you cant listen. Two sides of a coin
but they cant see each other, the head's so close to the tail
its got its eyes up its own bum. Is that the secret? Perhaps
that's to be your downfall. (*Pause.*) Scum. I flatter myself
I have the *mot juste*. As distinctive as the old school tie –
which you dont claim unless you're entitled to. *Cads* do:
but *I'm* genuine scum. I dont demand repartee: just the
odd insult. You wont oblige? No matter. I do brilliant
imitations. The only think I learned at school. Cut lawns

– oak panels – mullioned windows – tradition like bloodstains in the cloisters – libraries bulging with the wisdom of dilapidated books – and I learned the arts of a low comedian. (*He imitates* DODDS. LEONARD *walks away*.) 'I have prepared this piece of paper. I've lined up the dots with a ruler and counted them. They're all there. You can sign'. (*Imitates* DODDS *in Gilbert and Sullivan*.)

'*I am Dodds the dots – dots – dots*
I am Dodds of the dotted line'

(*Imitates* HAMMOND.) 'Trust me lad and I'll peel the skin off your back and flog it to you for wallpaper. Hate me, and we'll sit side by side on the same cadaver and share the same bone.' (*Brief shrill laugh. Imitates* LEONARD. LEONARD *moves away but he follows him*.) 'Mr Wilbraham this is young Master Oldfield. Im king of the castle! I want to be chairman! Only triple-scum would bring that up Wilbraham! Scum! State of the art scum! S for shit – c for crap – u for uckers – m for mess: scum!' Now for my *piece de resistance* – my imitation of myself! (*Parodies himself*.) 'Rightie-o young Oldfield! Jolly fine insulting weather! What's that you say? Bum? – no need to be personal. Rum? – I dont mind if I do. Slum? – my aunt used to own one! Dumb? Hum? – tis a mite pongy, could I scrounge the loan of a pair of socks? O *scum*! – Scum! Scum – scum – scum!' (*Weeps*.) And who's the weeping – who's that imitate? The world, the whole bloody bloody world! (*Slight pause, stops weeping*.) I shouldnt have drunk. Fancy that! O god was that me? I was looking forward to a nice normal weekend away from the London alley-louts, harmlessly shooting birds out of the sky. And now I've been a reformed drunk at night and a lapsed drunk in the morning and we still havent shot the birds. There's no limit to my vileness. Its a conspiracy against the world – certainly against myself. I listen to my imitations to find out what they say about me behind my back. They say Im scum. Utter scum. Yesterday I ruined your life, now Im ruining your weekend. What scum!

OLDFIELD *and* BARTLEY *come in.*

OLDFIELD (*to* BARTLEY, *pointing to the AS42*). Put an empty magazine on the gun.

BARTLEY *kneels by the AS42 and loads magazines. He puts one on the gun.*

OLDFIELD. I hope you're comfortable Mr Wilbraham? If you need anything my servant will look after you.

WILBRAHAM. Delightful house. Reminds me of my aunt's.

OLDFIELD. I wonder if you'd mind finding my assistant Dodds?

WILBRAHAM. Where should I look?

OLDFIELD. He's around. I'd be most grateful.

WILBRAHAM *waits a moment and then goes out.*

OLDFIELD. For god's sake what made you invite him? The man's absolute scum. If he's not careful one day someone will tell him.

LEONARD. I felt sorry for him.

OLDFIELD. You're so naive. I dont like you mixing with his sort. Reeks of failure.

LEONARD. He's in trouble.

OLDFIELD. Im not surprised. Any other weekend I wouldnt mind if you invited Bedlam and Pentonville for their annual cricket match. You know Im putting on my little show with the AS42. Over the years its become a ritual with a new gun. A celebration for friends. Its certainly the most innocent use it'll ever be put to. Now I feel like a clown performing to a stranger. Why you –

LEONARD. Shut up! Its stupid to waste – (*Stops.*)! Does it matter? Be a clown! (*Tries to be calm.*) I shouldnt have brought him. *He's* the clown . . . (*Angry.*) But its my house too! I might have something to celebrate!

OLDFIELD. What? (*No immediate answer.*) Well what? (*Pause.*) Was I going on . . .? *You* know the man's irritating. I made a resolution not to quarrel. I had a special reason for wanting a good weekend. I wasnt going to tell you till the evening. I'll put you on the board.

LEONARD. You changed your mind.

OLDFIELD. Not straight away – I'll approach the directors over the next few months. They wont oppose. You'll come on as trainee-director. I hope that's what you want?

LEONARD. Yes.

OLDFIELD. So you *have* something to celebrate. Frankly this isnt how I wanted to do it. You're impetuous – of course you cant see it, but its what you are and you have to come to terms with the consequences. With a gun you test and discard and the tears go on the drawing board. With people, they learn by wounding themselves – or others: though that tells them about guns not wounds. (*To* BARTLEY.) Find Dodds. With any luck that fool's got lost in the fields. (*To* LEONARD.) You're responsible if he strays in front of the guns.

LEONARD. Why didnt you tell me before?

OLDFIELD (*to* BARTLEY). Leave that – I want Dodds.

BARTLEY *goes out.*

OLDFIELD. You've begun to pull. If I hold you in you'll get – fractious . . .

LEONARD. If you'd said this – you passed me in the house every day with this in your head – why didnt you – ? – as if we were cars passing on the street! –

OLDFIELD. Would it've made a difference?

LEONARD. No – when you know what you're doing nothing does. (*Sudden change.*) You can still chuck me off, old lad!

OLDFIELD. The board hires and fires.

LEONARD. Hostile board – I fail – out! Rid of me!

OLDFIELD. Are you being bloody minded – or is it lack of

confidence? I've done what you wanted! (*Conciliatory.*) I took you by surprise. Well at least we can look back – our lives havent been without their strangeness – and see how we survived. Your first parents left you on a doorstep. I've opened doors. What would you say to them today?

LEONARD. I'd ask them to forgive me.

OLDFIELD. You mean you'd –

LEONARD. No – I mean *that*.

OLDFIELD. Would you try to find them? Give them money?

LEONARD. Mother burned the rubbish I was found in. Might've been a clue. D'you ever wonder about my father?

OLDFIELD. No – I've always had a very clear picture of him in my head. The reality you see in – O, doll's houses and gravestones.

LEONARD. Yes, but we're talking about strangers.

OLDFIELD. Children are born with nothing. I gave you things because I have them – its how I made you mine. Women are different. Your mother had to strip you to make you hers. Dont begrudge her her bonfire. She had a withered womb. I'll tell you something I – but she's been dead long enough now . . . She ate nothing for days (I found out later) and then swallowed a colic – a violent mixture of bitters. I came home. I thought at first it was the burglar alarm, not working properly. Her whimpering was drawn out like a scream. Real pain and fear. She pretended to give birth to you and you almost killed her. She tore the sheet with her teeth – along the top – holes and rents. She'd smeared you with something to resemble blood. I dont know what it was. You were beside her on the bed sleeping naked.

LEONARD. Cosier than a doorstep.

OLDFIELD (*controlled*). God you can be icy-blooded. You'll listen with respect when I talk about your mother. After she got well you werent a gift I'd bought her. There was

something between you. You'd given her fear and pain:
you were hers. And you gave me a new woman. I didnt
know she had such tenderness in her – that it was in
anyone. She became all I wanted, and I lost her. She was
a stranger – like your father in a way: a doll. Its precious
– you're happy its yours – but it cant be changed – you
take it as it is. (*Explains.*) Though your father was a
fiction. Not real. – You're right, dont pry into the past.
The detectives cant earn their fees. Put your arm round
me.

LEONARD. Bartley – he may come in –

OLDFIELD. Does a child found on a doorstep worry about
such things? – You should be at home with all doors. Sons
put their arm round their father. Do it today. You're my son.

*They stand side by side, their bodies barely touch, and put an
arm round each other's shoulder – they are like two dummies
each with a human arm.*

OLDFIELD. There. Our pact. (*Hand-pat on* LEONARD's
shoulder.) Strong. Not my flesh – but good. I was strong
once. Now its your turn. Our talk of birth makes me think
of death. No rituals can take *its* place.

LEONARD. Rituals?

OLDFIELD. Naked on your mother's bed. Your ritual birth.
Its hard to care for others as they deserve.

LEONARD. We have – we know what we should do.

OLDFIELD. And my gun! You must use that! Have to! Yes
– have a go! Bang it! Bang bang bang! (*They part.*) The
press office have hired a photographer!

DODDS, WILBRAHAM *and* BARTLEY *come in.* BARTLEY
has OLDFIELD's *coat over his arm and carries gloves,
mittens and a scarf. He goes to the AS42 and finishes loading
the magazines.*

DODDS. I've sent off the beaters trucks. Havers said to give
him twenty minutes.

WILBRAHAM. You must be proud of your new gun Mr Oldfield. I hear you're putting on a show? Just the normal shooting? – or do you juggle with it?

OLDFIELD (*to* DODDS). Mortingham turned up?

DODDS. No.

OLDFIELD. Ha ha all his land and the old scoundrel's jealous! He's had his chauffeur in and out his garage ten times this morning! He'll come – never miss a shoot! Watch the envious old bugger when he sees my gun! The ermined old faggot rang up the Game Conservancy to see if it was legal! The pettyness! He doesnt know I know!

DODDS. You should put a shot in him.

OLDFIELD. I'll wear my coat Bartley.

BARTLEY *goes to* OLDFIELD *and helps him to dress.*

LEONARD. Are you a good shot Wilbraham?

WILBRAHAM. The world's worst.

OLDFIELD. We cant all be good at everything.

LEONARD *picks up the AS42 and starts to demonstrate it.*

LEONARD. The new generation of personal weapons: sniper and assault rifle combined. Weight four kilogrammes. Barrell thirty-three inch. Calibre standard NATO 7.6. Muzzle velocity 2900fs – 860ms. Gas operated.

BARTLEY (*to* OLDFIELD). I brought a choice o' lined gloves or gun mittens.

LEONARD (*aiming at various targets*). Out performs the rival SSG69 Manfred Schöner with RWS match rounds. Ten shot groups of under forty centimetres diam at eight hundred metres. Thirteen centimeters dispersion at four hundred metres. The salesmen boast that guarantees a killing.

BARTLEY (*to* OLDFIELD). Shall ah put the gloves in your pocket?

DODDS (*to* WILBRAHAM). If you want to get into history Willy get shot by that. You'd be first.

OLDFIELD. So far its only put down pigs. (*To* BARTLEY.) Dont fuss.

BARTLEY. I was wrappin the gloves in the scarf so they'd nae go lost.

OLDFIELD (*to* DODDS). Make sure they ring the office for messages before they bring down our lunch.

WILBRAHAM. Whenever Im on a shoot I dread being peppered by someone who's an even worse shot than me – if there is such a thing. I wouldnt mind being put down with *that*. Die in the forefront of technology. Not like dying – more like enlisting for the future. When I see –

LEONARD (*aiming*). Image intensification using the wavelength of visible light and an infra red facility for seeing in night and mist. Image controlled by voltage on the plate. Two cheap torch batteries.

BARTLEY (*almost to himself as he watches* OLDFIELD). Mittens must be pulled on tighter than gloves.

OLDFIELD (*to* BARTLEY *as he starts to push the mittens down on* OLDFIELD's *fingers*). The head gamekeeper can be photographed with it. No one else. I dont want the crowd clowning. They may be the elite but they're like a coachload of borstal escapees when they've got guns. Send one of me out with a press release. I dont want to pick it. They complain I choose the unflattering ones.

LEONARD (*aiming through the sights*). The feather's on the blackbird's back. The line along the tips. A grey hair in the sea. So clear. You dip your finger in the pool in the trees a thousand metres away and wonder why it isnt wet.

BARTLEY. Pardon sir.

BARTLEY *goes to* LEONARD *and unclips the magazine from the AS42. On the way he drops a mitten.*

OLDFIELD. What – ?

BARTLEY (*to* OLDFIELD). Its nothin sir. (*To* LEONARD.) Beg pardon sir.

OLDFIELD (*pointing to the magazine in* BARTLEY's *hand*). Give me that.

BARTLEY (*throws the magazine into the case. Under his breath*). Nothin nothin nothin.

OLDFIELD (*going towards the case*). I will –

BARTLEY (*jerking passed* OLDFIELD *to get to the case before him*). Will yous leave the bloody – ! Its nothin sir. The guns are ready. Ah believe ah heard the beaters – (*Stops. Slight pause. He stands between the case and* OLDFIELD.) Ah dropped your mitten. Tch tch.

OLDFIELD *goes to the case, takes out a magazine and examines it. He wears one mitten.* BARTLEY *watches him.*

OLDFIELD. Loaded. One round.

BARTLEY. Och well I was in the middle o' loadin when – (*Stops.*) That's nae the magazine wor on the gun.

OLDFIELD (*magazine*). Dodds kindly confirm this round.

BARTLEY. That was nae on the gun.

OLDFIELD (*to* DODDS). It was on the gun. (*Goes to the AS42 and rapidly checks.*) With the safety catch released.

BARTLEY (*explaining firmly*). Now sir. Three magazines – and the one in Mr Dodds' hand I'd started – wor loaded. The empty magazine's in the case.

WILBRAHAM. Good lor' have we all been in danger?

OLDFIELD. Mr Wilbraham please confirm that you witnessed the gun loaded with that magazine.

WILBRAHAM. O guns guns I know nothing of guns. Depend utterly on my loader.

BARTLEY (*quietly explaining to the others*). If he'd'nae snatched – an mix em up – such a terrible awkward thing t' – like an old wuman wi a weapon in his –

OLDFIELD (*to* BARTLEY). Get your things together. Dodds see a waggon runs him to the station. (*To* BARTLEY.) You're dismissed with a month's salary. (*To* DODDS.) Warn the security guard in London to accompany him the whole time he needs to remove his things. (*To* BARTLEY.) Go. (*To* DODDS.) Go.

BARTLEY. Ah dinnae understand – Mr Leonard – ?

LEONARD *stands holding the AS42.*

OLDFIELD. Your irresponsibility might have caused a tragedy. And burdened my son with guilt. You're partly to blame Leonard. The magazine's provided with a transparent view strip. However I suppose one round is easily missed. (*Starts to turn away but turns back.*) And you were aiming. I wanted to stop you but I'd've been told I was treating you like a child. (*To* BARTLEY.) He's still there! Cant he move? Has he shot *himself*?

WILBRAHAM (*quietly singing Gilbert and Sullivan*). 'O Im the dots dots dots and Im underlined'.

BARTLEY. Sir –

OLDFIELD. If the magazine wasnt loaded why did you snatch it from the gun?

BARTLEY (*immediately*). I though ah heard Havers hoot oot the yard t' say the beaters wor in place.

OLDFIELD. I might have reconsidered but after that blatant affrontery I wont. All employees are issued with the Company Laws. Careless handling of weapons-stroke-rounds: instant dismissal.

BARTLEY. Och that does'nae apply t' domestics an such type o' –

OLDFIELD. It applies.

BARTLEY. Anyway I wor nae mistook! Ah swear t' god ah –

OLDFIELD. You're in no fit state to swear to anything. You rarely are. Its my fault for – (*Stops.*) Mr Wilbraham did you have something to say?

WILBRAHAM *stops singing.*

OLDFIELD. Its my fault for asking you to load.

BARTLEY. Well in that case ah think its –

OLDFIELD. I refuse to stand and argue with an ex-employee! You're on my property! And drunk! (*He reaches out and takes the flask from* BARTLEY'*s jacket.*)

Like the magazine this flask has a viewing strip – so the owner's not caught with it empty – as it now three-quarters is!

BARTLEY (*appeal*). Mr Wilbraham – ?

WILBRAHAM. I wouldnt know the lethal end of a pea-shooter.

BARTLEY. This is unfair unfair unfair. Will none o' yous speak for me? (*Blunt, angry resignation.*) Ach t' hell wi' the lot o' yous!

OLDFIELD (*flask*). Take it. I shant be short of evidence. The cupboards will be full of empties.

BARTLEY (*under breath*). Yous bastard. (*Apology.*) Ah'm sorry sir. If ah accidental clip on the wrong magazine that's cause ah wor sent oot in the middle o' loadin. Ah'd've check. Ah'm like a hen: check check check. I check when Mr Leonard had it up in the air. Ah'd never've let ma governor oot the door wi' nae check. Take your mitten sir. Its just that – (*Stops and turns to* WILBRAHAM.) Mr Wilbraham its nae right t' treat any man like this. (WILBRAHAM *starts to hum 'Dot' tunes.* BARTLEY *tries to edge* OLDFIELD *aside.*) Man yous know fine why ah carry the flask. Hoo many times've yous seen me in the bushes gi' the gentlemen a wee nip when their fingers's numb? Ah *need* my job. Please take your mitten. Its kelt oot there. (*Indicates* WILBRAHAM.) Ask yon what he took for breakfast an wor he got it. It wor liquid but it wor nae oot the udder.

OLDFIELD. I've been waiting for a chance to dismiss you and by god you've given me one. Any doctor will confirm you're an alcoholic. I should explain Mr Wilbraham, he was courtmartialed from her majesty's navy. I gave him a chance – I hoped he'd been taught his lesson.

BARTLEY *turns on his heels and goes out quickly.*

OLDFIELD (*to* WILBRAHAM). Sorry about this. Must be firm, y'know. Christen a gun with accidental death –

imagine the effect on the minds of men going out to kill! We all know the military are superstitious. If the procurement came down to a fine choice *that* could tip the scales against us. Now promise me you wont let this spoil your weekend Wilbraham. Fortunate you were here! I may need a statement – though I dont think he'll cause trouble. Went off smartish! – fraid to lose his sack-money. You recall how he insulted me? – not so much words but tone. He swore twice and was over-familiar.

WILBRAHAM *hums.*

OLDFIELD (*to* DODDS). See him off! Is the whole world coming to a halt? (*Takes the AS42 from* LEONARD.) And bring back my mitten – he tried to make off with it. (*To* LEONARD.) Bring the rounds. – My dear Eric I cant believe this about you being a bad shot.

WILBRAHAM. You soon will.

OLDFIELD. We'll get you a good loader. Wrong chap ruins the sport. If Mortingham didnt bring his own I'd give him one with aftershave – ha! (*Going.*) Dodds!

OLDFIELD *and* WILBRAHAM *go out.*

DODDS. I'll bring Hammond's assignment to your room before dinner.

DODDS *goes out.* LEONARD *follows with the case of magazines.*

Unit Five

Derelict House

The only piece of furniture is a traditional wooden kitchen-chair, with a curved back and a support across it, a cane or drilled-plywood seat, and a strengthening hoop between the legs. Beside the chair there is an empty bottle and there is a small bottle in a corner.

LEONARD *sits on the chair.* BARTLEY *has a blanket. Both wear shabby trousers, shirts and raincoats and muddy shoes.*

BARTLEY. Lyin prat . . . yous got money . . . your ol' fella would'nae cut yous off . . . get your hands on a fortune . . . stop wor us: yous pay . . . malignant bastard . . . What d'yous want? What d'yous want? . . . Have a few bevvies one night, see black in my head: kick yous t' pieces! . . . If ah had money ah could get oot this coffin . . . you could help us . . .

LEONARD. If you had money you'd –

BARTLEY. Booze it! Ay but that would'nae last. Scroungin every penny t' drink *drives* a man t' drink, yous dinnae have the strength left t' kick it . . . You think yous can live wi'oot money! Few months doon this hell, you'll murder for money! Why must ah suffer till then? . . . What d'yous want? What d'yous want? If ah knew that . . . God ah could murder a drink . . . Ah'll settle yous sonny: next time you're drunk you'll come to in a empty hoose! – cope on your own!

LEONARD. No one goes while they can still screw you.

BARTLEY. Is that right? I'll maybe teach you different laddie! . . . My god there must be somethin else! Sat here persecutin each other! . . . Ah wonder if its nae me wor's cruel? . . . If ah knew what yous want! . . . If you left yous have t' come t' your senses. Nothin t' stop yous, not even a door on the hinges . . .

LEONARD. You'd be running after me before I was round the corner.

BARTLEY. Dinnae be too bloody sure! Ah'd be better off shot o' yous even if you are rollin! Im still nae but the skivvy! Wouldnt slash your wrist if ah was'nae here t' swab up!

BARTLEY *stands, goes to* LEONARD *and grabs for his wrists
– * LEONARD *pulls away.*

BARTLEY. Ah'll bloody look man! (*Unwinds rags from*
LEONARD'*s wrists.*) No gangrene in my place! Stink o'
that on top o' your spewed up guts! Worse'n sewers!
(*Examines* LEONARD'*s wrists.*) Pathetic! Look at it –
scratches! Cant even open his veins! I hate yous bloody
amateur suicides – messin wor other people have t' live.
(*Goes to the corner and picks up the small bottle.*) Next time
tell the skivvy. 'Cut my wrists Bartley there's a good
man'. Ah'll do a proper job! Leave yous t' swill oot the
gutter. Leonard man shall ah tell yous somethin? (*No
answer.*) Is this how wor t' live, stuck starin at scabs? –
If ah telled yous would yous listen? D'you know why the
navy chuck us oot?

LEONARD (*Flat*). You lied to me father.

BARTLEY. Ay – but it wor a good lie: it stop him checkin up
the real reason. Why should ah tell such nonsense if its
nae true? I came t' the interview wi' a cock an' bull story
work oot: Victimized by wor officers – the *lie* came t' me
while I wor talkin. Ah start off tellin him bout the sub –
anthin nuclear, people are fascinated. (*Iodine.*) It does-
'nae hurt on whole skin. Hardens it magic. You'd need
a stone mason t' get in those veins noo. Ah thought it
policy t' stress the danger. I said in every chamber o' the
sub that has t' do wi' weapons there's a truncheon hangin
up. If someone goes beserk – or acts peculiar – yous beat
the laddie's brains oot – that's if he has'nae beat yours
oot first. Official yous give him a wee tap an a tablet
when he comes round. But when the master-at-arms (O
they worship titles!) instructs yous in the use o' truncheons, its 'Beat the bugger's brains oot – nae loonies in
my sub!' Your ol' fella's sat there listenin. There was
dead silence. Uncanny. He give the impression he's asked
a question an he's waitin for the answer – but he has'nae

asked. Then the lie came t' me. I swear it wor in his head
first – an ah told him the lie he wanted me t' telled him.
His mouth wor set – like a stone – but a bitty open – like
the gob on a wee angry ol' woman – an then ah said it.
It wor like lip-readin a corpse. Ah said on christmas
mornin ah went roond t' every truncheon an put a
condom on it. Shall ah tie these rags back on? The
wounds – if they deserve the name – dinnae need it but it
stops the iodine gettin rub off. Its expensive stuff. The
girlie in the chemist thought ah wanted t' drink it dilute
wi' water. Nuclear sub – under the atlantic – christmas
mornin – wi' novelty decorations. Ah says the captain
took it personal: ah wor callin him a prick. When wor
got home t' Faslane – court martial. Is that what we got
wor hands for: for t' cut wor wrists? Ay well, none o'
that's true – 'cept the court martial – the discharge – the
nae pension – an the poverty. Ah almost told him I put
a condom on the weapon-officer's trigger – the one he uses
t' fire the rockets. But that's kep lock away in a safe:
behind its own wee flies. So ah stops meself an thinks:
yous'll have t' settle for the truncheons ol' fella. Where'd
ah get thirty condoms on an all male sub that's been
under the sea for eight weeks? He did'nae think t' check
the mucky beast.

BARTLEY *goes to his blanket.*

Ah could teach yous a lot. Ay. Ah've blowed up the world
hundreds o' times. Five years in the service: eight months
shore, four months dived. Every few days, London order
– fire. Captain knows its practice. Wor dont. Everytime
could'a been real. They cannae tells us in case wor says
no. The deterrent works on the ignorance o' the rank an
file. Afterwards wor knows it was'nae real cause wor still
alive. If wor'd fired, wor rockets 'd've telled Ivan where
we wor: he'd've turned us int' human krill for whales –
if wor rockets had'nae killed him first. If they had wor
officers would've killed us.

HAMMOND *comes in.* LEONARD *and* BARTLEY *dont see him*

Once we'd blew up the world we'd be spare bodies wor nae world left t' blow up. The lads might feel bad – turn on the officers – or just fancy bein in charge for wor few days left. In the last war jerry used prisoners t' gas the yids. Every so often they gassed the prisoners. Had to – they can'nae trust lads wor did work like that. The crew of a nuclear sub's like the prisoners: same work, same pay. Yous owe us for the iodine: ah made a note. People reckon when the war comes t' forces'll kill the civvies – an then be the ones t' survive. Sheer ignorance. The captain has his orders – an if he did'nae have em its still: bang bang bang. He could'nae risk keepin wor alive. (*Sniffs fingers.*) That lassie was on t' somethin: the smell o' my iodine-fingers gi's us a thirst. The captain's a prat – but he'd run the sub wi' his officers for the wee while left till the grub ran oot an their time's up. Or maybe the poor ol' sod'd just put a bullet in his own head? The crew would've shat oot o' every orifice when the rockets left the tubes – the blood when he shot us – the air conditionin could'nae cope wi' the stink o' carnage.

LEONARD *is staring at* HAMMOND – BARTLEY *sees his stare and turns to see* HAMMOND.

BARTLEY. Chriss a brown ghost . . .!

HAMMOND. I came on my own. We can talk. No one'll interfere.

BARTLEY. Who's that?

HAMMOND. It doesnt seem right in this hovel: but congratulations. You're the first to get the better of me in a long time. I always allow for an element of chance. Oldfield might've had another son – gone bust – war been abolished. Far fetched but you cant tell fact from fiction when it happens to you. But I didnt allow for this.

BARTLEY (*penny drops*). Dodds!

HAMMOND *gives* BARTLEY *a bottle of whisky.*

Ah. One? Wor's the crate?

HAMMOND. One for the moment.

BARTLEY. One? I want more than bloody one! I told Dodds a crate! What bloody moment?

HAMMOND. Later.

BARTLEY. There is nae bloody later! My pals'll blow the world up before bloody later!

HAMMOND. I thought I was home when I had your undertaking to give me control of Oldfields when your father died – assuming he wasnt immortal. Instead you've deliberately run yourself off the rails and got yourself disinherited. That's what I call determination. You're a fanatic.

BARTLEY (*drinks*). O yes – the right stuff – fair dues. Will it be a crate o' this?

BARTLEY *drinks.* LEONARD *sits with his wrists tucked in his armpits.*

HAMMOND (*after a moment's silence*). Shall I go?

BARTLEY. Stay there! (*Goes to* LEONARD *and hisses at him.*) By god ah took trouble t' fix this – yous spoil it an ah'll give yous hell. That man's money – you respect him! (*To* HAMMOND.) He's listenin mister. (*He stands in the doorway.*) Nae one passes me till ah'm paid. What sort o' cheapskint d'yous think ah am? I dinnae betray a pal for a bottle – ah want my crate!

LEONARD. Why d'you want Oldfields?

HAMMOND. Would it change your mind to know?

BARTLEY. One bottle! – an ah drink it! Ah've known the time ah'd've chuck it in his face! God ah've fallen!

HAMMOND. Im in clothing – transport – construction – but mostly in food: the biggest chain of supermarkets in Europe. Half the world's starving but they cant afford my stores. That ought to upset you.

BARTLEY (*drinking*). They call em coffin ships. Lads have coffin dreams. Medically recognised condition! Wake up screamin – all o' em! 'Let me oot!' In the middle o' the ocean!

HAMMOND. Im supposed to be too European. The trade says it takes two generations to change what people eat. The food in the bellies of kids running round the streets is the same as the food in the bellies of their parents lying in the grave. But things are changing even in food. We could adapt. Its the governments that wont let us in: not desperate enough.

BARTLEY (*drinking*). Been roond the world more times than the sun! Chriss! – niggerland – chinkland – yankyland – saw nothin – not even the sea – (*Swig.*) – only the inside o' wor subs – pipes an tubes – an laddies crawling on em like maggots in their own guts.

HAMMOND. The governments say they cant afford to eat *and* arm. Guns or butter. So they tell the people to starve. You cant afford to eat but you must be able to kill: that's history. Sacrifice.

BARTLEY (*waves bottle*). Shut it! Shut it! You're one good reason t' press the button!

HAMMOND. These days the West cant afford to make arms for itself unless it exports them. But they're expensive for the third world. They tried making their own – not much cop and no R and D. So all the time they're getting into debt. Soon so many'll die it wont look like sacrifice anymore: just bad government. Then they'll be desperate – and I'll make my offer. Let my stores in – and I'll sell you arms.

BARTLEY. One bottle an ah cannae drink that in peace!

BARTLEY *goes out.*

HAMMOND. If I sell both I can sell cheap. But the margins'll be low. So I cant afford to buy in arms to resell. I must make my own. That's why I want Oldfields. I'll start in a small way: guns – mines – PGMs – then educate the consumer – branch out. The next century will be a great gaping mouth – wide as a continent – with rows of missiles for teeth. Out of that mouth there'll come a great roar for food – as loud as the fire-storm from a burning city, a great wind so loud it'll make the screaming of bombs sound like the whistles of errand boys going home on their bikes. People must eat. First its need – then greed – then fear – and then you're back to need. That's why people will always want weapons. I'll feed them and arm them – and if they pay I'll transport them – house them – build their shelters – amuse them – dress them: and I'll make their civvies as bright as they like, they'll still be battledress – because they'll all be in the front line. Harsh? The old myth of peace is harsh. Peace caused more misery than all the wickedness of war. Peace was the time when people trembled – went without – and sweated to arm themselves for war – that's more history. Now I'll make life easier for them. I'll provide swords and ploughshares, tanks and tractors, and do it cheap. Once it was guns and butter. Now it has to be both. They can never be parted again. That's the Great Pieta I see for the twenty-first century: guns *and* butter. No government can refuse it: the starving wouldnt let them – and more important, nor will the rich. Old men make plans, young men see visions. I shant live to see it – but you can. Im offering you the sales franchise on a century. All you have to do is go back to your father.

LEONARD. I havent got a father.

HAMMOND. I know your sort. If anyone lets you in you tangle up in their bowels. That's why Oldfield had enough. A man wants his guts to be his own. Im offering you more than I've offered anyone else. What do you want? I've come to this ruin like a door-to-door salesman

trying to flog you the twenty-first century. I dont know
why. (*Slight pause.*) One of my sons makes clay pots.
Ones a specialist in grass. The rest do business. There
are five thousand species of grass – more. Someone
couldnt make up their mind. (*Shrug.*) I talk to so many
fools, perhaps its the novelty of talking to someone who's
only mad . . .?

LEONARD *still sits with his hands in his armpits.*

LEONARD. Tear up the paper I signed.

HAMMOND. No its my only hold.

BARTLEY (*off*). The bloody – bloody – bloody – bloody – (*A
crash.*)

HAMMOND. What the – . . .?

LEONARD. Cellar. A fit. Lasts five minutes. His brain sucks
in alcohol like a live sponge.

HAMMOND. You think you're still young enough to play
games. If you stay here you'll crack up for real. Pneumo-
nia or drink. What d'you want from me? Tell me.

BARTLEY (*off. Crash, roar*). That – that's doon wi' yous
laddies – come on! – naebody messes me! – ah'll smash
the – ah!

HAMMOND. Shouldnt we . . .? (*No answer.*) There's no
middle road between us. You can break rules and change
facts, but hunches are like the laws of fate: they cant be
changed. You've got the gift of hunches or you're in the
herd: I've got it, so've you. You wont end here.

BARTLEY (*off*). The stairs – he threw the stairs at me – the
railings tore the – a hole! – a hole! – is that hair? – or
people? – its seethin in the – no no no! – I didnae do
wrong! – the people in the hole! – let them oot t' die! –

LEONARD. Machines: my father's workshop. Little metal
arms with rows of snapping teeth making prehistoric
reptiles. We become human and make tin dinosaurs.
Why are people scared of death? A bit of pain and then
– peace. A statue picking up a sheet to use it as a cover for

itself. It never has to take it off. Its never tired of standing there. Never even feels the weight of the sheet. The linen turns to stone. And no sculptor can prise him out of it. Death is the last thing to be afraid of. Its our living monument.

BARTLEY (*off*). Agh! Agh! O! Help me! Leonard! The bricks are turnin roond – the light beween the bricks – the walls turned in t' teeth! (*Crash.*) Gi' me back my bones!

HAMMOND. There's no romance in squalor. Dirt and drunkenness are dirt and drunkenness. Dodds says your father wants you. He's got no one to hand on to. He blames his stubbornness. You dont have to ask – just walk in.

LEONARD. I could've done so much. I was strong. Fit. I was like a child who always had its arms open. What had I done to deserve so much hatred? I knew there were enemies. But why were you waiting to break my back? What had I done to you? What machine made you in what swamp? I didnt even check. What you offer – you break everything as you hand it over. People massacring each other – faces screaming at TV cameras – soldiers' hands blotting out the cameras – why should I be interested in their suffering? – turn the sound off. Give them power and watch them torment their tormenters. Airmen bombing little children. Would they stamp on their faces? The answer doesnt interest me. Women making bombs. If you gave them a bonus they'd make them in their womb. D'you think that can go on? They learn nothing – not even the numbers tattooed on their arms. Who says Im doing this – this is on my hands? They say they're not doing it while they do it. Words mean nothing to them: they communicate with signs with blood on their fingers. And then they celebrate. Parties and parades. Corpses wanking in the grave to kill the time or fill their loneliness.

HAMMOND. You shouldnt say those things.

LEONARD. Go away.

HAMMOND. You wont get one penny from this! All this spite
will be wasted! . . . Im rich, I can afford defeat: but
when I want I get! I'll get Oldfield's when he's dead. The
rubbish'll move in – not class! That's when I get! – I can
hound you sonny! That lunatic! – five minutes – under
lock and key and soaked in carbolic.

LEONARD. You'd be doing him a favour.

HAMMOND. Why did I come here? What d'you want from
me? Tell me? (*Plea.*) Dont sit there, your arms curled
up . . . you look like some crippled foetus. Let me fetch
you clean clothes? I cant leave you here. What d'you
want? If only I knew. I stand here like a servant begging
for scraps of attention. I dont know why. Come with me.
If you're ill, lean on me on the stairs. I've hurt you . . .
maybe harmed you . . . Now I'll take you away from
offices and paper, where no one will hurt you, quiet, and
make you well, and my life will be cured by your wounds
and make amends as if I could wash the greyness out of
hair like common dirt, which no one can . . . of course
its not to be. But I can do a simple act of kindness, that's
allowed. I'll take you where you can think, and there –
in that place – you'll tell me what you want. I'll get it for
you. Anything. Im rich. I can afford one folly. If things
worked out I'd make you boss of Oldfield's. And there's
my companies – if things worked out, if there was an
interest. But dont ask me to destroy my paper. I must
have my paper. It was a hunch. Dont block it. Its the one
thing I couldnt humour. Its not allowed. No doubt I
shouldnt tell you – its a bad mistake. You'll find a way
to use it against me, wont you? Dont. Dont. Dont lad.
Please dont. Let it stop here. Im older, I know where
these things lead. One day we'll all be dead. Is it worth
struggling in the meantime? I wonder more and more. I
need my paper – to get me through the time. (*Slight*

pause.) I dont think you can listen. A pity. Now I'll tell you something different: People are hard, so the rule is: be harder on yourself. Say no to me – I'll drive off and I wont say no to myself fifty or a hundred times: one no will be enough with me. (*Slight pause.*) Five thousand sorts of grass. – So you'll send me through that door alone? You wont exist. The door wont exist. You wont even be dead – you never were. A stain in an abortion clinic. The last time? – no. If I had your blood on my hands I wouldnt even see it as I washed it off.

HAMMOND *waits a moment, then turns and goes out.* LEONARD *fiddles with the rags on his wrists.* BARTLEY *comes in with the empty bottle. He is blind drunk.*

BARTLEY. I have come up wi' my empty bottlesh: it floatsh. (*He raises the bottle in front of him and holds it there.*) Not all drunk. Much slop. 'S'plenty damp dust if yous thirshty. 'S rests gone – 's way of all watersh 'n runny thingsh thash flow. Ah have exhaust. 'S no more bottlesh? – O god ah'll gesh sober an real – ish – the predic – immensh! (*Holds out the bottle to the side.*) You crushify me wi' one hand an let me hang! No bottlesh! No money! No nailsh! No nailsh – in all t' world – t' decent hang a man!

BARTLEY *crashes unconscious to the floor.* LEONARD *fastens the last knot with his teeth and free hand.*

LEONARD (*to* BARTLEY). I swapped the mags. I tried to kill my father. I'd've killed him as sure as two sides of a coin. Its easy. Extra sugar in your tea. A slight sense of self-indulgence. Shouldnt something defend us from ourselves? There was nothing interested enough to stop me. No hand out of the cloud. Then you spoke – that silly stupid voice. (*Imitates* BARTLEY *and* OLDFIELD.) 'A moment sir – I think your laddie has a loaded weapon pointed at your head'. 'You're sacked!' 'Ah'm innocent!

Unfair! Unfair!' 'Out of my house! You'd steal the fingers from a man's mittens!' – frothed and waved his arms and you'd tried to save his life! (*Laughs shortly and stops.*) You were down for sacking anyway. And he'll die sometime. (*Sings and makes Black-and-White Minstrel gestures.*)

> O de camp town races five miles long
> O de camp town races sing this song
> Ready to run all night
> Ready to run all –

He continues making the gestures and silently mouthing the words – and then he adds little puffer-fish choo-choo breaths in the song's rhythm. Stops. Silence. BARTLEY's *eyes are shut – stiff as a signpost, one arm rises and points at* LEONARD.

BARTLEY. Why yous starin at us for?

LEONARD. Your eyes are shut.

BARTLEY. Sub-men see in the dark. (*With his eyes closed he feels for the bottle, finds it, holds it to his ear and shakes it.*) Jees. Would yous look-see if its empty? For ah cannae open my eyes – nae even the one.

LEONARD. Yes.

BARTLEY. All that drunk? He didnae bring my crate? – god bless the man that spared me that. Was ah oot long?

LEONARD. Five minutes.

BARTLEY. O god that's bad when its short. My head's in another world. I'd have t' droon in the stuff t' get any lastin benefit.

LEONARD. The boards boom when you walk on them. Dust crunches like icing sugar.

BARTLEY. I wor happy once. At sea. M'be that wor wrong? – just satisfied wi' the servility? Ah'll never be happy noo. Its all pretend pretend an gettin old. A rat drownin in a puddle cause its roond like the door o' its hoose – he thinks he's inherited a palace. I dinnae tell yous why I was discharge. I'd like t' telled yous if you'd listen: ah dont

know why. There's no education in it: only officer
stupidity. I was eatin in wor mess. A ratin cut his arm –
quite nasty – an come through rollin up his sleeve t' keep
it oot the cut. He stop t' get his breath – leant against the
table an steadied his-self wi' the flat of his hand on top.
The blood ran doon his arm. Its no on t' show sympathy
on a nuclear sub: its no but an underwater raft for
murder. I went on eatin. Some fella crack a joke. The cut
man went on t' the sick bay. Where his hand had rest on
the table there's some spots. Some wingey drops o' blood.
I had a little-bitty bread ready in ma hand. I dipped it
in the blood – t' mop it up – an ate it. No special thought.
The blood was red – the bread was that stark white – they
seemed t' go t'gether. I should explain we wor encouraged
t' be clean. Are yous sure yous listening? They're
fanatical for cleanliness in all that water: dirt's a capital
offence – an bein sick – an wor gear oot o' place – they
have machines t' purify the air. So my hand cleaned up
the mess. It did it on automatic pilot – an drop it doon
me gob. Wor cook was squintin oot the galley. He telled
the captain. He telled the MO. I did his tests. Blobs on
paper. Would yous credit it? Blobs. Ah felt ashamed –
like a kid had mess its briks! Ah cannae see what ah did
wrong. Can yous? That fuss 'bout a wee-bit-bread-roll
dip in blood? It was bread so ah ate it. In wor hoose you
learned yous dinnae waste man! You'd think ah'd dip my
hand in the laddie's pocket – or lift his wallet oot his
locker. He did'nae complain ah'd pinch his goods – if his
blood's so precious why's he flitter it on the walls? – he's
nae jasus chriss ah'm tellin yous. Ah give the cook squint:
jab the bugger's eye wi't the handle o' wor breadknife.
Fightin on a sub on active service: *oot*! Yous wrong cause
yous innocent. Will yous hold my hand noo Lennie-man
while ah open my eyes. (LEONARD *holds his wrist.*) Ah'll
be all right. (*Kneels.*) Steady it is. (*Opens his eyes and
crouches down with his face to the ground.*) Jees-jees-jees.

The light blinds yous but wor need it. Ay – ah can see.
(*Straightens up.*) Ah'm goin t' be all right man. Jees. Jees.
(*Looks at the empty bottle.*) Terrible. Nothin. An ant
could'nae lick it oot.

LEONARD. You spilt some.

BARTLEY. Was ah away below? (*No answer.*) O god one day
ah'll tear up the foundations o' the hoose an the roof'll
jump doon on wor heads. (*Pause. Tries to remember.*) Was
that yous singing when ah come roond?

LEONARD. Yes.

BARTLEY. Lenny go away. Dont be offended noo. Let go
o' me. The two o' us are nae good t'gether. Its a hunch.
If yous left, ma ol' ruin'd be as snug as a fortress-hoose.
By the time yous get your money ah'll be dead. What is
it yous want? (*Pause. Cries.*) I dinnae want t' die in a
mac. That's the worst death of all. Ah could'nae show
me face in another world. M'be ah cannae die – is that
ma problem? If ah could die ah'd've been dead long
since. They shovel the dirt on me – I'ld lick it off like a
street-dog lickin its jaw. (*Silence.*) Singin – he kep that
quiet. Your singin, my mouth organ – should get a pitch.
Make a bomb. 'The Man Who Blew Up the World a
Hundred Times an the Poor Millionnaire'. Could catch
on. (*Stands and covers himself in his blanket.*) I need a pal
t' push me under a bus an bugger his scruples – then ah'd
see if I cannae die. If I cannae, we'll put it in wor act.
Yous reek o' piss an iodine. Gi's that bottle – we'll get it
filled. By chriss ah could drink the booze oot a dead man
if ah could find a tit. (*Points to the other bottle.*) An that.
One each fella.

BARTLEY *pulls the blanket tighter round him.* LEONARD
picks up the other bottle. They go out.

Unit Six

'The Two Armchairs'

A room in OLDFIELD's *House (as in Unit One).*

One of the two armchairs is covered in a white dust sheet.
OLDFIELD *dozes in the other. He wears a pale dressing-gown.*

LEONARD *is standing in the doorway. He wears the mac and
the other clothes he wore in the ruined house, but he has brushed
them and smartened himself up. From time to time he pulls his
sleeves down over his hands and then pins them against his palms
with his second and third fingers.*

LEONARD. Father.
OLDFIELD (*sees* LEONARD.) What d'you want?
LEONARD. I woke you.
OLDFIELD. Money.
LEONARD. The house is quiet.
OLDFIELD. I'll authorise my accountant.
LEONARD. I have to talk to you.
OLDFIELD. Leave me alone.
LEONARD. Five minutes.
OLDFIELD. No. (*Silence.*) I cant. Im tired. Its not your fault
  – its age: the fight with Hammond took more out of me
  than I knew. It was hard to get on with my work when
  you left. Now I've settled down. Please leave me alone.
LEONARD. Im sorry if I hurt you.
OLDFIELD. Young people must turn against their elders,
  everyone knows that. I didnt know that understanding,
  patience, regret have nothing to do with it. They fight
  each other to the finish so they can get away from each
  other. Its like a curse on us.
LEONARD. I have to tell you why I left.
OLDFIELD. You dont even know. I thought we could end

our constant quarrelling. Then suddenly you're gone. No luggage – your jacket hanging on a chair – you dont use your bank account: were you supposed to be dead? – a hostage? – amnesiac? I read the daily listings from the morgues and learned how terrible the city I've spent my life in is. Three months later Dodds finds you in a hovel sharing the grudges of an ex-employee. Are you drunk? You've come to rob me?

LEONARD. Father when I've told you I'll go away for good.

OLDFIELD. Im not your father. Dont pretend. A poor man might have made you his son. From the street to this house – the distance is too far. When you went I loved you as a son. Now I feel nothing. I stare at you and there's nothing. You no longer give me pleasure – and you cant hurt me.

LEONARD. That's how fathers talk.

OLDFIELD. Go away.

LEONARD. Criticise their sons and kick them out.

OLDFIELD. *You left*!

LEONARD (*shrugs*). I made a mistake.

OLDFIELD. I dont condone the right to make mistakes – that's modern cant. Your natural parents made mistakes. If that's what you want, go and find your mother: dont waste time looking for your father – even your mother couldnt help you there.

LEONARD. That's jealousy.

OLDFIELD. Jealous of people who abandon an infant?

LEONARD. The day after they left me they probably went dancing. That's what you envy.

OLDFIELD. You're mad.

LEONARD. Shall I get you a drink?

OLDFIELD. Is that your way of scrounging one?

LEONARD. I've been to the street where I was left. I dont think she knew the house. She came a long way – crossed the river by bus – walked miles – then turned into a gateway where there were lights. I must've had her tears on my face every day I was with her. Her arms would've felt light – unnatural – after she'd carried me for days. The street's pulled down. New blocks. My doorstep's rubble under a motorway. I walked on the pavement – that's still there. If the doorstep had been there I'd've touched the stone that touched the back of her fingers when she put me down. I hope it didnt graze them. Every few years your whole body changes. There isnt one part of me she's touched. Every bit of her child's gone. Dead skin flaked off. If she saw me now she'd see a ghost put in its place. The stone would be the same if it hadnt been pulverised for rubble.

LEONARD *sits down in the armchair covered by the dust sheet.*

OLDFIELD. You strung me along for years – an inherited trait – but you finally showed your true self. Dont try it on anymore! All you needed was a little patience – a little cunning – to wait till I died. You've come to tell me the truth? Lie. The only way *you* can help anybody is to lie. Why didnt you leave me the comfort of my foolishness? I was happy. You only had to tell a few more lies . . . Suppose you came back here? Yes it would be companionship for me – you're the nearest I had to a son. But it would be another lie dragged into the open. Sons inherit: but would *you* leave your life's work to a drunken wastrel – a tramp? No one can trust you anymore. If I made you my heir you'd have *this* quarrel with your own son – he'd object to you just as I have, for the same reasons. You'd learn the quarrel from the other side and find how bitter my role is! (*Flat.*) No no you're not coming here. I accept my legal obligations – Im not vindictive – I'll pay. But that's all. My wife's dead. I dont have friends. I dont even need a servant. We couldnt look each other in the face. The constant self reproach: 'Have I been unfair – should I change my mind?' All the old

horrors. Im not up to it. Let me live in despair. Each time
I tried to help you I damaged you. I dont understand. Im
afraid of you. When you came in I thought you were from
a dream.

LEONARD. I went away to be ill. The only movement I made
for days was shivering. My eyes and tongue seized up –
stopped like print on a page. Even my bowels. I heard
breath going on inside me like a little animal leading its
own life. I saw the light on a broken window – brighter
in the cracks. And rags – the weave comes through when
they're worn. Everything was beautiful. I wanted to put
the rags and dirt on and let them make me beautiful. I
felt sad – a sorrow – for the air. Why doesnt it struggle
in our mouths – choke us as if we're dragging it down a
filthy corridor to an execution shed? Our lungs are
charnel houses, mausoleums. If they were cities we'd pull
them down. The air takes all the filth away. It stinks of
us. Yet lets us breathe. I thought when I could move I'd
cut my wrists: I held the knife against them – but I went
to see the doorstep. My parents arent survivors – dead,
not lucky people. You're my father. I didnt deserve your
kindness when you took me in. I wasnt anyone – I lay in
my shit and cried. You werent kind to *me* – I was a *thing*
in the way: something's in the way of a bullet – I was in
the way of kindness. But I survived and grew up and
made it mine. I dont mean I have a legal right. *This* is a
law that can only be made by crime. I grabbed. I shut
you inside my body. The body shuts up tight – like iron
in cement. My mother left a ghost. I found you. You're
in every hair I've got – every bit of flesh. And what I didnt
shut in I shut out. Everything outside's in the same
prison. You cant escape from outside. We're in the same
prison – we're just on different sides of the wall. It made
me ill, and then it made me well. I've come to confess.

OLDFIELD. You're in trouble! I knew it! Something shady!

LEONARD. You know I took over Wilbraham Engineering?

OLDFIELD. The accountants found out. An impetuous waste of money! Dodds tried to speak to Wilbraham – the bounder wouldnt!

LEONARD. I was tricked. There was a debtor with a death-grip – perhaps you should have a drink?

OLDFIELD. Go on!

HAMMOND. It was Hammond.

OLDFIELD. Hammond? My Hammond? (*Rapid thought.*) Is he – he sent you! He's manipulating you! Still after my company!

LEONARD. He tried to force me to give him control when you died.

OLDFIELD. Yes?

LEONARD. I couldnt turn to you –

OLDFIELD. What?

LEONARD. You couldnt help me –

OLDFIELD. Of course! Of course! I'd've bought him off! Anything! My company's at stake – still! What's the situation? What's –

LEONARD. Listen! Listen! Listen!

OLDFIELD. I dont understand.

LEONARD (*short laugh*). No – you dont. You said it again just now, you're always saying it: no one could ever trust me. So if I'd told you what a mess I'd made of –

OLDFIELD. Yes?

LEONARD. – you'd've disinherited me: its what you *have* done!

OLDFIELD. Of course – so? So? For god's sake Leonard! – we've got more important things to deal with than your future. My company! Yes yes of course your future's important but we can settle that any time. *Has Hammond got a hold on me?*

LEONARD (*wearily*). Would you believe me if I told you?

OLDFIELD. O god he's impossible! Impossible! Totally impossible! Self! Self! Self! The everlasting whining! *What's my position?* (*Silence.*) It doesnt matter. I apologise for betraying an interest. (*Slight pause.*) Fancy – some nights I sleep in this chair to spare myself the journey to bed. I take my meals at a dining club. One gets used. So you found the house quiet? My lawyers will tell me in the morning. They may have to trouble you with a question or two – I apologise.

LEONARD. I didnt sign his paper.

OLDFIELD. Are you sure? You might've signed when you were drunk. (*Silence.*) I'll never understand. You wait three months! God knows what Hammond's been up to!

LEONARD. There's no more.

OLDFIELD. How could you know? Hammond twists boys like you round his finger. You put me in this terrible situation and then have the temerity to *reassure* me! – as if your opinion could ever be worth anything! That's gall even from you!

LEONARD. You see.

OLDFIELD. No. Whatever we see isnt the same – thank god! You'll stay here tonight. In the morning we'll try to limit the damage. Dodds will arrange a meeting – lawyers – accountants – we'll call in private detectives – a Grand Council! Not that I look forward to it. I cant even enjoy the fight – with you involved there can only be alarms and fiascos!

LEONARD. I have more to tell you.

OLDFIELD. O god now it'll be interesting. He's sold my organs for research. Hammond gets my eyes transplanted so I can watch him counting my money when Im dead.

LEONARD. If I'd signed you'd've died without knowing. An easy lie! When I was trapped one thing became clear – it surprised me. I'd betrayed you – you'd driven me to it – but it was difficult to hurt you. For the first time I felt what it is to be a son.

OLDFIELD. Well – that's handsome of you – and Im sorry if you had –. But three months! You put everything in jeopardy – then take three months sick leave! Couldnt you have managed with a week – or come to me first like a proper son? Hurt me? You destroy me! Even now you come out of office hours!

LEONARD. And I betrayed you on the day you beat Hammond. Imagine! – you were going on about new beginnings and I was buying nails for your coffin! Now you can use them in mine.

OLDFIELD. O dont despair – Im sure we can find you a suitable profession. You show all the talents necessary to a member of a minor soap opera. (*Calculating to himself.*) Its unlikely but Hammond may have stepped outside the law.

LEONARD. And what's worse, you loved me as a son.

OLDFIELD. Not more self pity! You disgrace yourself – put my company at risk – go on a celebration (for all I know) lasting *three months* – then talk of love! You certainly demand patience. Love is responsibility to others, above all those you dont know. Its not meant to give us satisfaction. Or pleasure. What it gives us in compensation for the suffering it causes, I dont know – something we need to make us put up with the folly! Whatever it is its like the old names of gods: it cant be spoken. If we could get away from our bodies so that our minds were pure – unbiased – aloof – then we could deal with the squalor. The body creates problems and stops us solving them. – Let others judge: I carry out my responsibilities. I know what it costs. And all those who've ever been anyone's victim, will know if they should be grateful . . . We're as alone as statues and pictures in a gallery. We stare at each other and see nothing. But isnt that the shrine? – the memorial to *some* sort of civilization? Perhaps its the distance that keeps us together. – Not one word of apology. Im even blamed for your blunders. You make me sad. A man accepts responsibility for his actions. Go to your room – try to imagine how others see you. If you cant it might've been better to leave you on the doorstep. I begin to think it was cruel to pick you up.

LEONARD. Dodds works for Hammond.

OLDFIELD. O?

LEONARD. Dodds drew up the paper to hand me over to him when you're dead.

OLDFIELD *gets up from his chair, goes to* LEONARD *and stares into his face.*

OLDFIELD. Have you gone mad? Is this revenge? I cant smell drink. Im at a loss to know how to handle you.

LEONARD. Dodds is on Hammond's payroll.

OLDFIELD (*tense bemusement*). You've come to set the house on fire. You offered to get me a drink so you could poison it. My god is there nothing he wouldnt stoop to? They cant wait for the fathers to die – they make them visit their graves! Touch the spade! Watch the earth being thrown! You come here and in that quiet tone say monstrous things – lower your voice as if you're going to pray and utter profanities! You have no secrets to flaunt at me! I will not be patronised! Dodds is my friend! I tell him everything! He knows all my secrets. Never never never will I believe what you've just said about Dodds! Dodds is Dodds! Not a drunken – rip! I insist you tell me it isnt true! (*Slight pause.*) O Im being stupid. You're treating me to my own medicine. Because I said you had the talents of a soap opera (*Claps hands twice.*) – you're playing this terrible joke. I deserve it! Hammond – Dodds – everything you said since you came . . .? (*No answer.*) You're telling me I must believe it? No Leonard dont – this is not good for my head. I shouldnt go through this. You're turning me into a circus animal! – dragging my past behind me like a monstrous tail! I'd be aghast to try to live with what –. (*Stops.*) The liftman takes bribes – the secretaries work for the KGB – but not Dodds!

LEONARD. I must be firm with you father: you've been as

gullible as a schoolboy. Its important you own up to it. Dodds must be trapped. Im sorry I told you quietly. All this is sad for me. It was hard to come and confess – and harder because I knew it'd turn into an accusation: you rejected your son and crawled to your enemy.

OLDFIELD. You'll say this to his face! I'll get to the bottom of –. (*Calls.*) Dodds! Dodds!

LEONARD *jumps from his chair, goes to* OLDFIELD *and literally puts his hand over his mouth.*

LEONARD. No no dont!

OLDFIELD. Ah! ouf! He's stiffling – ! Help! My throat!

LEONARD. Father please. No. You're putting your head in the snake's mouth. I've got more to tell! (*Releases* OLDFIELD.) Dont betray me. Not now. Please O god I didnt know he was here. Im shaking. Let me help you. O god father I see you on the doorstep and me bending down to pick you up. See how frail you are. Your face in my hand. Let me be your son for one day and everything will solve itself.

DODDS *comes in.*

DODDS. Leonard.

LEONARD (*arm round* OLDFIELD). The prodigal returns.

OLDFIELD. Yes. Leonard's . . . as you see.

DODDS. How nice. It's been a bad time.

OLDFIELD. So I thought . . . drinks? . . . Dodds – would you mind? Some whisky?

DODDS *goes out.*

OLDFIELD. His tie's straight. There's no blood on his face. Dodds, Dodds . . . (*To* LEONARD.) But you're not deceiving me.

LEONARD. Why should I?

OLDFIELD. To make me doubt? Dont dont – no matter how much it matters to you. You'll regret it. Running a

company's like walking a tightrope in burning shoes. You
cant do it if you doubt. Blind foolish faith – let me keep
that. Let me have my illusions. I dont know what you're
up to. There's some scheme. What is it? I feel you must
want something. I look so foolish – all this bewilderment
over a colleague. The company's my life. My legs are
trembling. I've no right to put on this suit. How stupid.

LEONARD (*explaining*). Dodds is to be told you know about
Hammond. I'll tell him I kept his *own* part secret so we
can both rook you – he has more experience.

OLDFIELD. Yes yes if that's . . . I'll be in control tomorrow.
I could believe you cheated me – you're always change-
able. Sometimes I paraded you – to show you off – you
didnt know – but you found a way to spoil it – always –
it seemed like spite. But Dodds was always Dodds, the
faithful servant. Now I have to watch him like a common
spy.

DODDS *comes in with three glasses of whisky.*

DODDS. We'll all have a restful night at last. – Your father
was very worried.

OLDFIELD. Yes – Dodds . . . these are worrying times. (*To
DODDS.*) Your health – old friend.

DODDS. To Leonard.

LEONARD. To father.

They drink. DODDS *starts to go.*

OLDFIELD. Stay, stay . . .

DODDS. You two must talk.

OLDFIELD. Yes Dodds – you're right, as always . . .
Goodnight – till the morning Dodds . . .

DODDS *goes.* LEONARD *listens at the door.*

OLDFIELD (*whisper*). O god he's bugged the room.

LEONARD (*whisper*). No need, you tell him everything.

OLDFIELD. What have I done? God knows the damage

he's – ! And not one sign! Yet there were mysterious – I thought I'd slipped – coincidences. Thats why Hammond almost beat me! . . . Since you left he stays late. Snooping in case I got his scent.

LEONARD. Im here now. It'll all be gone into.

OLDFIELD. But we're acting as if he cheated me for years. We know one slip! And you're as much to blame – I warned you you were gullible! Im thoughtless – I push him too hard. Do I pay enough? You dont think he's being blackmailed? Dodds could never do anything to give a – but if he's betrayed me he's capable of anything! Such infamy under my own roof!

LEONARD. O before you go to bed: put me on the board.

OLDFIELD (*groan*). Not now.

LEONARD. You cant trust Dodds and you need someone to –

OLDFIELD. All right – yes! God knows you've earned it – by moral right and force of arms!

LEONARD. Cheer up! Paper isnt sacred. The hand that writes it can tear it up! But I think you'll make a new sort of decision from now on . . . you'll be bound by your word.

OLDFIELD. Yes yes when you're on you'll stay. I shant live to see the changes. I need my bed. This is more than tiredness. We must leave the rest till the lawyers open their offices.

LEONARD. Goodnight.

OLDFIELD *goes out.* LEONARD *sits in an armchair.* DODDS *comes in.*

DODDS. Why?

LEONARD. The smell of iodine. He knows about Hammond – I had to explain my 'break down'.

DODDS. You didnt say he has the rights?

LEONARD. Fool . . .!

DODDS. You scared Hammond. He said you were destroying yourself to spite him. I said no one's so stupid.

LEONARD. He was right: I found I could destroy myself to *get*. Im on the board, tomorrow I'll fix his will: I'll get Oldfield's when flesh and bone pass to time's grave . . . And Hammond can use his paper in the loo. I'll have to give him something to stop him going to my father: twenty per cent – his proper incentive. Do the paper work at the same time as the will. That leaves Dodds-is-Dodds.

DODDS. You and Hammond can go to your father: so can I. Anyone call tell the truth if they'll put up with the inconvenience.

LEONARD. Why did you hand me over to Hammond?

DODDS. Greed. (*Shrugs.*) If you want another reason: fear of poverty? They say when a dog's whipped it bites everything except the whipper. No, it bites everything except the whip. If it sees the whip chucked in a corner – the tip doesnt even flicker – it howls. The power of the tool: me. You're the dog who's learned a few elementary tricks. Two things you mustnt trust: god and the servants. They know too much about you. So, the tool has the power of god – if that's not immodest? While Im drawing up Hammond's paper I'll draw up another one in my favour. We'll talk about it tomorrow – in office hours. Your father doesnt pay overtime.

LEONARD *goes out.* DODDS *picks up the empty glasses and goes out after him.*

Unit Seven

Oldfield's Office

At the back a tall Georgian window with small panes. In front of the window a desk with a desk chair and a desk lamp. In front of the desk, left and facing into the room, an office armchair.

DODDS *sits at the desk with* OLDFIELD's *will in front of him.* OLDFIELD *comes in.*

DODDS. Going through your will. A duplicate of the one you tore up. (*Stands.*) To be signed by you and two witnesses in your presence and the presence of each other. The lights?

OLDFIELD. Desk lamp please.

DODDS *switches on the desk lamp.* OLDFIELD *sits in the armchair.*

DODDS. I'll be in my office.

OLDFIELD. Working late?

DODDS. Checking the Zaire report.

OLDFIELD. Zaire.

DODDS *goes out, leaving the will on the desk. A few seconds later* LEONARD *comes in. He wears a business suit, dark tie and shoes and a white shirt with conspicuous white cuffs.*

OLDFIELD. He was sitting on my chair.

LEONARD (*picks up the will from the desk*). I've checked it.

OLDFIELD. Have it photocopied. There'll be interpolations – invisible ink that comes through when he sprinkles my ashes on it. Turns black into white, honour into how much!

LEONARD (*half musing*). I wish you werent so absurd.

OLDFIELD (*not hearing* LEONARD). . . . sitting at my desk, fingering my will. He'd charge you a hiring fee on the knife he sticks in your back. I must not be bitter . . . In my chair like a spider spinning a hangman's rope!

LEONARD. He's a little man.

OLDFIELD. They have big ambitions. They make the ruins we live in – and we spend our lives struggling not to be rats. Give it here! (*He takes the will from* LEONARD.) I'll sign it.

OLDFIELD *sits at his desk, silhouetted against the window. As the sky and the room darken only* OLDFIELD's *hands, the will and the pen are seen in the pool of light from the desk lamp – and, caught in the reflection,* LEONARD's *face and white cuffs.*

LEONARD (*unscrews the top of the pen*). Your pen father. (*He walks away.*) I've something else to confess.

OLDFIELD (*murmur*). Im reading.

LEONARD. I must tell you now you have the will. You'll sign, but you must do it when you know.

OLDFIELD (*reading*). . . . whatsoever goods and chattels I may die . . .

LEONARD. I'll tell the truth. Dont leave – or speak – or make a sign. Perhaps you'll want to *keep* it secret? Its your truth as well as mine. The two halves of a code come together – and there's the meaning. Truth's a 'one off' – like losing your virginity or getting conceived. You only tell it once. Afterwards you're changed – you cant get away. When you tell it it may ruin you – and you have to live off your attempt to tell it.

OLDFIELD. Sh. Later.

LEONARD. Suppose a child before the age of speech – in a kitchen or a shed with a woman who's afraid to look at it – if it spoke – with all the inflections of a lifetime's experience – you'd listen. Even if it only said good morning you'd listen as intensely as the dead would listen to the living if they could.

OLDFIELD (*reading*). No Leonard please . . . Im doing my duty to you. Sole beneficiary.

LEONARD. I cant stop. If a cliff as big as the world was leaning over it'd be as silent as if nothing was happening – but nothing could stop it. When it hits the ground everything will change.

OLDFIELD *turns a page.* LEONARD *is sitting in the armchair with his back to him.*

LEONARD. I tried to kill you. I would've done it. You can hear it in my voice. You're listening to a recording of your killing. (*Sudden collapse.*) No! – its not! I should have to . . .! (*Stops.*) Still! Still! Dont move! . . . I changed the magazine. A strange gun – an accident was plausible. That was my first advantage. It was as if the gods were smiling at me. They were far more cunning than I could ever be. I meant to shoot you in the fields while the photographer snapped me – that was the second advantage, no one poses for photos while they're committing murder. Dont move! Still! Its our only chance! – I would've aimed well. A clean death. – I can tell you: its going to be all right. Words are like things. That helps. They share the responsibility. Just prod with them – they're little bits of iron or stone. I considered wounding you so you'd live for a few minutes – in case you had something you wanted to say. Then I saw that was an insult. Who'd condescend to speak to the living when they're being handed over to the dead? So I'd make it a clean shot like a diagram on a shooting chart. I promise you you wouldnt even wince. Then I had another bit of luck. The third advantage. I could kill you indoors. I couldnt miss! The whole sky was grinning at me. The loaded gun was in my hands. I aimed at different things. Then I focused on you through the sight. The optic dragged your face so close – you were bending down to kiss me. The technical virtuosity, the gun's workmanship – astounding. I could count the stubble on your chin. Measure the thicknesses. Your pores were old bomb craters. But no smell. A world of glass between us. Only Wilbraham's stink – his breath – armpits – crutch: a corpse sprinkled with eau de cologne – the scent brought out the stench of his dried sweat, that no movement would ever bring to life again – the wells were dry. I counted. I was a war-machine registering hundredths of a second. You were so close to death and didnt know. I

lived your last seconds for you. Filled them with life.
Stretched them. They were as long as all the time you'd
lived before. I gave you a long life. But the clock's looking
for the last second. It'll find it. Children putting away
their toys – turning their heads to look for the last piece
– the little fist comes down. All children are giants. You
werent in the morgue but the morgue's in you. A handful
of gravel thrown at the wind: it gathers it to a stone. In
a moment you'll be dead. You'll fall – go down. Your
hands will wave above you as if they're trying to pluck
the bullet from your brain. And now you think: Bartley
spoke – an idiot reprieved you. No, it was a bird. In a
bare tree. Leaves would have blanketed the sound – a
fraction of a decibel – but I was living in millionths of a
second. The bird sang in the tree. So innocent and clear.
The time to die had come and you were saying –
something irrelevant, when its all irrelevant. Your voice
grating like stones on the bottom of a *maelstrom* – that's
the word. You couldnt say no. The word would fall into
the gap between the millstones. The grating roar. An ogre
had cut its throat. There was blood. A lot. And then I
saw your words – I told you words were things. A red
carpet stretched between your mouth and the gun. The
words were moving on it. Ghosts. The air movement
behind a jet. Or the wires that guide a T.O.W. to its
target – something like that. A great suction comes from
your head to draw my bullet to it. The trigger's curved.
My finger. Millions of fingers – crawling from the mud.
The filth. The nails were eyes: they cried to wash away
the mud. Anything should be pitied if it lies in its
own tears. The rags of skin. The claws. The rot. Decay.
And so I thought, as Im a kindly man, clean and well-
educated, sent to sit among the wise, like my sort – the
bird must sing. If you shoot it flies. Rattles up through
the trees – a whole army looks up – the food drops from
its forks – their footprints in the mud – the crying bones.

There was only the bird's sound. The metal sheets in a shipyard. Iron wings. Music – but exact, precise, a total grammar – that said nothing. So I let it sing. (*Pause.*) Then I couldnt kill you. It would've been a tactical mistake. Two incidents with a gun? – and I had a motive. If the idiot had spoken on his own: bang! I'd've said his lurch to grab the gun had startled me. It was the bird – that's all between you and death. Think of it when you hear one sing. Im glad you know. It wasnt difficult to tell it. I'll never try to kill you again: I've set us free. One last thing. This time I must say it all. I said I didnt kill you father. That's a lie. I did. You're dead. So am I. I wont hide it from you. You walk about and breathe but I killed you even more than if we'd been buried together and I killed you in our coffin. I made you the living scene of a crime. The embryo of everybody's death. We keep it secret by parading it in the streets. Everywhere you go – every cup you put on a saucer – every crumb you brush from your trousers – tells everyone I killed you. I couldnt have killed you – got through your last seconds – on my own. You had to help me: Im a parasite on your death. I got inside your dead skin to kill you. That's where Im sitting now – and your bones are in me as if they'd been wrapped up in the wrong parcel. And as that's so, what do we do? How shall we go on? The dead must think of the future. Take stock. I have to give you a good reason why I killed you. One you can respect – that makes sense of your life. Then we can go on living. I killed you to prove Im fit to take your place. I'll live for you. Your successor had to be aggressive and patient – the disciplined patience that's a sort of knowledge. A man who kills to *get* proves his aggression. A man who waits to let a bird sing – proves he knows. Who else can you trust your company to? – only your killer. I've earned the right to your place. Well?

No answer.

Every other father would envy you. I prove myself by killing you and let you live to share my inheritance. Im a worthy son – you must prove you're worthy to be my father. That's the catch: I set you free, chucked you out of prison. Of course you hesitate. Its sudden. But you must choose.

No answer.

If you get it wrong it shows you have a weakness that's infected all you've done – so you've only got second hand goods to leave me. What son wants that? I told you truth was dangerous.

No answer.

(*To himself.*) I've untied the riddle. I killed – now Im giving life. Im father and son. (*To* OLDFIELD.) We cant pretend I havent spoken. (*To himself.*) If you choose properly you're the father I wanted: we'll live together as brothers. (*To* OLDFIELD.) I shocked you. You'll get over it. They used to wound god in the side to make him live. (*No answer.*) Im being inconsiderate. I've tired you. These last few months I've made you old. Let me hold your pen. Dont be a child father. Someone may come. This is the one time in our whole lives we must be alone together.

LEONARD *stands, goes to the desk and picks up the will.*

You signed. Im grateful. (*He puts the will on the desk.*) Father.

LEONARD *shines the desk lamp in* OLDFIELD's *face.*

Why dont you – ? (*Touches* OLDFIELD.) He doesnt –.

LEONARD *goes to the centre of the room and stands behind the chair. He turns to face* OLDFIELD *and clasps his hands together.*

He's dead.

LEONARD *goes back to the desk and lurches across the top to peer into* OLDFIELD's *face.*

Dead! Dead! The cunning bastard! The wicked – cunning – ! I told him all that – and he – ! The shit! (*Starts to go, talking to himself.*) No he wont get away with that. Im not so easy to beat! Right! You want to play dirty! There are machines – life support! (*Goes to the desk and kicks it.*) You wont get away with it you bastard!

LEONARD *goes out. Pause.* OLDFIELD *slumps from the chair and goes out of sight behind the desk.* LEONARD *and* DODDS *come in.*

He's gone!

DODDS *switches on the lights.*

DODDS. Is this a joke?

LEONARD. O god he's turned into a ghost and walked! No no! – not dead! Tricked me! He's hiding! I'll teach that shit to play his jokes on – ! O god he's gone to the police! (*Picks up the phone on the desk.*) It's dead.

DODDS. Miss Shrewsbury's gone home. (*Sudden thought.*) The will.

LEONARD *finds* OLDFIELD *behind the desk.*

LEONARD. Ah!

DODDS. What?

LEONARD. There! Fell! (*Starts to pick up* OLDFIELD.) Help me!

DODDS (*examining the will*). You bloody fool!

LEONARD. What?

DODDS. Incompetent bloody fool! Look! Half a signature! – he wrote half his name and stopped!

LEONARD. Is that – bad? O my god – what's he up to? What's he doing to me?

DODDS. Quick – the chair – it may be a stroke – not dead. He must sign the will!

LEONARD *and* DODDS *set* OLDFIELD *in the desk chair.*

LEONARD. Yes yes not dead – air came –
DODDS. His mouth – I saw it – gasped –

OLDFIELD *sits in the chair.* LEONARD *flattens the will on the desk in front of him.*

DODDS. Mr Oldfield its Dodds here. Dont die before you sign the will. Leave us with happy memories. (*To himself.*) The lawyers' fees on a half signed will! O god *Hammond*! (*Aloud.*) Mr Oldfield – please.
LEONARD. Father!
DODDS. Pen pen pen! He cant sign without a pen!
LEONARD. He had a – ! Where's the bloody – ! He must've knocked it when he –. (*Calls.*) Miss Shrewsbury my father needs a –
DODDS. Miss Shrewsbury's gone home!
LEONARD (*going*). There's an office full of – !
DODDS. The same pen! The same pen! D'you want to finish it in red biro?
LEONARD (*searching*). Pen . . . pen . . .
DODDS. There!
LEONARD. – ? – Ah!

LEONARD *gets the pen.* DODDS *takes it from him and holds it upright in front of* OLDFIELD. LEONARD *flattens the will on the desk.*

DODDS. Mr Oldfield Dodds begs you. A last gesture of farewell. (*He puts the pen in* OLDFIELD's *hand – it falls out. Dodds turns away with the will.*)
LEONARD. But breath came from –
DODDS. Wind – when you kneed him in the belly. The dead are always belching and farting. That doesnt make it the day of resurrection.

LEONARD. He's hot!

DODDS (*studying the will*). Gone to hell – making a take-over bid!

LEONARD *watches* DODDS *as he walks away with the will. Behind them* OLDFIELD *falls out of sight again.*

DODDS. At least he didnt tamper with the text. Fool! – fetching me – he was probably still alive. You could have made him sign – told him no doctor till he did – (*Shrugs.*) under the circumstances. To think the company's in your hands! (*Stops.*) Why should he go to the police?

LEONARD. He's dead – what does it matter?

DODDS. Of course the police matter if he's dead.

LEONARD. O my god he's gone again! (LEONARD *and* DODDS *look behind the desk.*) He's trying to get up! The kiss of life!

LEONARD *heaves* OLDFIELD *onto the desk top.* DODDS *pulls* LEONARD *back.*

DODDS. No! You've done enough harm! He might've heard what we said! What did we say? Its impossible to think with a dead – or dying – man in the room! He always kept the big decisions to himself – now he leaves us in the lurch! We mustnt go to pieces! Mr Oldfield is it better if we let you live or finish you off? What an absurd question! (*Looks closer.*) Well he's come to a firm decision on that: he's dead.

LEONARD (*sits and cries*). O god what can I do? What'll become of me! I'll never get away from him! No one can help me! He's unfair!

DODDS. Im sorry I shouted, I didnt mean to make you cry. I lost my grip. I'll finish his signature. He taught me to do his hand for minor documents. A simple bit of forgery is far less complicated than the kiss of life. We've had the kiss of death, and if you ask me we got the best of the bargain. (*Pushes* OLDFIELD *aside.*) Clear a space. (*Signs the will.*) There. A baby's hand patting its mother's cheek couldnt be more sure.

LEONARD (*crying*). What can I do?

DODDS. Spare me the hypocrisy. We'll say he signed his will this morning. He'd better be found out of reach of pens and desks. He collapsed in the corridor and we carried him to the VIP reception room. Leonard.

LEONARD *helps* DODDS *to pick up* OLDFIELD's *body. He is still crying.*

DODDS. I believe your tears are genuine! Death plays funny tricks – no one's safe. The suddenness after a run of shocks. I could cry with relief. (*A flurry of tears.*) People say I have no feelings – but when I think of all that could've gone wrong! (*A flurry of tears.*) But you came back in time – Hammond stuck to his guns – and I was on hand to forge his signature! That's a lot to be grateful for! And if the truth's told he's better off dead than having to live with Hammond – and you – and me! (*A gush of tears.*)

DODDS *and* LEONARD *cry as they carry* OLDFIELD *out.*

Unit Eight

The same

Next day.

LEONARD *sits in the armchair with his eyes shut.* BARTLEY *comes in. He wears his mac and the other clothes from the ruined house. He walks to* LEONARD *and stops.* LEONARD *opens his eyes.*

BARTLEY. Ah come through the wall. You're wore oot. Countin the loot? Ah saw the old sod's death on telly. (*Explains.*) Servant's key. – Have ah been the bloody fool!

BARTLEY *sits at an askew angle on the top of* OLDFIELD's *desk.*

BARTLEY. I could'nae figure oot why yous come t' my hovel. The scratches on them wrists'd fool nae'body. What's the laddie want? Is he m'be sorry for us? – pourin oot the ol' sunny-treacle for his pal? You're nae'body's pal. You're a bastard. When ah got the sack ah'd supped a drop, ay – but that never put a man wi' my stomach in a state o' homicidal confusion. It was nae'body's confusion – it was your cold cunnin calculation. You switch the mags – yous tried t' kill yous dad. Then yous stuck t' me t' see if the penny drop – if it had you'd've murdered me! When yous saw ah wor too innocent t' guess – you was away. Well ah've guessed noo! Ay. Ah'm too smart for yous laddie. Nae'body's fool me – ah'm tellin yous. If yous want t' catch me yous dont get up early – yous dont go t' bed! And noo yous'll pay. Ah'm nae drunk – ah walked oot that pub an left a full jar – less one gargle – stood on the table. Nerves o' steel man! Do ah go t' the police? I cannae prove wor ah knows – but others can: they've got the money t' prove the world's flat. Plenty o' that sort like t' see the back o' yous. Two times ah wor kick oot – once by toffs an once by offal: an yous'll pay – for your old man – the navy – the whole bloody world – ay for every crick o' my cradle: they even rocked that wi' a boot.

LEONARD. I envy you. You want so little.

BARTLEY. Little? Ah want the bloody lot – murderer!

LEONARD. You stupid bastard! I could've killed him! – knew who I was! Knew what I'd done! You stopped me! Now you come and shoot your mouth off! Too late!

You should've come a month ago – yesterday – and told him! He'd've made you rich – so would I! Your stupid voice . . . had more in it than all the wisdom of philosophy. It stared you in the face but you did nothing. (*Shrugs.*) Isnt that worse than murder . . .? How can the world be so cruel? Because you're its servant and help it do its stupid tricks. No you're so stupid you're the master.

BARTLEY. Ah-ha, ah-ha! – the police are on t' yous kid! Ah'm your man. Ah swear an oath ah loaded the gun accidental. Ah'll swear anythin. But yous pay first. Ah'm nae the skivvy noo – ah'm in wi' a chance o' partnership. A hundred thousand in the bank.

LEONARD. There's no police.

BARTLEY. Then what? – By god I'll murder yous an then there'll be police! This bloody hoose – yous bloody people! Ah'd get some peace in prison! Ah have t' twist an turn an try an be degraded for every penny o' my share! Wait on murderers wor practice cuttin throats on their own wrists! (*Calmer.*) No matter – ah still know, an yous'll still pay.

LEONARD. The middle drawer.

BARTLEY. My money? My big moment? (*He goes to the front of the desk and opens the drawer.*)

LEONARD. The will.

BARTLEY *takes out the will.*

LEONARD. I got everything. It needs one more bent witness. Dodds is hunting the clubs for Willy. (*He reaches a hand for the will.* BARTLEY *gives it to him.*) My whole life would be different if I'd sat in another chair. I heard the page when he turned it: as if a piece of paper could sigh at what was written on it. But he said nothing. Why? If you could tell me that . . . Perhaps he didnt hear a word I said. Concentrated on the will and died by coincidence. Or did he stop to listen and then die? But why no sound? Perhaps he wasnt shocked – stopped because he didnt take me seriously, but I went on pouring my poison in his ear, and he slipped away in confusion, as if he *found* that he was dead? Or was the shock so deep he *couldnt* speak – a fist screwing him up inside and throwing him down through his own anus? Or was it malice? Or something I dont know? There's no life after death. No voice to tell us anything. The worms swallow us up and go off on their journey as if we were their luggage. Or we're burned and our smoke drifts off in the air, which is full of waves. Sound waves, shock waves, radio waves, light waves, time waves, quantum waves. When we're dead the waves pass through our dust and ashes drifting in the air. The dead carry the news of the living. The chatter from radios, threats from satellites, children's crying, the banging of hooves in the slaughter house – they all travel through waves. That's science. The laws of physics: a joke really. They even carry the past. Once something happens its recorded – voices, events, spectacles – its all recorded and goes out to the edge of the universe and then begins the journey back. The dead are always speaking the laws of physics. Our last words grind backwards and forwards over our first cries. Jokes and shouts from the holocaust, the orders to shoot and the pleas for mercy – all passing through each other in silence. The axe keeps falling. Mothers keep pleading, fathers cursing. The waves that guide missiles are full of human voices. Our ignorant little acts are dragged round and round the universe – they never lose their ignorance – and deepest space goes on shuddering at things we did millions of years ago. The waves recorded what my father heard and why he died. But they can never tell me. The dead spend eternity telling the truth and no one can listen. The dead dont even know they're talking. No wonder living in such brutality we die. Bartley I told the truth – and no one listened. I've come to the place where we stumble over the dead and their skeletons sit up and spit at us and dribble down their chins. The dust uses us for a little while and then the wind blows us out of it and howls. And that's all there is.

BARTLEY. Is that gabble supposed t' put me off? Im one ahead laddie. Ah know ma bit o' truth an (*Imitates bouncing coins in his palm.*) it chinks! Sacks an sacks an sacks o' it!

LEONARD. My father and Hammond. I couldnt beat two of them. If he'd left one sign – one thumbprint – to show he'd heard – I'd've had to spend my life pondering that. No. Old men with long beards waiting like children for their questions to be answered. I wont live like that. I think our trouble is we're never born. If he came to the door now and tried to tell me, I wouldnt listen. There's nothing to say.

BARTLEY. Whist!

LEONARD. What?

BARTLEY. Door. (LEONARD *shakes his head.*) The door man! My servant's ears! Dodds has a key. Ah'd better see.

BARTLEY *goes out.* LEONARD *puts the will into his inside pocket.* BARTLEY *comes in with* WILBRAHAM.

WILBRAHAM. Forgive me. Dodds left messages – Hammond wants to see me here.

BARTLEY (*to* LEONARD). Did ah do right?

WILBRAHAM. So sad. Deepest sympathy. You know Im scum so you wont be offended if I change the subject? I've gambled heavily. I made my bank send out a notice they wouldnt honour my gambling debts. The clubs said (*Imitation.*): 'Gamble old sport. You've lost so much old cock you must win!' They've turned me over to the mobsters. My pocket's ripped. I put talcum on my eye.

BARTLEY. The bloody vulture beggin before your da's buried! Let me thrash him Lennie!

WILBRAHAM. Yes yes despise me. Thank god decent people

still know scum when they see it – even if we do have to depend on servants to keep up our standards. The streets are full of buses. I cant throw myself under one. The passengers would stare at my body. Being dead wouldnt make it easier to bear their pity. I dont mind anger – Im *used* to angry servants – but I wouldnt even pray to god for pity – only his anger, which I deserve in the full majesty of its diapasm. My immediate debts are ninety-five thousand. Thirty would call the bullies off.

LEONARD. No.

WILBRAHAM. Why should you? But you're so rich its like being immortal! The first time we met I asked you to help me – you wouldnt. Look what happened to you! Im asking you to help me now. Fifteen thousand?

LEONARD. No.

WILBRAHAM. Then its over. I cant hide. I'll turn up at some club. Its my destiny to be thrashed to encourage the others – so the owners can get the pennies out of the pockets of those who still have any. Ten thousand? – a pittance to you, and me in my days of glory.

LEONARD. No.

WILBRAHAM *kneels.* LEONARD *ignores him.*

BARTLEY (*amazed*). He drop doon like a turd!

WILBRAHAM. Would you pay for abasement? I've knelt before. I had a regular appointment with an eccentric in the city. The panelled office – churches peeling by the river – a ritual from the middle ages. It was his price. To be fair he knew he'd never see his money. People bewilder me. What do you want? This posture is ridiculous. The thugs are waiting in the street. I cant kneel to them – they kick you when you're down. (*Crouches forward and hides his face in the ground.*) Pity me. Pity me. I've come to that at last. Have pity on me.

LEONARD (*to* BARTLEY, *going*). We must hurry.

BARTLEY. You'll nae leave this shit here?

LEONARD. We'll get your money on the way. (*To* WILBRA-
   HAM.) Tell Dodds I'll be at Bartley's dosshouse. You're
   ugly –

WILBRAHAM. Yes yes odious!

LEONARD. – because you're innocent. That's why you're
   punished.

WILBRAHAM (*face on ground*). Dodds – Bartley's doss – *any*
   service I can render –

   LEONARD *goes out.*

BARTLEY. You touch any o' this I'll break your fingers.
   Your thuggie-pals'll look like holy sisters! Yous wont
   have knees – yous'll crawl on your belly. All this is mine!

WILBRAHAM. Thank you thank you. Implicit trust. I'll wait
   quietly for the clubs to open. I'll enjoy the peace.

   BARTLEY *goes out.* WILBRAHAM *gets up and looks at the
   armchair.*

Unit Nine

The Cellar of the Ruined House

Empty. A bracket on the proscenium arch.

LEONARD *comes in carrying a rope. He looks round, goes to the
proscenium arch, sees the bracket and turns back to the centre of
the room. He ties a noose in the rope.*

BARTLEY *comes in carrying the kitchen chair.*

BARTLEY (*chair*). What's it for? (*Stops and sees rope.*) What's
   that?

LEONARD (*points to the spot under the bracket*). There.

BARTLEY (*sees bracket*). Ah'm nae gettin in t' this. O no.

LEONARD. There.

BARTLEY. Yous nae right in the head.

LEONARD. Money.

> BARTLEY *places the chair under the bracket.* LEONARD *gives him the rope.* BARTLEY *hesitates.*

LEONARD. Money.

> BARTLEY *climbs onto the chair and fastens the rope to the bracket.*

BARTLEY (*as he works*). Ah'm nae doin this. (*He finishes fastening the rope and steps down from the chair.*) Is that for yous – or one o' your pals?

LEONARD. Test it.

BARTLEY. That'll hold.

LEONARD. Test.

BARTLEY. I bloody tested it! I bloody tested it!

> *Slight pause.* BARTLEY *gives the rope two savage jerks.*

BARTLEY. Now yous play on yous own. Gi' me my money. Ah'm off.

LEONARD. Kick the chair.

BARTLEY. Yous nae serious?

LEONARD. Money.

BARTLEY. O nae. I've done some stupid things. But ah kep a little innocence left t' live on. Yous nae draggin me doon t' your cess. Give me my money an ah'll away.

LEONARD. When Im dead.

BARTLEY. Dead! (*Grabs chair.*) I'll beat your bloody brains oot! Then I'll take me money!

LEONARD. Dont rob – earn it.

BARTLEY. I'll rob – an keep my self respect!

LEONARD. You can take my watch.

BARTLEY. Watch?

LEONARD. Yours is a joke.

BARTLEY. Yous cruel bastard! Rich scum! Yous wont get away wi' it! There's some justice left!

LEONARD. The man who blew up the world.

BARTLEY. O ah'm nae so easy beat! When yous up there
ah'll cut the rope – get a knife an – bite it wi' my teeth!
I'll take my money – an leave yous on the ground! You'll
kick yourself back t' life! That'll settle your hash!

LEONARD. Knock a chair over for fifty thousand pounds.

BARTLEY. My god what monster are yous! (*Starts to leave.*)
Stick your fifty thousand pound! Get your pals in – they'll
offer yous a discount! (*Stops.*) Fifty thousand pounds.
How do ah know yous didnae drop it in the gutter when
us left wor bank. Your idea o' a sick joke – me workin
for nothin!

LEONARD. In my pocket.

BARTLEY. What d'yous want? An audience? Ah can roond
up the wino's – junkies – kinks – every sort o' crap an
prat! Pack the room! Gi' us the money – ah have t' pay
em. Ah guarantee some'll be wide enough awake t' know
what they're watchin – honest man!

LEONARD. I'll tell you when to kick.

BARTLEY. Yous'll kick when yous hang – kick the bloody
chair for practice! No no Lenny please. No son dont. Its
nae necessary – none o' this. Yous stand there lookin
soaked and its nae rainin. I dinnae mean ma brutality.
You're no a bad lad Lennie son. Come away – wor'll still
find us some laughs. Ah'll show yous how t' live – not help
yous t' die. O my god – the door! (*He goes to the doorway
and listens.*) Dodds. People wi' him.

LEONARD *stands on the chair and puts the noose round his
neck.*

BARTLEY (*sees* LEONARD *and points at him*). O god look at
that! He means it! A harmless little blackmail an ah end
in this shit! God if ah come away sane I'll never take
another penny from another man! Lenny show a bit o'
pity! What yous puttin me through'll drive me t' drink
myself t' death! Im standin here in hell! How can you do

this t' yoor pal? Kill yourself fine – but why must ah suffer? They're off up the stairs – the missin treads 'll hold 'em up. I dinnae know what you hopin oot o' this – but I reckon yous in for a colossal disappointment. – Fifty thousand quid! Ah'd be free for life! Yous got your money through stark wickedness – put it right by doin good! Lift me oot the gutter! You'll never spend a better penny. The best flowers for the hearse lad, an ah'll live a credit t' you. Ah'll swear ah'll never touch a drop! The holy saints'll pray t' me! Lenny think o' the shit-hoose world you're leavin me in! Im nae better'n an orphan! For the sake o' the good times pal!

DODDS (*off*). Mr Oldfield.

LEONARD. Soon.

BARTLEY. O god they'll break ma bloody neck for helpin yous! We might as well swap places! Shall ah go an telled em yous ran off? Then yous can take wor time. Dont let em rush yous in t' it. No – they'd find yous body and ah'd be for the high jump – innocent or not! Jump Lenny – there's nothin else for it! Jump for god's sake! Let me get my money an go!

DODDS (*off*). Oldfield I know you're up there.

BARTLEY (*hovering in the doorway*). Jump jump jump! Are yous a bloody coward! Its a disgrace standin there so ah have t' plead. Jump!

DODDS (*off*). Dont do anythin rash. I've fixed the will.

BARTLEY (*hovering in the doorway*). They're comin back t' the hall. They'll come down here. Jump! (*Wringing his hands.*) Have yous no shame! Do it Lenny! Yous promised! Ah *need* that money! Jump!

LEONARD (*flat*). Soon.

BARTLEY. Jump! You little cock-teaser! You're an insult t' wor manhood!

LEONARD. Fifty-thousand pounds.

BARTLEY. Jump jump jump! Ah'm pissin meself wi' suspense!

HAMMOND (*off*). Oldfield.

BARTLEY. Hammond . . .!

LEONARD. Now.

> BARTLEY *creeps towards* LEONARD.

BARTLEY. Ay so ah will. There's nothin reckless in it . . .
its on request an a clean rope, not second-hand.

WILBRAHAM (*off*). One could try the garden – the gardener
seems lax!

BARTLEY. Hark at em bellow – an here's a man aboot t'
hang hisself assisted by his pal an they do nothin – nae
notion o' the urgency they're in. Ah'll top yous an be off.
I know a hole wor goes up t' the street. Shant even meet
em on the stairs t' stand aside an let em through. This is
where I allus wanted the boss – an ah almost miss ma
chance for wor little voice o' conscience they would'nae
hear anymore than you will when you're dead.

HAMMOND (*off*). Oldfield – you down there?

BARTLEY. Yous arms! Wor should've tied yous arms – shit
– you'll reach up an grab! The struggle'll be shockin!
They'll cut yous doon alive!

LEONARD (*puts his hands in his jacket pockets*). They're gone.

BARTLEY. Bloody keep em gone! (*Suddenly stops to listen.*)
Ah dont believe it! (*Goes to the doorway.*) They're havin
a conference. The ineffectual bastards! Captains o'
industry! No wonder wor in us mess! Shall ah go up an
get em organised? They'll be oot on top o' the roof pigeon-
spottin! Hup – they're comin! (*Goes back to* LEONARD.)
Goodbye pal!

LEONARD. Wait!

BARTLEY. Wait! Wait! Bloody wait? – when ah've screwed
meself up t' –

LEONARD (*hands the will to* BARTLEY). Teeth.

BARTLEY. Teeth? – Does he want me t' take his false teeth
out?

LEONARD. Bite. Blood. Gag.

BARTLEY. Gag? Blood? *Teeth*!

> BARTLEY *puts the will into* LEONARD'*s mouth. A noise outside.* BARTLEY *runs off and vanishes into his hole.* LEONARD *stands on the chair with the will in his mouth, his hands in his pockets and his neck in the noose.* WILBRAHAM *comes in very bored.*

WILBRAHAM (*calls back immediately*). 'S empty.

> WILBRAHAM *slowly waddles round the room, looking for a place to sit. He mutters to himself.*

Up and down broken stairs. One could break one's neck. So pleasant in that armchair. Anonymous. Cosy. Peace. Nice. (*Starts to go, but loiters.*) Better make it look as if I searched – had the floorboards up. (*Taps foot.*) Blue magazines. Hot rod cars. Shit. Filth. Greedy old man. Moronic youth. Lascivious insects. And so Rome fell.

> WILBRAHAM *starts to leave.* LEONARD *coughs through his teeth clenched on the will.* '*Huh-humph*'. WILBRAHAM *turns, sees* LEONARD, *walks a few steps towards him and stops.*

Good lor.

> WILBRAHAM *looks away, hesitates for a moment, adjusts his tie-knot and goes out. Immediately* BARTLEY *runs out of his hole.*

BARTLEY. That's it! Ah'm nae leavin tuppence for that toerag! Its my life's wages! See yous pal!

> BARTLEY *kicks the chair from under* LEONARD. LEONARD *hangs.* BARTLEY *searches in* LEONARD'*s pockets.* LEONARD *reaches up and grabs the rope with both hands to take the weight of his body from his neck.*

My money! My money! Will yous keep still – wrigglin like a bloody tart as hadnt had it up for a year! (*Finds the *wad of banknotes.*) Dear god ah hardly dared t' hope the world could be so good t' me! Halleluja! Fifty thousand quid! It is! It is! (*Starts to count the notes.*) One two three four – O god let it be there! – yous would'nae cheat me at a time like this pal? – four five six – nae! – six seven five – och I should o' listen more at school! – what the shit ah'll have t' take his word! (*Starts to run out. Stops.*) 'The watch!' 'Yous can afford a hundred watches!' 'It was the laddie's last request!' 'You superstitious prat!'

BARTLEY *runs back to* LEONARD, *rights the chair, stands on it, and starts to undo* LEONARD's *wristwatch.* LEONARD *is clasping the rope with both hands.*

Will yous – you said yous – get your bloody hands off – yous stubborn git – you'll spoil the mechanism!

BARTLEY *gets the wristwatch, jumps down from the chair and starts to run out again.* LEONARD *gets one foot onto the chair to support his weight.*

O god son ah hope that's nae too painful!

BARTLEY *stops, turns and across the distance mimes shaking* LEONARD's *hand in farewell.*

Yous turned oot trumps pal! Ah'm sincerely grateful for all yous help!

BARTLEY *goes out through his hole. For a moment* LEONARD *teeters with one foot on the chair. He takes huge breaths and then kicks the chair away.* HAMMOND *and* DODDS *come in.*

HAMMOND. Hanged. I told you: reckless. I'd've run a book on something like this!

DODDS. The dirty little wrecker! Years of scheming thrown away! The sheer bloody-mindedness! Burned the will or put it through the shredder!

HAMMOND *and* DODDS *come down to* LEONARD.

HAMMOND. What made you leave a valuable document with him? You knew the lad suffered impulses. God knows he gave us warning.

LEONARD *(jerks)*. Yrgh!

HAMMOND. If it had been deposited in my safe in the proper way we'd be laughing. A man of your experience making elementary mistakes. Its downright diabolical.

WILBRAHAM *comes in and hovers round* HAMMOND *and* DODDS.

DODDS. I think you're totally unjust. How could I know he'd destroy the will? He was the beneficiary. There's usually some twisted logic in what he did – but this?

LEONARD *(jerks)* Yrgh!

HAMMOND. An avoidable blunder. I hate bodge.

WILBRAHAM. Er –

DODDS. If you foresaw calamity would strike, it would've been a help if you warned me.

HAMMOND. You're paid to know not be warned.

WILBRAHAM. Er –

DODDS. Its been a difficult day. The cigarette smoke in those clubs has given me a headache. And now I see Im to have my feelings trampled on. However, I do of course apologise.

HAMMOND. Excuses are always late and apologies never meant. I dont accept either.

WILBRAHAM. Excuse me I do apologise but – *(Points to* LEONARD.*)* he's alive.

HAMMOND *and* DODDS *look at* LEONARD.

HAMMOND. What's that in his mouth?

DODDS *(takes the will from* LEONARD*'s mouth)*. The will.

LEONARD. Hrg – hrg – hrg –

HAMMOND. I suppose he wiped his bum on it? That lad's

sense of humour contributed to his downfall.

WILBRAHAM. If we had a knife? (*Going to* LEONARD.) We could take the weight from his legs so –

DODDS *violently pushes* WILBRAHAM *away.*

DODDS. Fool! We've got the will and he lived to inherit! Let him hang!

LEONARD *is still.*

HAMMOND. The pair of you give over. Anyroad its too late – he's a gonner. Best call the police. We passed a phone box on the corner – if its not been rifled by some spark taking a crash course in private enterprise. And get an ambulance – it'll look good. (*Pen.*) Wilbraham if you'd be so kind. And for god's sake dont shake lad. They might not know you're alcoholic and think its fear. No point in stirring suspicions.

WILBRAHAM (*signs*). Anything anytime anywhere. Could I mention the sum the chap with the Mohican haircut hissed in my ear as he twisted it?

HAMMOND (*examining the will*). As efficient a piece of perjury as we can expect in the present slapdash company. (*Pockets pen.*) Look sharp – or must I draw a map?

DODDS *and* WILBRAHAM *go out.* HAMMOND *picks up the chair.*

HAMMOND. 'Scuse me lad. You wont object if I borrow a loan of your chair? Its yours by rights. Always yours. If that doesnt make you sole proprietor nothing will.

HAMMOND *sits on the chair beside* LEONARD. *His head is bent over the will. He mutters to himself as he reads.*

Getting short-winded – which you'll understand is an affliction. Dont mind telling you I can do without too many of these days – will or no will. (*Reads.*) Have they spelt my name right? These modern hussies use their imagination when it comes to names. If you're Smith they put down Jones. Brazen.

LEONARD's *left hand comes from his pocket, with smooth silent jerks. There is a pistol in the hand. Slowly and smoothly the arm jerks sideways and upwards, as stiff as a blindman's stick searching for a wall.*

You did me proud lad, according to your lights. Not all I wanted but plenty to build on.

LEONARD's *arm falls silently and swiftly to his side.*

(*still muttering as he reads*). As to the rest, Im sorry. I warned you. I distinctly remember. 'Say no to me an you're a dead-un'. (*Looks ahead of him and contemplates space, caressing his jaw with one hand.*) Wouldnt heed – couldnt heed. Strange lad. You moved me to the bowels. Didnt know I could still be touched. Wont happen again. (*Goes back to reading the will.*) It was a nice dream and they're bad for you. There's a lot to be said for grass. Five thousand sorts and no questions.

The arm has silently risen again, in smaller jerks. The rest of LEONARD's *body is still. The pistol searches till it finds* HAMMOND *and then stops – aimed.*

(*Suddenly sucks in air through his teeth*). Ysssss: grass! Might the fuzzy-wuzzies start to eat it and and shut my shops? Put a stop to that: root it up! No no – worrying for nothing. (*Ruminates over the will for a moment.*) . . . The world changes. No bridge between the ages. The shores move further apart.

A shot. HAMMOND *jumps up, sending the chair flying. He darts to the centre of the room, frantically looking round to see who shot. The pistol fires into the ground.* HAMMOND *retreats to the back wall and stares at* LEONARD *in shock. The pistol falls to the ground.* DODDS *comes in.*

DODDS. – ?

HAMMOND. He shot me!

DODDS. Are you – ?

HAMMOND. A dead man tried to kill me!

DODDS (*looks at* LEONARD *and then at* HAMMOND). Well he missed. Typical. Death hasnt improved his aim.

HAMMOND. Then he shot the earth!

DODDS. Now now, the onset of rigor mortis – a spasm jerked the gun. (*Slight sneering amusement.*) Im surprised you didnt forsee it.

HAMMOND. We'll wait outside.

HAMMOND *and* DODDS *start to go.* HAMMOND *goes back to* LEONARD *and kicks the pistol away from under his feet – it slithers along the ground.* HAMMOND *and* DODDS *go out.*

LEONARD *hangs dead.*

September

September was written at the request of the World Wildlife Fund for Nature. It was first performed in Canterbury Cathedral on 16 September 1989 with the following cast:

CHICO MENDES   John Kane

O   Maggie Steed

A BEGGAR   Assam Mamodeally

Directed by Greg Doran
Designed by Jenny Tirahani

CHICO MENDES *comes in. He wears a short-sleeved shirt and slacks.*

MENDES. I am the Brazilian Chico Mendes. From the age of nine I earned a living tapping rubber trees. Not an efficient use of resources by the standards of your economies. Millions of trees to give a living to a few thousand poor tappers and two hundred thousand Indians! The forest was great. It seemed as everlasting as living granite. Then the rich saw it. The great companies moved in. They sent workers to tear down the trees with chainsaws and bulldozers. They burned most of them, some floated away in the rivers. And armies of poor settlers followed the rich. They were hungry. They burned more trees. Ranchers brought cattle. When trees sheltered the soil it was wet. Now sun dries it and cattle tear up the grass and their hooves hammer the soil and it dies and the cattle are slaughtered and made into your meat and the settlers move on and burn more clearings and more cattle follow them. They drive the Indians before them, they steal their hunting grounds and in return give them their diseases: the Indians die of measles and chicken pox. Well Indians have been dying for years. No one worried. And then a miracle! Rich people in distant countries found that our forests are the rain forests that hold the world's climate in balance. Rubber drops from the slashes I make in the rubber trees – but rain drops are far more valuable! Imagine! – the great industries, crowded cities, motorways, arsenals, atomic power stations, stock exchanges – it all depends on our forest. Its as surprising as if you discovered the little children's games were as important as the laws of governments and the movements of armies and the prices of shares. Even the sky needs our forest. If gods live in the sky they must water their gardens with our rain. For years I fought for the Rural Workers Union and the Workers Party. We demonstrated. We stood in the paths of bulldozers. The rich had many of us shot. My life was threatened. Still no one bothered much. Till suddenly I was famous. My face in foreign newspapers. I won a prize. I was fighting to save the world's forest – so the rich could get richer and go on polluting the air and kill the forest anyway and the poor would stay poor. These days the rich dont just exploit poor people's bodies – they exploit their spirit. (*Shakes head.*) We had many problems.

One night I was in my kitchen with my police guard. I wanted to use the toilet in my garden. I lifted the backdoor latch. It clinked like a safety catch being freed on a gun. The gunman had waited all day. Strange to wait all day in a man's garden to kill him. My silhouette in the lighted doorway was like one of the cutout men your soldiers use for target practice. He couldnt miss. Im dead. I shouldnt be talking to you. (*Shrugs.*) I wrote a message not long before I died. I mustnt waste this chance to tell it to you. I wrote: Attention young people of the sixth of September two thousand and twenty – the first centenary of –

O *comes in wearing a white mask and grey kimono with longish black hair.*

O. The dead must be silent!

MENDES (*shrugs*). I upset authority even when Im dead! – Attention young people of the –

O. Dont! Its dangerous to say that. Its why you were killed.

MENDES (*amused*). Now Im dead I can tell it to anyone who'll listen.

O. Each time you tell it you must pay.

MENDES. That doesnt matter to me now.

O. It does. You should trust me. I killed you – paid the killer.

MENDES. Young people of the sixth of September two thousand and twenty – the first centenary of the world socialist revolution. The revolution that united all the people of the earth. My one ideal is my belief in the socialist unity that will rid the new society of all its enemies. Then all that will remain of the past will be the sad history of pain, suffering and death. I am sorry. I was only dreaming when I wrote these things. But I had the pleasure of the dream.

O. Now you must pay.

MENDES. The dead cant suffer anymore.

O. You will see. This is *my* statement.

All creation is a struggle between all things. There's no judge: only the Law. The Law is that the strongest survives. I am the strongest. I *am* the Law. The strongest is the best fighter. All I know is the fight. I *must* fight – conquer – subject – exploit. When human beings became lords of the beasts we couldnt live together in peace. That would have been against the Law that made us lords. Instead we made weapons to kill each other. Then we made the most powerful of all weapons: money. Money buys all other weapons. I am part human and part money. Everything anyone does must obey the Law. Every act leads to the survival of the fittest – the strongest. When you fought for your forest you were only preparing yourself for your killer. You little people live your life backwards: you come out of your grave and spend your life wandering back to it. Im the only creature who knows what it does: you're the puppets pulling my strings. Now I'll kill you again. (*Points.*) Fetch the chair rope and gun.

MENDES. You want me to help you kill me?

O. You spent your life helping me to kill you. When you opened your garden door you were letting me in. The chair.

MENDES. No.

O. When you're dead its too late to play for time. Fetch the chair!

MENDES *goes towards the chair.*

MENDES. My feet are moving like machines . . . For the first time I feel what its like to be dead.

O. Now you're learning how you lived!

MENDES *starts to come back with the chair. He stops.*

MENDES. I see . . . children. Strange. Three. No – more behind. They're looking up. What's screaming? (*Panics.*) A man's thumb on a button. A plane. What is – ? (*Looks back.*) Children dont be afraid – its a dream – not happening! (*Sees more children.*) Ah! Fire! Children burning! Running boy! His shoes on fire! Her dress! Fire! Ah! (*Looks up at the plane.*) Stop! Stop! No! No! (*Looks round.*) There! Look! Bouncing! Black! On the road! Bouncing to put the fire out! Up and down! Or dead and cracking – snapping – in the flames! Not still alive! Yes! – trying to tear off bits of burning skin! – and throw it away! No! No! The screaming! (*Waves the chair as if he's fighting off wasps.*) The plane! The hand! In a metal room! A helmet! Grinning! Or screaming? Children run! Run! The man's coming back! Children run . . .! (*He becomes quieter.*)

O. Here.

MENDES (*bewildered*). Didnt you see the children? Burning! (*Points.*) The puddles in the road. Little streams. Black. Shining on the road. Were . . . Why didnt you help?

O. It cant be helped. It was the past or the future. The rope.

As MENDES *goes to the rope he mutters uncomprehendingly to himself.*

MENDES. A child. A black bundle bouncing on the road. A metalled – macadam road. Bouncing. Like a toy. As if its playing while it dies. (*Stoops to pick up the rope. Suddenly stops.*) Will I see more things?

O. You cling to your lives and others pay for it.

MENDES *starts to return with the rope. He stops.*

MENDES. Can I leave it here? (*No answer. He starts again to take the rope to* O. *He stops.*) Women running across a field. They stop and start again. Little dashes. Tired. One's digging. Tearing up the earth. Burrowing with her hands. What's –? She's found a bit of cloth. Blue. A little squeal. Her. All the women crawling and tearing at the earth. Kneeling as if they're praying. Shoes. A cap. Children in the ground. More cloth. Mothers in head-scarves and old coats digging at the earth as if they're picking a giant's teeth for bits of their children. (*He holds the rope as if he were nursing a child.*) If I were alive I couldnt comfort them. (*He buries his face in the rope.*) They cry. And kiss the rags of all the children. One of them's found a patch she sewed. (*He hands the rope to* O.) I dont want to see. I'd rather be dead.

O. How weak you are! (*Points.*) The gun.

MENDES *goes towards the gun. He stops.*

MENDES. . . . Will there be any more? (*No answer. Sullenly.*) Yes – children sitting on the ground. So thin there only seems a few of them – that so many can seem so few . . .! Faces. White.

O. Starvation.

MENDES. Perhaps they're dead – at least their minds dead so they dont suffer? Flies. Walking on their faces. Black flies on white faces like the markers madmen use on war maps to show the movements of their armies.

MENDES *gives the gun to* O.

O. Tie yourself in the chair.

MENDES *ties himself in the chair while* O *speaks.*

O. A few people suffer for a few moments and you're ready to die? I've seen dead and dying piled as high as the Tower of Babel – and couldnt tell if the babel was the cries of the dying in the tower or the grunts of the builders piling them there! I saw atomic bombs split open two cities and fire spurt out like blood as if the earth had been disembowelled. If every tree in your forest was a stake with a victim tied to it – I've seen more tied to stakes to be shot or burned. And the victim is always more innocent than the executioner – because at that moment the executioner learns nothing. I'll die one day. When the fittest has destroyed everything else it must destroy itself. I cant stop destroying. That's the Law. One day I'll meet my last enemy: an army so modern its become prehistoric. We'll destroy each other and the ground under our feet and the sky over our heads and the wind in our sides.

A young BEGGAR *walks in almost like a sleep-walker. He is barefoot and wears half a sheet loosely wrapped round him like the skirt of a sarong, a vest, an African skull cap – all dirty white – and a bright crimson Victorian military jacket. The jacket is too big for him and the epaulettes, buttons, one of the two hip pockets and most of the braid are missing. For a begging bowl he carries an open food or soft-drink can.*

O. A beggar. Too weak to sing or speak. Shakes his empty can – and it makes no noise.

The BEGGAR *stops before* O *and holds out his begging can. He shakes it a few times.*

O. He's too clever to beg from you.
MENDES. He cant see the dead.
O. I brought you back to life. That's why I got you trussed up. He doesnt beg from you because you're powerless. These beggars see everything. He saw a mile off I

wouldnt give anything. He wont stay like that long. He's just using the excuse for a rest.

The BEGGAR *goes out.*

MENDES. Shoot me now.

O (*suspicious*). Why dont you struggle? Plead!

MENDES. The children and women I saw in the dreams – their suffering was terrible. But I knew how people suffer. And I know – the people I lived with taught me – that the rich are crueller than the poor – and that means more ignorant – and that means weaker. With all their power the rich are weaker than children. They're like your executioners: they cant learn. My people's children – every one of them – gives us a new chance. The beggar wasnt a dream like you. He'll grow up and have children and when the time comes there'll be people to read my message.

O. That little gutter rat! – change the world?

MENDES. Yes.

O (*laughs*). Your Indians werent running from the bulldozers they were running from your stupidity! Wager your life on that child?

MENDES. Wager?

O. I'll give you some bread. Get him to give you half. No – a mouthful. No – a crumb. If you do that I'll let you go home and fight for your forest. You'll have changed the Law. If you fail I shoot you – and you stay dead. And I warn you – if you fail you drive him deeper into his own corruption: he'll have refused a man in need.

MENDES. Call him.

O *holds up a piece of bread. Almost immediately the* BEGGAR *comes back, hurrying in a curiously careful way, as if he doesnt want to seem to be hurrying – it would attract others' attention to the bread. He stops in front of* O *and stares at* O*'s face.* MENDES *has untied the rope.*

MENDES. I know how hungry you are. I've been hungry. So have my children. But we can do better than a bit of mouldy bread. My house isnt far. I'll take you home. My wife will find something for us to eat. She'll be so pleased to see us there'll be a feast!

The BEGGAR *gives one quick glance at* MENDES *then goes back to staring at* O's *face.*

You'll live with us – be part of our family. I'll feed you every day. Teach you. Get you a job. It'll be a good life. But first you must give me some of this bread. If you gobble all of it you'd be punishing your greed – you'd lose all the good things I'd've given you. Eat this.

MENDES *takes the bread from* O, *breaks it in half and gives half to the* BEGGAR. *The* BEGGAR *eats it in the same rapid, careful way he came back.*

(*Shudder.*) Ah, he's so hungry he blinks when he eats . . . (*To the* BEGGAR.) You saw how I smiled when I gave you the bread. My smile showed I enjoyed giving you bread. I want to give you lots of things. If I'd wanted to cheat you I'd've eaten all the bread, wouldnt I? Now I know you have to be sure when it comes to so much bread: so I give you half of what's left – so you can be sure Im not cheating – and you give me the other half.

The BEGGAR *nods.*

So much more depends on you than you know. You promise to give me the bread?

The BEGGAR *nods.* MENDES *hesitates.*

O. Give him your bit to prove you're not keeping the best for yourself.

MENDES. I must be sure you understand. What's your name? Where're you from? (*No answer.*) If I can go home I'll be able to help many people. They'll eat and be

clothed. I'll save their jobs. They'll owe all that to you!
You wont have to beg – they'll all help you.

MENDES *breaks off half the bread and gives it to the*
BEGGAR. *The* BEGGAR *eats as before.*

Is this my piece?

The BEGGAR *stares at* MENDES. *Silence.*

You're so hungry – how can you think of people you
havent seen? But you see my face. You see how much I
need you to . . . If you dont give me the bread I'll be shot.
You can see the gun! . . . A little piece of bread. I could
see my children. My wife. When my friends saw I wasnt
really dead – the joy, the joy . . . I could do so much. –
I know what Im asking. This scrap is a millionaire's
ransom to you. Starvation's eating your body – your
bones could be chopsticks and your flesh the bits of rice
left in the bottom of the bowl. And now I want even that!
That I dare to ask tells you I must. Share the bread with
me. Please. I beg you.

The BEGGAR *is staring at* MENDES.

. . . What can you say to a child like that? (*Turns to* O.)
Tell me! One little defeat – one slip up on a dirty little
road going nowhere – who'd see? You'd lose nothing. My
death isnt worth even a crumb to you. (*To* BEGGAR.)
Look – (*He breaks the bread again and gives a piece to the*
BEGGAR. *The* BEGGAR *eats as before.*) Half a mouthful
left. Your chances are running out. Dont be a fool. (*Holds
the bread in front of his own mouth.*) Say eat. That's all you
have to do. All I –

Suddenly the BEGGAR *makes several swift grabs at the*
bread. MENDES *backs away.*

MENDES. How can I help him?
O. Break his arm.

MENDES (*to the* BEGGAR). You fool! Fool! – Perhaps he
doesnt know what a gun is. He's walked over Africa or
Asia and now he's so tired he's forgotten. No – the
journey would remind him! The milestones are guns.

O. Break his leg. He'll give you the bread so you dont break
the other one.

MENDES (*to* O). You tricked me! You bet because you knew
he was starving.

O (*offering*). Threaten him with my gun.

MENDES *goes to the* BEGGAR *and embraces him with one
arm. With the other he holds the bread in the air away from
the* BEGGAR.

Poor child. They starved you. Now you think I want to
rob you. Your parents would do what you're doing.
Anyone as hungry as you would. Im not angry . . . Two
strangers, a miserable bit of dirty bread and a leering
ghost: that's our world. Help me.

As MENDES *speaks and embraces the* BEGGAR, *slowly
behind* MENDES'S *back the* BEGGAR'S *hand steals up to the
bread.* MENDES *sees it and violently pushes the* BEGGAR
away. The BEGGAR *totters.*

You little bastard! Got you! You're not so smart! Look
at him – is he tottering or dancing? (*The* BEGGAR *falls.*)
Get up! – there's nothing wrong with you! Thieves dont
go hungry! I'll break your *back*! (*He crouches in despair.
To himself.*) I'll force him. I'll thrash him. How else?

O. The weak fight and the strong watch: their desperation
gives us tips.

MENDES. If I could give it to him. Say eat and see even that
bit of hunger go – wipe even a few dry tears from his face.

The BEGGAR *starts to crawl towards* MENDES, *making little
placatory grins as if he's given in. He doesnt take his eyes off
the bread.*

MENDES. No – its mine!

The BEGGAR *crawls towards him.*

Mine! For my kids – not swine like you. Mine! I'll find a way to save myself without you!

The BEGGAR *reaches* MENDES *and stops.*

Mine . . . You even smell of hunger – like dry wind. There, you saw how the man who smiled got angry. He's no better than you. Has no more right than you to bread. Why should you help? Who did you any good? But you're all I can turn to. Save my life. Let me take your hand.

MENDES *takes hold of the* BEGGAR'*s wrist. In his other hand he holds the bread in front of his own mouth and puts the* BEGGAR'*s hand on his own wrist.*

MENDES. You see – I trust you. The bread's almost in your own hand. Put it in my mouth. Then everything will be changed. (*They stare at each other.*) I'll eat for both of us. Please.

Suddenly the BEGGAR *grabs the bread, crams it into his mouth and bolts it down.* MENDES *jumps up with a cry. The* BEGGAR *grabs his can and starts to run.*

O (*pointing*). A crumb! A crumb!

MENDES *and the* BEGGAR *stare at the floor. Moment's silence. The* BEGGAR *sees the crumb. He dashes for it.* MENDES *dashes for it.* MENDES *throws the* BEGGAR *aside. He gets the crumb and holds it on the tip of a finger an inch from his mouth.*

MENDES. The crumb's on the end of my finger! Feed me! Feed me! Please please please!
BEGGAR. Kill him kill him kill him!

O *shoots* MENDES. MENDES *falls dead.*

O. Clever child – you saw through him: all take and no give.

The BEGGAR *falls on* MENDES' *body, clawing at his fist and making little isolated animal sounds.*

What're you – ? The crumb! The starving child picks the crumb from the dead man's fist. The dead grip hard. No – rigor mortis cant have started. He's dead but his anger's living inside him like an animal waking up in winter. That's what's clenching his fist.

The BEGGAR *opens* MENDES' *fist and takes out the crumb. He stands with the crumb in his cupped hands.*

Eat your crumb. Celebrate. You've earned it.

The BEGGAR *goes to* O, *kneels, crouches down and offers the crumb in his cupped hands.*

What d'you – ? I dont want it. I wont take it. (*Measured.*) No no. Its yours. Eat it. (*The* BEGGAR *doesnt move.* O *moves off a few paces.*) Go away! You order me to kill kill kill? I'll kill you! Forcing your filthy trash on me! It stinks of your starvation! I eat the best – they serve me the world! (*The* BEGGAR *doesnt move.* O *turns away and holds the back of the chair for support.*) Why did I stay? Why why? Stupid bets. Stupid charades. I stay and let a tramp stop me and ask me to account. I didnt know it would come so soon. I thought I had all the time I'd stolen from everyone I'd killed. Tell me your name? Your name! (*No answer.*) So hungry he's forgotten his name. He doesnt know who he is or I am. Tomorrow you'll wake up – mornings are always beautiful when you're young – and set out to find me. I work in the night – or in just enough daylight to see to murder and go to market. Give me the crumb. (O *takes the crumb. The* BEGGAR *lowers his hands but makes no other movement.*) You've made a contract. I have to pay with what I value most. (*With one foot* O *pushes the gun along the ground towards the* BEGGAR. *With*

one hand the BEGGAR *draws it closer towards himself.
Otherwise he doesnt move.*) Please. Eat it. (*No response.*)
There are two extremes in you. They could only live in a
body as frail as that. Total selfishness – and yet you'd
throw yourself away on a chance. That's the power of
nothingness. You're a picture hanging on a missing wall.
I thought my last war would be the bloodiest – armies in
the sky and the whole world crouches and covers its head.
Perhaps we'll bump into each other on a street corner and
the world wont even know what's happening any more
than children know when they're conceived.

O *eats the crumb. No sign of revulsion.*

Bitter. I ate the crumb but you'll eat the dirt of your
grave.

The BEGGAR *remains crouching.* O *picks up* MENDES' *body
and holds it waist high with one arm supporting his back and
the other his legs.* O *carries* MENDES *through the spectators.*

Roll up! Roll up! While the show lasts! See Chico Mendes
and his killer! Buy your tickets now! Wallets gentlemen!
Ladies open your purses! Kiddies raid your piggy banks!
Grandma be nice to granddad and he might dig up his
cash box! I guarantee a show worth paying for! The
Family Show! The Great Circus! The Trailer for the End
of the World! For a small consideration one of my lady
assistants will snap you standing between me and my
corpse! Show your friends the snap of you with your
killer! You'll all be in the Last Show on Earth!

Roll up! Roll up! I killed Chico Mendes!
Roll up! Roll up! I killed Chico Mendes!

O *shouts and carries out* MENDES' *body. The* BEGGAR *is
alone. He has stood up and looked for more crumbs – none.
He stands awkwardly holding the gun at his side in one hand.
With the other he holds out his begging tin to the audience.*

Slowly he moves the can once from one side to the other, intently studying the audience's faces with all the politeness of beggars.

He goes out through the stage entrance.

Notes on Post-Modernism

Notes on Post-Modernism

1.   These notes concern the history and present state (known as post-modernity) of the relationship between people, technology and authority; and the way in which theatre and other arts are part of that relationship.

2.   People organise themselves into societies in order to fulfill their needs more efficiently. They experience the social as the private. Because of this the relationship between them and society does not develop mechanically. The development is reciprocal – as a plant helps to biologize the soil and climate in which it grows.

3.   The human mind's capacity is greater than that which people would use if they only fulfilled their needs individually. This over-capacity makes possible the ramifications of society and culture. The total capacity is invocable in immediate experience and so the mind is radically interrogative. No answer stops it because the capacity to interrogate engulfs the answer. For this same reason of over-capacity societies interpret their needs not in relation to their locality but to the world. People cannot live in society without interpreting the world.

4.   Meaning cannot be derived from the world but must be given to it. The world is the boundary – the cosmic world. The boundary is unknowable and is a fact without meaning. In the way in which societies use it it does not exist.

5.   Because of their mind's over-capacity people must interrogate the nature of the boundary. Even children do this. They ask the questions of philosophy. Why? What? Whence? Whither? The answers to these questions must unite the lowest human functions and behaviour with the highest culture.

6.   Authority claims to speak to and for the boundary. The boundary is seen as the source of meaning and value.

7.   When people organize themselves into societies some of them exercize authority in the organisation. The organizers may be stronger, wiser, more devious and so forth. I shall call them the 'authority'. Authority organizes society to use technology in the seemingly most efficient way to meet the common needs. In the course of doing this the relationships between people and authority, people and the boundary, and authority and the boundary, must be interrogated. Belief and consent are forms of

interrogation in which the same questions are constantly repeated. That they are forms of doubt is concealed by the prohibition (by self or state) of other questions. Belief is a form of boredom.

8.   The threefold model of people, authority and boundary can be used to understand the history and present state referred to in note 1. The three elements are not as mutually exclusive as the model suggests but it is able to throw light on their relationship.

9.   The boundary is unknowable. Its mystery is analogous to the mystery people know as their 'self'. Light plays on exterior things but not on the self and its thoughts, passions and dreams. The things of the world have analogues in the structure sensed in the self. It is as if the exterior boundary had knowledge of the interior boundary, but not the other way around. The interior is contained in the exterior but encompasses it in ceaseless interrogation. Society depends on the natural world to meet its needs. But accidents, the hazards of the seasons, natural disasters, all threaten society; so it propitiates, induces and thanks the boundary. Authority stipulates and regulates these practices and rites.

10.   Authority relates people, technology and the boundary to each other. In speaking for the boundary and interpreting the relationship authority increases the humanness of the human mind. This is the reason for optimism. Authority does not derive humanness from the human mind. Humanness is socially, culturally created within the mind's excess capacity. (So its characteristics cannot be acquired genetically.) The mind's consent to authority's story is part of the process by which humans create their humanness. Authority partly represses people but at the same time it must increase their collective humanness. In time repression of people greater than that needed for technological efficiency forces them into interrogating authority. The mind creates its humanness by living in the threefold relationship. In this way even barbarism is a source of humanness, though barbarism is not necessary; it is a disharmony between the social and the individual's perception of the social. Authority's story – its account of the threefold relationship – is false: the boundary has no story. So it is as if the rabbit believed in the conjuror's tricks.

11.   Authority may use force as well as or instead of its story. As the human mind must interrogate, authority itself eventually becomes a barrier. This happens in slave and prison cultures and under all forms of social exploitation. Authority secures power,

privilege and prestige more easily if it tells a story which wins willing consent.

12. Authority is not free. It declares the meaning of the boundary and so of people but is coerced by the necessity of meeting people's needs. Technology disturbs social relations and this stimulates interrogation of the boundary. As the technology by which needs are met changes, so authority changes its story or gives way to the next storyteller. Authority cannot return to the beginning. It inherits a story which legitimizes human needs; needs are then seen not as coming from the individual but as being given to them by the boundary. Raw need is culturally legitimized. It is the legitimizing of needs and not the fulfilling of them which gives authority its greatest power: people will sacrifice their needs to preserve their legitimacy and will sacrifice their lives to preserve their icon of the self. Authority inherits a story which legitimizes the existing humanness of the human mind and it must develop the story. The new story can only be understood as a further episode in the story from the past – as if the new story were an episode in a serial novel. The new story must enable people to recognise themselves in terms of the humanness they have come to believe of themselves; the belief has become an essential part of their economic and cultural life. These beliefs and practices are – together with the interrogation of them – their humanness. If this were not so it would be as if we had to tell a story before we had learned a language.

13. It is important that in its relation to the boundary authority uses the boundary to legitimize people's needs. Ultimately the legitimization depends on the need of the mind's over-capacity to interrogate. Authority's story tells why people are entitled to their needs, how having them is evidence of their humanness. People relate to their needs in accordance with the boundary's approval or condemnation of their needs. Authority legitimizes both needs and interrogation; and interrogation even subverts needs, turning fulfillment into need and need into what is desired; in this way interrogation justifies the answers to its questions, giving them the authority of questions. Legitimizing authority cannot act arbitrarily; its story is defined by people's needs and the possibilities of technology and organisation. Even tyranny cannot be arbitrary for long. Corruption of people is not arbitrary but is defined by the virtue it excludes; and to this extent it serves virtue's ends in the dialectical changes in the threefold relationship.

14.   Throughout history much human behaviour remains the same. People must meet the needs of their physiology and these change little. They must eat, sleep and multiply. But humanness changes radically. This is because technology and social organisation change. To eat, for example, is a constant need, but the generalization of the behaviour by which needs are met creates each society's culture and so each individual's culture.

15.   Instincts are commonly misunderstood. We learn our instincts when we learn our social roles; but they are not rational and easily corrigible. They are learned in the context of social stories, especially in the versions told to children – told not only verbally, but shown in uniforms, agendas, punishments, architecture and so forth. Children are dramatized by their induction into society. Instincts do not determine culture. On the contrary, culture gives instincts a social character. Instincts are not biologically determined but culturally manipulable. This removes them from the private to the public. This is true even of antisocial instinctive behaviour. That behaviour is the objectification of the tensions in unjust society. The tensions need not be consistently abrasive and may be emollient in the way they manipulate sentiment and even in the norms of behaviour they encourage (as in the chaos of a shipwreck there may be order). These distortions – which give us the wrong reasons for our instincts – are unavoidable because of the vulnerability in which children grow. It means, however, that in contesting their own antisocialism people should not think they should repress their animal nature and feel guilt for their self-assertion: that may be provocation or at best expedience. Instead they should criticise society – the mind's need to interrogate is their natural ability to do this.

16.   Individuals have the instincts of their social roles, just as they do their language; and their own *use* of language – in Saussureian terms their *parole* as distinct from their *langue* – is also derived from their social role. Individuality has the same origin as class generalisation. The former is the shape of the fragment chipped from the block of the latter. Individuality is authentic but it cannot be expressed or understood outside its class context. Individual diversity comes from class uniformity and class experience is derived from individual diversity. Individuality is the product of generality. The private is how the public expresses itself – the statue embraces its sculptor. Hence the instability of class roles. They are not instinctive, or even politically determined except in shifting generalities; so that if self autonomy is to be achieved there

is need not only for political understanding but also for self understanding. Both forms of understanding are the subject of drama. If individuality is discounted in politics, then need is stripped of legitimization; authority cannot then increase the humanness of mind; it attempts to take the boundary's place and any authority which does that becomes a barrier; it has stifled or, worse, diverted into regimentation, the need to interrogate.

17.   The individual is dramatized because the over-capacity of mind makes him or her a spectator of his or her self, which is (by analysis) a spectator of himself or herself in society: an actor on stage. The combination of reason and the capacity for instinct dramatizes the child as it becomes a social agent.

18.   Understood in this way instincts explain much of the drama of knowing yourself to be human. We are not tools of instinct. Our reasoning, interrogating mind severs instinct from the natural world and our instincts are not our birthright but are donated to us in the drama of childhood and our later need to redramatize that drama. Instincts and cognition make up a whole, like weft and warp; neither exists nor changes without the other. Instincts are humanizing since they help to make the mind interrogative; if they are corrupt that is because they are wrongly thought. But thought does not control instinct, it creates it – sometimes as Frankenstein created. All pleasure is the satisfactory – that is, precise – asking of a question: because the flesh is made literature. But we cannot remember the question, only its interrogative form. The question is lost in its first dramatization in the child; redramatizing the drama means understanding the new situation and letting the old answer – which we cannot remember – serve as part of the question; then our ignorance teaches us and our knowledge of the new may be precise – we have no need of lies and find no security or comfort in corruption. Plato is wrong in saying we learn only what we know. What we know is the truth – but the facts are against it. The facts are the new. They must change the truth – and that is the redramatization of childhood necessary to maturity; the new must constantly be integrated into the old so that the truth may become fiction. We would die without our trauma.

19.   We can only think of society in our role as spectators of the boundary. The corruption of instinct is ultimately derived from society. But as drama precedes rational understanding, culture is in two respects founded on falsehoods: the child's and authority's.

In the rationality of drama instincts can elucidate their humanness – or in the corruption of drama they turn interrogation of authority into belief and obedience. Belief is the constant reiteration of the same questions in order to avoid answers.

20.   This account of instincts is compatible with theories of mind as diverse as Locke's and Chomsky's. A modular understanding of the brain must allow for information and performance ultimately to be generalized in the cortex and so in experience. Otherwise we would in effect be working on other people's memories. We do not have *other people's* memories even of the times two multiplication table but *our own* memory of it, and this would be true even if the table were innate knowledge. I am not making the simple point that knowledge is what we think of it or need it for, but what the things we know keep secret from us.

21.   Authority does not discern an existing story but creates one. God does not speak till he is spoken to by authority. Authority does not pray. Just as people create – in submission or resistance – their humanity in their relationship to authority, so does authority in relationship to the boundary. It believes it knows its story just as it knows the language in which it tells it. People do not necessarily lose their humanness under tyranny. They lose it only when authority with their consent replaces the boundary with itself as barrier; usually this happens only when authority delegates authority to subordinates in a way which (through fear or prestige) prohibits interrogation – it creates a chain of vavasours. Then the child's philosophical birthright is lost and the functionality of the good citizen is produced.

22.   Madness unlike officiousness is not corruption. Madness, when its cause is not chemical, bodily etc., occurs when the questioner turns on himself or herself in fear – not in self-questioning but in the process of questioning the boundary; then the individual haunts the boundary as if it were no man's land. The exterior is internalized and questions become answers; yet the madman or madwoman does not have the sanctuary of belief (which depends on outside authority) but must constantly fantasize reality.

23.   Some changes in the threefold relationship are culturally more important than others. Their importance is that later developments have to take account of them – they cannot rescind the earlier humanness but must incorporate it into their own.

24. Early cultures related people to the jungle, veldt or desert in which their society lived. For them the world was not mapped beyond the community's tracks. It was the demesne of spirits and animal-spirits. The natural was seen as the supernatural. Authority's story described the spirits and controlled the rituals that ensured good relations between them and society, so that needs were met. The totem animal might be eaten and actors might be sacrificed. (The first actors were killed at the end of the performance but this is no longer done in modern theatre.) The iconography was of animals and humans and their symbiosis. Ritual and theatre can only be combined in such primitive societies. Politics hardly existed because it was synonymous with culture and wisdom. Opposition came from without, from the boundary which was alien and malevolent.

25. The tendency of greek society was discursive not ritualistic. The boundary was partly literalised by asia on the greek frontier – not a jungle inhabited by animal spirits but a place of barbarous political darkness. And technology had changed. Slash and burn and hunting were replaced by husbandry and herding. Plato's ideal world had a perfection absent in this world. Yet people were victims of the ideal world. In Plato's myth of the cave people are bound like slaves. The world was imagined as controlled by gods. The gods were frivolous. Judged by human standards they were mad. The boundary was fate – and perhaps fate was even the graveyard of the gods. In greek drama human suffering was enormous and served no natural, totemic purpose. It was – amazingly – endured for the purposes of the inner boundary, so that it might interrogate the outer boundary. The drama of people and animals was replaced by the drama of people and gods. But people achieved their humanity in defying the gods. Their ability to choose to submit to fate was a moral condemnation of its arbitrariness. A judgement on it. The radicalness of the greeks in doing this has not been surpassed. In the greek world authority was not free to create culture by its interpretation of the boundary, founding its power on fear of the world. The gods were judged, the world was explored and new maps were made. Culture was divided into the poetic, the philosophical and the administrative. The division meant that ritual was once and for ever excluded from theatre. In the past ritual had increased the humanness of mind. In future ritual would function as a politics that excluded understanding; ritual is without interrogation. Philosophy interrogated authority's institutions.

This openness produced self knowledge that later cultures would have to take into account. In greek society answers were not dictated but came through discussion. Even oracles were ambiguous, not out of sacerdotal cunning but out of respect of the questioner: ambiguity was not a trap but a dialogue. Of course the institutions were imperfect, and when the oracle was acted on, the hand came off with the glove. But it meant the gods did not know – or did not respect – the truth. The greeks were not the chosen people but the people who chose themselves. Their statues showed the gods as superhuman, heroic and harmonious even in discord; but drama showed them as arbitrary, entangled, inhuman. The first is the human utopia, the second is the reality. The function of any religion is, in order to explain the boundary, to create gods who in their dealings with this world are able to behave worse than human beings could in that situation. If human beings behaved as badly they would lose their self-respect and destroy their icon of humanity. Religion does not idealise our goodness but licenses – in the acts of the gods – the worst in us. Gods are not sacrificial scapegoats, either, but the actors of *Realpolitik* in the world of ethics and emotions. Their miracles are only a moral figleaf. We misunderstand god because we have not understood ourselves.

26.   There were flaws. The greeks could not have achieved their openness and still have organized society if they had been truly democratic. Democracy could not have been created without the support of slavery; greek technocracy was too primitive to allow humanness to be generalised. The economy needed slaves – two-footed cattle. In this matter the greeks were forced to be as frivolous as their gods. Plato's story of the cave is political not metaphysical.

27.   Slaves cannot accept their master's evaluation of slaves. They cannot be corrupted in this way; but free people are corrupted by accepting their masters' description of freedom. Authority cannot have the institutions and forms in which slaves can question it and so it cannot give slaves answers that increase their humanity. Slavery cannot be legitimized for slaves, at best it is endured in resentful fear. Slaves must question the boundary directly and that is the advantage they often have over the free. They create their own culture, which is the way they answer their questions. But if the masters seem technologically competent the slaves might adapt their masters' culture to their own ends. This means that in order to escape from slavery slaves will lose some of their freedom. That is part of the drama of being human, the way the psyche is enmeshed in politics; and why we can only live by

human law when our humanity does not depend on the legitimizing of our need to be criminal.

28.   Slavery was the classical world's weakness. ('If all slaves were dressed alike they would see how great was their number and murder us.') To accept that all people were equal before the boundary would have weakened authority and made the administration of technology too hard. Greek society's discursiveness was not a viable model for the organisation of ancient technology. Christianity resolved the resulting crisis between psychic tension and political efficiency. Christian authority spoke dogmatically for the boundary. Dogma was the price of making god human. The new freedom was based on a rigidity which must in time become a prison – when god will turn into the devil in order to escape again from human beings and make machines his chosen people.

29.   Societies migrating to new lands or developing new economies often seek dictatorial leaders. Judeo-christianity created the single god as a moral counterpart to political need. When humans became political ethics had to replace ritual. As christianity made everyone equal before god it was not in the common interest to see gods as frivolous: that would have devalued the equality of humanness. The frivolity of the greeks' gods had seeped through into the relation between masters and slaves; what a culture cannot use as a strength becomes a weakness, a corruption of the state. In fact the christian god's acts were as frivolous (or were as bound by fate) as those of the greek gods. But they were monotheistic, tyrannical, ineffable signs of love: god became moral and jealous. He was not to be defied and judged. Perhaps in criticising the gods Euripides abdicated human responsibility for them. We must accept, with all their faults, the gods we create; we create their faults because we need them; the gods have a graveyard but they must not go to it too soon. Greek drama had to accept the criminality of the gods so that the utopian heroic greek statues could dance in the orchestra of dionysus.

Christianity could not accept responsibility for its god and he was not to be interrogated though he redeem the world with murder. Christianity closed theatres because they cannot exist without questioning. It closed the arenas because they were the scenes of its martyrdom. But they were also the scenes of the martyrdom of heathens. The church closed the arenas less to prevent victims' sufferings (it inflicted suffering on its own kind) than to prevent the spectators' delight. This was wise, because to the state pleasure is more dangerous than suffering; when people suffer a tyranny already begins to control the authority that will replace it. To be human drama must be fiction, not real. Otherwise people behave like gods and that is not how to become human. To put it crudely, our gods do our dirty work for us and allow us to keep our human icon. Its often thought that gods are a projection of the best in human beings, the utopian. But gods are created to do what human beings would find it inhuman to do, but which (at the time it is done) must be done if authority is to administer technology and the economy and still legitimize the human mind – which means to increase its humanness. The moral accountability which people are supposed to have to god they really have to authority: god keeps the hands of the police clean. Gods are our moral slaves and combine ethics and *Realpolitik*. When we created tools we had to create god to take responsibility for the effects of their use. If we look at it analytically we see that we create gods to drive our machines.

30.   Christianity's drama is in the past in the days of conception, golgotha and resurrection; but it is also timeless and always at its moment of crisis. The church-state administered culture as an open wound. Theatre must question the boundary, and so authority replaced theatre with ritual, the constant making and healing of the wound. But christian ritual is different from the early ritual of people-and-animals. *That* combined ritual and theatre; god had not yet chosen martyrdom for his son and so taken ritual and theatre out of history – and so in primitive ritual real martyrdom (real even when symbolic) was still repeatedly acted *as theatre*. There was no functional difference between the stage in the mind and the stage in society. At each ritual performance the god was re-won; there is no prayer in ritual, only invocation and presence and the question is erased by blood or chant. But the christian martyrdom of god occurs only once. This enables authority to control dogma, within limits extending it as necessary to meet the remapping of the world and to enable society to change technology efficiently to meet new ends. In fact technology did not greatly develop, but many different technologies and ways of living in different climates and terrains were brought into economic contact and administration was extended. The administration of souls meant the overseeing of these new technologies and the start of turning the map of the world from a rune into a market diagram. Doctrine involved politics but was outside history. The church could adapt its foundations without destroying its edifice; till in time it would be shown a map it could not survive.

31. Fiction must be built into the threefold relationship and the purposes of fiction respected. Otherwise stages in the mind and stages in society become confused. Finally you cannot stage in society what must be staged in the mind, without corrupting the humanising process. It is not that the stage is a way of avoiding reality. We cannot have the facts of reality – survive them – unless we teach the facts our fictions; a knife has no morality, a machine has no appetite – yet they are martinets that instruct us. The child is both murderer and murderers' victim – many times – and because of its vulnerability it must be so; the emulsifying of instinct and reasoning is tragic and dramatic. When the process is understood the stage in the mind and the stage in society can be used to increase our humanness. Drama uses a dead language which, although it cannot be known, corrupts unless the facts of the new are clearly articulated in the memory of the old. This is true also of politics. That is why politics must not be confined to administering and ordering. We speak of the dictatorship of the proletariat: but we need the *diction* of the proletariat, the anarchy of the party and the dictatorship of (I mean from) the self. Like golgotha, the nazi parade ground and the lager appellplatz were real stages where the fictive ought to have been; and perhaps golgotha was a fiction? – as fictive as the resurrection. But golgotha was dogmatized as real. At least, unlike the nazi sites, it was creative because it freed slaves. The nazi sites were prisons. The problem set christian authority was how to make golgotha a prison, and it did this by declaring it to be a place of love.

32. Where there is no theatre society is the dramatic stage. What the theatre cannot stage must be staged in reality. Christianity's story is a drama of family and state. It legitimizes criticism at many levels but turns it into a means of repression. The son-god was born into a poor family. He dealt with earthly authority patronizingly and destructively. He dealt with the god of the boundary submissively. His mother is made pregnant not by god but by the son-like Gabriel; as if the unborn son made his mother pregnant. Oedipus fathers himself on his mother and treats his father as his son. The son is punished with crucifixion. Death becomes birth. Punishment becomes love. And forbidden love becomes love of the world: how else could it be concealed? By these contortions an elemental drama is suspended over people and state. Authority rewrites the story in which the child was originally dramatized and the psyche produced as the scene of drama. As children grow up the first story must be rewritten so that children can make the new practical; so that the victims can use technology

and become citizens and perhaps victimizers. But as the private can only think the public, children rewrite the story collectively as classes; the child's memory of events which did not occur are transmuted into mystical 'facts' of his or her culture. Unfortunately the old may be fictionalised as the new – the frequent cost of being human. Whenever organization must change, authority can enter the gap between the child's story of childhood, the story of events which did not take place (but which are remembered) and the new facts of the present world – which then become facts about the old story. Culturally it is the job of the individual to return as detective to the scene of the old crime with a bagful of facts from the new (the present) and litter them about the place – where they become clues of a crime that did not happen. Thus the present makes the past real so that the individual (murderer and victim) may take responsibility for the present: in this way childhood becomes maturity, with the moral mandate of that word or with the obedience of a good citizen whose soul is the taking of orders. The psyche is a plot; the stories of epochs are at the same time domestic dramas.

33. Catharsis is not the evacuation of emotion but the means by which inhuman acts of *Realpolitik* are legitimized, in the face of needs, as part of the human icon. Culture is graffiti written on the wall at the boundary; graffiti, because doctrine is inventive and made 'on the run' as authority responds to crises. The wall does not exist but is actualized by the graffiti. Later, doctrine slowly changes into dogma and the boundary becomes a barrier and is actualized in bureaucracy, financial devices, schools, police cells and so on.

34. In christianity all are equal. The authority of church and state speaks for the boundary. People may shut themselves off from the love of god and lose their place in society: a great garbage bin is set at the edge of the world, hell. Authority punishes heresy in the name of the boundary. In this way authority achieves administrative competence but legitimizes (as part of the human icon) its right to coerce when its other means fail. It legitimizes its violence in the same process by which it adds humanness to the human mind. Christian authority increased the humanness of the human mind by the story it told of god and his people. The individual's need to interrogate was co-ordinated into authority's power. Conflict stems from the injustice of the real world, but so long as authority can administer technology (which often means, so long as there are no leaps in technological development) conflict

may be acted out in terms of the story, not in terms of ownership. Authority donates humanness both to believers and heretics; heretics turn authority into a barrier; and this means turning authority's story of the boundary into a barrier. Heresy speaks directly to the boundary and so creates a new boundary which may humanize the mind. Provided it is not reactionary (reaction is nostalgia for the dramatization of childhood; it treats the events which did not happen as if they had, and brings the dead past into the present as clues: nostalgia is the utopia of the sexton; in submitting to his condemnation Socrates died of nostalgia for his childhood) interrogation itself is humanizing.

35. Christianity removes drama from the stage to reality. Drama is turned into ritual. Ritual is not cathartic. Saints and sinners are constantly coerced with their unworthiness, impurity and sin. Because it abrogates interrogation the church's iconography is static; the soul must be an invalid. A god in movement forbids images because they immobilize; a static god allows images of martyrdom, disease, weakness, torture, captivity. At first christianity created other memorial martyrdoms, not merely because of the conflicts involved in the conversion of a continent – it used the inevitable and turned what would have been repressive into creation. Later as more of the world was mapped and marketed there were more martyrdoms, for the same reasons. The martyrdom of golgotha was replicated till its shadow fell everywhere and the memory of it sank into the stones of cathedrals and the proceedings of chancelleries and the angelus became the victim's wail in the fields. Only the market place was untouched. When there were enough sites of martyrdom the martyrdom of the orthodox ceased; since authority had now changed places with the past, the holy act became a crime. Now martyrs went to hell not heaven.

36. Christianity combined rigidity with flexibility. It severed doctrine from administration and legitimized state violence; but it restrained violence so that it did not become so tyrannous that it could not represent the boundary and still legitimize need and add to the humanness of the human mind. Christianity's flaw was that it freed the soul and legitimized slavery. That is a common paradox in the dealings between state and people.

37. Christian ritual allows people direct contact with the boundary but only through the mediation of authority. In its ritual (which is without theatre) communion with others is achieved through isolation from them. People experienced social unity only

by accepting their isolation. Ritual which creates community, as it once did in earlier times, is no longer possible because ritual cannot co-exist with theatre and the interrogative. Kierkegaard showed that christian fellowship is isolation before the holy. Ritual is possible only in a static society which does not have to treat the new as clues because there is no new and the present is eternal; for christian ritual to *tell* the new it would be necessary, say, to change the number of nails used in the crucifixion. Only theatre (and other fiction) has a hold on reality strong enough to do that. That is why christianity is foolishness to Oedipus and all greeks.

38. In times of radical change the mind anticipates and (so to say) experiences the future. When it does this the mind still works materialistically: it experiences changes that *will* occur by its experience of past and present change; in the same mental event the mind is public and private. It is because the mind is materialistic – that is, a unity with the body's needs – that fiction and imagination are possible for us; their reality is created by the gap between the public and private, and the old and the new, which is opened and bridged in every act of thought. Because the mind anticipates the future, to understand what happened in the threefold relationship we can consider the renaissance and reformation together.

39. Authority's story changed in the Reformation. There was a new map of the world and the rate of change of technology increased. To use the new technology in ways which seemingly best met human needs social organisation had to change and so had the humanness of the mind. Individuals had to accept more self-authority, which meant to become more complicated to themselves (and thus to know themselves less). The existing authority of church and state could not adapt because its own humanity (and its privileges) were invested in a particular arrangement of the threefold relationship. The state freed itself from this arrangement and claimed to speak directly to the boundary. Authority's change (though part of the forces of change could not yet be institutionalised in authority: that could wait for the eighteenth century bourgeoisie) increased the humanness of people's minds. It brought people and machines closer together. The relationship of people and state can be seen as that of a statue that carves itself with a mallet and chisel – but to understand the human drama we must see that the mallet and chisel are made of dust from the stone – and also see, in the end, that just as god was imagined as making men from clay we make our machines from the statue's dust. What

is iron, is the will. In the new world technology intruded more and more into natural cycles and more utopian dreams were disciplined on paper and in statutes, maps and literature and so ceased to be utopian and began to be the autopsy of births. Authority could not completely rewrite events; many of the changes of mind must be resolved in the mind; the watchdog barks at itself and does tricks to entertain itself in the mistaken belief that it is already the master, and soldiers are seen eating their uniforms.

40.   The puritan conscience broke away from the state. It questioned authority's interpretation of the boundary and spoke directly to the boundary itself. So the state could not exercise authority and administer technology and the economy so as best to meet needs. This led to civil war. War is a ritual and therefore an aberration in civilization; it takes over the proper role of god (to act out and take responsibility for our humanity) and so is always pagan. For this to happen the necessity must be dire; war is the clumsy attempt of human beings to make a miracle. It follows that god must always be on the wrong side in war. There are no good wars, but, like accidents, they cannot always be avoided. War cannot close the gap between ritual and doctrine and so war and utopia become each other's illusion.

41.   The Reformation disturbed the feudal settlement. Afterwards christianity could never be a doctrine (which imprisons in order to free) but must be dogma. Instead of imprisoning society it imprisons itself; mentally it passes to torturing the psyche. Modern christianity turns it back on society except in its fantasies.

42.   Because the Reformation questioned authority's story theatre again became necessary. Theatre interrogates and so cannot be confined to ritual knowledge of another world. Theatre deals with mental and social changes which the existing mind and society cannot deal with. The mind could not go on experiencing society in the old way. Administration and the economy were disturbed by new energy from coal, water, minerals, maps (scripture accepts new maps only by fantasizing itself). The new energy was both mysterious and astonishingly practical: a machine has all the chief characteristics of the human soul *and* of the utopian image of heaven. It was as if the mechanical clockwork of animated idols were turned inside out and the gears and pulleys worshipped for themselves – as if the simulacrum of the human form which masked god was ripped off and behold there were the gears and pulleys which were the real workings of nature and

history. Truly the puritan god moved among his people, not in rural grottos but in workshops and market places. Even now faced with a new machine we become a little hysterical; and machines are still the true sublime. The new theatre had to create an iconography to serve as social plan, psychological diagram and invocation and legitimization of the new forces (perhaps the legitimization was not legality but danger, not order but offence) to build the plan. Once there had been a theatre of people and animals, then there was a theatre of people and gods. Now there was to be a theatre of people and the devil.

43. Jacobean theatre's one chief study is the devil. The first operas dealt with Orpheus's descent into hell; but, after the classical model of loss and defiance, Orpheus loses utopia. The new theatre reversed the story. The devil was brought out of hell. Oedipus unknowingly offends but gains self-knowledge; Iago is the unconscious agent of evil but never knows himself (the name is like a squashed fly). Iago is the true soldier, the doer. Othello is a toy soldier. He murders Eurydice not after looking back – as all men desire Utopia – but after spying on her. Othello is black and should (in the iconography of that time) be the devil (and in Shakespeare's first play the devil *is* black). Iago had to be the white devil (though conventionally with dark hair and eyebrows, as if to authenticate him his own shadow flitted for a moment across his face) because the new machines are owned and worked by whites. People had looked upon the iron guts of god and seen the devil – and it was good: the devil is a white mechanic. Shakespeare's history plays try to establish a Reformation without industrialism. They offer a patriotic political theology for modern feudalism, as if people could build great factories in which to carry on cottage industries. In the end of the history cycle, when the new feudal sovereign appears, he is accompanied by the new reality: Richard the Third is the devil. Theology fails in the presence of the new god. Richard's death cry for a horse is the complete strategy for the new world: I throw away the old kingdom if I may have the energy of the new – the symbolic horsepower, in which machines are still measured. All Shakespeare's next plays examine the new individuals: the creatures of machines and the devil. Evil is in all these plays and they are all studies of Faust. Shakespeare would certainly have written *Faust* if Marlowe had not already written it so well that there was no excuse to rewrite it.

44. The Reformation needed the devil for the reason the primitive world needed animals, the classical world needed gods and the

christian world needed one god: to increase the humanness of the human mind. God could no longer do it because the new technology took creation out of his (too human) hands. Machines do not need to be handled with piety and the experimental way of finding knowledge is not an approach to god: no one carries out experiments on god and who will wait for a miracle when they might have a machine? The new industrial satanic energy was not only humanizing in destroying an old authority and an old mind and creating new ones – it was a danger to the new. Theatre interrogated and created a new consciousness to bear new human responsibility. At the end of Othello authority calls for guards and torture not god.

45.   The Reformation disturbed the mind so radically that the mental energy involved in the change could not be contained in the change; it destroyed the old structures and ignited the anticipation of the new; the impulse became the goad, the need became the danger, and the future was presented in fate's hands – to pass through that sanely the mind had to treat the real as the mental: fantasize it – the world must go mad. And so the real drama of witch hunting and witch burning was created – an extraordinary craze of torturing, burning and hanging took place in the future lands of industrialism. The classical gods had behaved with human frivolity, the more draconian christian god showed human goodness (dangerous in such powerful hands because it sanctified *Realpolitik*) – the Reformation needed the creative anarchism of the devil. But its culture could legitimize itself only in terms of the humanness that went before it – the dignity of the greeks and the severity of the romans, among other things. One way of being the devil – allowing his energy to work in the mind – was to become the devil's persecutor: to come face to face with the devil is evidently an embrace in which you see yourself in the light of the devil's flames.

But puritanism punished the devil only in ways convenient for manufacture and trade; in harmless women too old to exploit for manual work and sometimes in children – and in a few token men. In this way puritanism harboured the devil as its living god; punished the devil where he had no political, military or commercial value; and exercised the devil in its own mind by violence and cruelty and so practised the mental energy it needed to wreck the old economy and build the new. The mental energy that created the industrial revolution could not be accommodated in its creators' minds and had to lead to either madness or theology.

The witch hunter knows – and so does not have to confess to himself – that as manufacturer he is the devil's agent, so it is vital that he always choose victims who are innocent: hence the old women and children. He must destroy the innocent because it is diabolic to do so. The confessions of the torture chamber, the bestial, remorseless torture to obtain confessions from the innocent, is really the witch hunter's way of keeping his own silence. He tortures others to perfect his silence. That is why he is merciless – he must be blinded by the torture's eerie brilliant light, as if satan were blinded by his own fire. The witch-hunter uses satan to sanctify the good works of his hands. There was no way other than torture to increase the humanness of his mind. We have our machines because he tortured. Is this so surprising? – later, when the need for religious adventure was past, the devil became institutionalised in the factory, survival wages, slums and the lottery of stocks and shares; the poor were degraded so that profit could produce the glories of enlightenment culture; and when whole communities can be barbarized in the name of the good, it will be good, enlightened, the voice of humanity, to legislate against the barbarity of burning witches.

46. It is not that there is no difference between good and evil. There is all the difference. Our icons do our dirty work for us, or permit us to do it; they legitimize our inhumanity; sometimes we call them good and other times evil – in the end they do the same work. It need not be so. There should be a time when people will accept responsibility for being human, for what they do, and then they will know what they do. Good and evil have only one suit of clothes and they take it in turns to go out in it. Sometimes to be human we have needed the devil. Perhaps the worst we do is to use the devil to remove tragedy from politics.

47. Jacobean theatre ended as abruptly as it began. It existed during the disturbance of the exercise of authority and the way the mind told itself it was human, when the existing relationship to the boundary broke down. A new authority which spoke to the boundary had to be established, otherwise technology could not be owned and administered in ways seemingly best to meet common needs. Puritans closed the theatres because they interrogate. The puritans also broke images. Drama was removed from the stage and went back to reality. But there were as yet no new rituals because they must be administered by authority, and authority represents the community in its relations to the boundary; but the protestant church could not revoke the puritan conscience

(humanness must be built on existing humanness) which itself claimed to speak to the boundary. In fact the self-autonomy created by this could be useful in a society of machines: authority could form an alliance with it and corrupted conscience into conformity and the taking of orders. The blood of the mass became symbolic and the orderly ritual became the Walpurgis day of the shakers and then the silence of the quakers. The new society's ritual would be factory labour – good in the sight of the lord. In the factory the relationship with the boundary will be forged and people will say what they are. That was the nearest society came to ritual, because it came from the economy as part of the threefold relationship and not from the story – *that* would have made it mere aestheticism. Industrialism replaced the witch hunt as a social discipline.

48. What causes the fanatical animus of all puritans against theatre? For them theatre is a torture chamber demanding that they confess. The restoration re-opened theatres to plays which did not tragically question the boundary. The king was resurrected and the constitutional monarchy became the Garden of Eden from which the serpent had been driven out. Restoration plays honour cynicism and give thanks for the stupidity of the poor. The boundary was the counting house. The factory existed outside Restoration theatre in the way slavery had existed outside the theatre of dionysius. Cynicism protected the individual; when the new institutions are more extensive they will need more support; cynicism will give way to sentiment and licentiousness to respectability in order that things may stay the same.

49. Some authorities survive upheavals. The Counter-Reformation used the old story to achieve ends which the reformation could only achieve by new stories. Old stories may be used in new ways but this does not give them a lasting truth. Generals may be buried in their uniforms but they cannot give orders. In history, eternity seems to come to an end every one or two hundred years or so.

50. Before the Reformation iconoclasm was always followed by iconography. The puritans broke old images but they did not make new ones. They would have had to create images of their living god, the devil, and no matter how assiduously authority worships and works with the devil it does not create images of him. Witch burning broke the devil's telltale image even as the witch-hunters placed it in its niche in the new mind. And as the puritans could not create a new image of their god they changed their clothes and gave christ to the devil as a doll.

51.   God does not paint pictures or compose music because they are static images. God talks, always as a poet or dramatist. That is because he comes from the child's first dramatisation. God is created by children and worshipped by adults. Talking is the foundation of theatre because theatre is interrogative. So when god talks there can be no theatre – no one is allowed to question god. Job questioned him for a time and might even have become a greek but he ended by loving god as he loved his neighbour.

52.   The industrial revolution settled much of the turmoil it had created in the human mind. Labour became ritual and the nonconformist conscience sober and diligent. Energetic struggle with the devil, necessary to make him a familiar and install him in the mind as reason and not fear, gave way to the administration of both conformity and nonconformity; authority which is establishing itself can at first use the antagonism it incites as a means of support – when a hoop moves over a surface parts of the hoop recede as other parts advance; only later can antagonism harden into political opposition (this is the story of Stalinism).

53.   Authority built the geomorphic body of the devil in the factory town. It needed to protect the physical body of satan, not the idea; the idea had become property. So heresey lost its use and instead morality, obedience, became politically important. Crime was invented to replace witch burning and the gallows was erected as satan's altar. Authority set about teaching god good manners. Satan, securely buried in the foundations of factory towns, was banished – a typical confusion of morality. Satan did not attack the mind but property (his claim to property was merely moral not legal). Crime became a public institution. (Really this was a return to the primitive: satan was constantly being hanged and then like the ancient corn god resurrected; capitalism cannot exist without crime, not merely because it provokes crime, or because crime makes it respectable, but because crime serves a religious function for it. If there were no crime capitalism would be forced to take on the responsibilities of tyranny.) The statutory list of capital offences was grotesquely extended and children were publicly hanged for petty offences. Theatre became melodrama, the ritual of the dying; and later the modern musical, the ritual of the dead. (I do not deny that the dying and the dead need consolations or even that they find their humanness in them.)

54.   Literary novels were (and most of them still are) written to be read by robots: members of society with established incomes

who need to cultivate their subjectivity to prevent them from doing anything about the state of things. 'Novel' really means 'conservative'. Unlike christian rituals novels do not create isolation in the individual; they create an elite confident that wherever it casts its pearls there will be swine. Novels are written by the devil after he has been reformed; that is why there is no poetry in them. God is a poet but the devil is a statistician.

55. Crime made it possible to remove interrogating drama from the stage. Reality was dramatized in prisons and hulks and on scaffolds. The scaffold does not exhibit the victim as possessed but as devil incarnate. Satanism became instrumental in rationalism – the dead rose from the graves and threw stones at the devil so that the state might administer the economy. Surely only the dead are interested in watching people being killed?

56. Fielding, one of the first novelists, was a magistrate; and crime was an obsessive subject for Dostoevsky, Dickens, Balzac, Flaubert, Tolstoy and others. The novel is a sort of bible of crime. Later, class relations became atrophied and antagonism could not be creatively shared between classes – and a vast social division was created, a fact that could never be destroyed or rationalised away or bought off; it will remain under every gloss and will have to be settled with. Authority lost its responsibility for the human image; this created the frigidity of modern capitalism, the rigor mortis of the living. A literary sign of this was the detective novel. One of Sherlock Holmes' first recorded remarks is his claim that if he had been listened to many more people would have been hanged. The detective novel offers no hope; its rigidity comes from moral sclerosis not sureness of judgement; it does not use *Realpolitik* to achieve (tragically or farcically) ethical action, instead it takes *Realpolitik* for the ethical; all we may do is administer fate; it reifies the child's first story and makes it into a suicide note; the blood which is always in it is sacrificial in the most primitive way; it is the pornography of the death warrant; it is nothing more than the diary of a corpse.

57. Crime serves a social purpose. Authority's aim in the threefold relationship is to establish and legitimize itself and contingently add to the humanness of the human mind. Authority uses the boundary to discipline the social discord its own injustice creates. This injustice derives from its economic and cultural privileges, which (it says) must be accepted by people as part of the all-important relationship with the boundary. Industrial

society's injustice promotes resistance. Crime develops from the puritan conscience's mode of opposition. But the criminal is more religious, closer to godliness, than the institutionalised puritan because the criminal speaks directly to the boundary but the puritan establishes authority as a false boundary: god is his constable and clerk. Crime, with its cynicism, desperation, viciousness and brutality is the purer religion because it is less corrupt – and its arsenals are smaller. Authority turns punishment into theatre; law and order isolates people from the boundary; and crime takes on the role first performed by christian martyrs and then by heresy.

58.   The state's increasing brutality undermined its authority. It transgressed against the humanness established in the mind by earlier stages of the three-fold relationship. Science was part of industrial technology; now it was used to codify resistance and the antisocial and it created the category of deviance. Authority sought to be more liberal and tolerant so that it could economically exploit its intricate technology more easily. Deviance could be dealt with quasi-medically (though more in apologetics than practice). Church-and-state gave way to science-and-state. People were not seen as the cultural creations of interrogation but as the products of scientifically studiable and corrigible determination. This led to conflicts with the historical development of humanness and cultural memory. Art was split off from science, theology and politics and pursued as an end in itself; this split culture from authority; and this removed responsibility for culture from authority and handed culture to it as something it could use. The politics and aesthetics of fascism became inevitable.

59.   Picasso's *Demoiselles d'Avignon* exemplifies the art that smashed the image. Modern art was iconoclastic in the way puritans were iconoclastic. The academic icon of human beings was destroyed because it no longer added to humanness: unlike the great art of the renaissance it was not a portrait of the scientist but a diagram of the object of instrumental science, a laboratory exhibition. It was potentially the icon of fascism. In this respect modern art was an attack on authority; but unlike puritan iconoclasm, modern iconoclasm was also iconographic; in the end in desperation it sought the new icon in the rubble of the old. The puritans swept away the fragments of the idols they broke, modern iconoclasm venerated the fragments. This process took place over and over again in many forms and to various degrees; it provoked counter formulations (the pretty and decorative) which served to

legitimize the original iconoclasm. Even authority was prepared to patronize iconoclasm; two icons were acceptable to it – the public academic art of monuments, portraits etc, and the private-public art of modernism: authority could seek to legitimize itself by patronizing both. The iconoclastic-icon disturbed the threefold relationship by creating an elite which claimed to have its own contact with the boundary. Often a new-icon god must speak in a half-gabble: as authority does not understand even its own role it cannot interpret the new scripture – and the artist wont or cant, because in the past he was part of the scripture and because in the present he poses on the boundary of the avant-garde. This made modern art a dictatorship without power; so that in time the ad-man could loot it. Children born in the ad-age are born with their parents' memories and so the new becomes part of the old and change is accelerated and made static.

60. The arbitrariness of dada, surrealism, the novel cut up and pasted randomly together, or the mathematical precision of some abstract art – all are icons of chaos. The cut-and-pasted novel functions in the same way as the bureaucratic form; both administer emptiness and find value in the act of administration: the street leads only to the office which reminds you which side of the street to drive on. The cut-and-pasted novel wants value without administration; administration wants meaning without value. Public and private are not related but the public is seen as the private; this over-values the individual by cutting him off from himself. The threefold relationship itself becomes the boundary; science an ineffable mystery; authority the administration of the mystery and not of knowledge; and the individual a thing to be studied scientifically. That is the foundation of modern pseudo-democracy.

61. In pseudo-democracy there is enjoyment as duty – or, for the bohemian or drop out, meaningless pleasure. The philosophical questions are corrupted; political movements seem to ask questions but see people as things and the boundary as history; and reaction sees the boundary as a wall that is a static dance of death. This reduces change to the contortions of administration and people are not free to question the boundary.

62. Reaction uses the social aggression caused by its own or past injustice to justify itself and its use of repression. Often progressive politics denies the subjective and so cannot add to people's humanness. People must be free to question the boundary and

accept the best answers they can give – even if they are mistaken; it is better if people pay for their own errors than for their government's errors. Humanity cannot be created in any other way. But because this is so humanity may even be created in suffering (though suffering should not be made a fetish) and happiness may not always create humanness. Good and evil, devils and gods, have changed roles many times. Puritans needed the devil to become more human. The greeks – being promethean – needed to defy their gods to become more human. In our time – for the first time – we have no need to murder to become human. That is the problem of post-modernism. What can murderers do with their idleness?

63.   Authority claims itself and the economy as the boundary. To administer science is more deterministic than to administer ethics. In the old language, its as if you set out to teach god morality.

64.   Science extends human purpose into the macroscopic and the microscopic and takes over god's territory. The sacred has become the commercial. In the past the threefold relationship was disciplined by the meeting of needs. Authority legitimized needs in the name of the boundary and this legitimized its own role. Need was the foundation of technology, organisation and morality. It led to the increase in the humanness of the human mind. But in post-modernity needs are met; or if they are not met it is a matter of mere interruptions or shortfalls in organisation and not because meeting needs is sometimes impossible because the boundary (seemingly) does not will it. Post-modern society is a society of wants. Wants cannot function in the threefold relationship as needs or be broken down into needs. The extraordinary consequence of this is that we can no longer have a utopian vision and so any mystery of any boundary cannot have any ethical content. It is as if instead of cultural development there had been a mutation in culture.

65.   In terms of the threefold relationship post-modern people live on the boundary. So we are in heaven. The point is not rhetorical. If there is no boundary beyond authority and people there can be no utopia. In heaven we lose all need and so the meaning of suffering, discontent and lack changes forever Their biological foundation is recast. The idea of imperfection in heaven is not new. Before he was cast out satan was in heaven. We cannot cast out satan because we are in heaven and the imperfections are part of it; changing it would be like trying to change our skin as we change

our clothes. Imperfections are to be dealt with by science and technology, but science and technology are the *origins* of the imperfections. Science and technology cause terror. Terrors arise from the proper working of technology: the waste of environment; industrial pollution; the disorientation of fact by the new media which disperse culture; the danger of nuclear weapons; political terrorism when the injustices inherited from the old world of needs are made more destructive and vehement by new technology; sabotage; hostages; city violence; glass in supermarket food; debt. We are in heaven but cannot get out of hell. We live by an iconography of perfection which is self-iconoclastic. Once we destroyed the images, now the images destroy us. The icon of goodness has become the lord of evil. We may, if we can survive it, stoically endure our situation; or we may create an ideology not of fictions but of the real. And that is the resurrection of satan.

66.   We are in heaven and so we do not need god. We live on the boundary and so there is nothing for him to do: if he existed he would become one of us. In the past people needed religion in order to have god and so add to the humanness of their minds. The devil was the contingency that explained the imperfections of god's world. In the post-modern world people have god because they need the devil; and in future god will remain absent from religion, like the image broken by the puritans. (Art can aestheticize rubble, but religion cannot make capitalism moral.) In post-modernity love of god is the pretext for worship of the devil. The substance of all post-modern religion is the devil; god is merely the spell that conjures him up. Why do the religious need the devil? To account for the terror created by technology. The devil has no practical work, as he had in the industrial revolution; he is the explanation created by frightened minds when they contemplate the stirrings of their insanity. The devil can no longer add to our humanness or improve society. He is needed only to account for the terrors in the post-modern world. He is its salvation. But if you found reason on fantasy, then reason itself works in a mad way – but without the saving weaknesses of madness. One consequence has been the spate of books – such as *The Clockwork Orange* and *The Lord of the Flies* – diabolizing children and young people. Such fictions are quite barbarous. The Royal Shakespeare Company has turned two of them into musicals.

67.   Wants cannot become needs and so cannot be a foundation for the threefold relationship which has been our means to humanness. We are in a world culture in which those who still seem

to have needs have only wants. A child starves to death in the third world not because it has needs, and because no one comes with bread and water, but because it wants luxuries. The paradox is that the child dies of wanting luxuries because it is in a world of wants and so is part of that world culture. In post-modernity the boundary moves for everyone. It cannot move for some and not others. And because for the affluent wants cannot serve as needs, the fulfillment of their wants cannot add to the humanness of their minds; their wants are fulfilled but not met and they are left 'starving' of fulfillment – and so the third world's starving and dying are, for the affluent, icons of their own psyche. The ultimate terror of unjust technology is that it pollutes the inner boundary and creates, there, desolation: it asks us to live with our own death – we are dead haunted by ghosts. In the post-modern world of wants human life cannot be sustained by either the have nots or the haves; and if the starving child were saved it would still be in the world of wants. Charity is no longer a gesture of humaneness. Acts of charity by the dead-in-want are fascistic just as post-modern love of god is really need of the devil. These harsh paradoxes make our post-modern world clear; in the end we are creators of a threefold relationship which substantiates our humanity. We are guardians of history and creators of the threefold relationship or we are not human.

68.   The child starves not because it lacks needs but because it has wants – does not *need* sustenance but *wants* affluence. Why do I say this? I say it not just because there is no place on earth not surveyed by satellites; not explored for minerals or cheap labour; not considered as a site for nuclear weapons or markets for big business; not even just because any starving child may be filmed for TV (the viewer is as helpless as the camera); or because its governments buy weapons so that it can die in freedom among friends; or because in our nuclear wars of freedom even the sky would be taken away from it – I say it simply because of the way the child's mind relates to the boundary and so to how its humanness is sustained. The affluence of the world is not a secret to the poor; we have created their boundary just as, often, our agrochemical industry and our politics have created their starvation. The starving no longer sacrifice or dance to their gods for food, and even if they wished to they have no strength to dance and nothing to sacrifice. The boundary has changed for all of us. The child wants a just world because a post-modern world of wants which is politically and economically unjust kills it. The dying

child knows that this is so – that it dies not because the gods are displeased but because people are unjust. Death has become more bitter. Perhaps the starving child knows the legend of the future, and perhaps only the starving have utopia? If that is so, we are the starving child's Utopia. That is why I say our charity is fascistic. We buy the right to be unjust and our good conscience and our self-esteem: and we would buy the Utopia from the dying if we could and hang it on the wall as a tourist souvenir. Those who need the devil make a pact with him.

69.   In the world of needs the boundary was always the site of Utopia. Utopia was presented either as desire or a fierce command. It parodied needs but also transcended them. In reality needs could be met but not escaped from and so their fulfillment was both total and partial. The mere fulfilling of needs could not have humanized the threefold relationship. Legitimizing needs – making them human – required a Utopia. Needs were met but Utopia was unobtainable. That was its function and it related needs to the radical interrogation produced by the mind's over-capacity. Utopia transcended need but was not a dream and had in it the grit of hunger, cold and mortality. Wants can have no Utopia – if you are in heaven you cannot have Utopia. What is wanted is more of the same or a new variety or fashion of the same. That is a radical mutation in our species; the brain has lost its main cultural activity. Needs (because they invoked Utopia in practical, daily, economic life, and in political and religious dealings, and because they made interrogation ethical) were the means by which we created our humanity – in the teeth of our inhumanity, which, certainly, needs also created. We could not have the first without the last. Wants cannot be such a means and so they alter the *nature* of the threefold relationship. If we invented god now he would not be a poet; I refrain from saying what he would be. We have lost the icon of our humanness. *We* are the image that has been smashed and we cannot find a new image in the debris of commercialism. Our society is a frenzy of media and ad-imaging, of cutting up and refashioning – but we only catch glimpses of ourselves in the blades of the scissors and knives. Post-modern iconoclasm destroys the icon maker.

70.   The threefold relationship has developed so that now neither gods nor devils can add to the humanness of our mind. If we destroy ourselves it will not be because we do not fear ourselves enough or lack good will but because we did not learn to be human in the new world of technology and space. We cannot keep the

humanness we inherit from history without adding to it. It is really a technical question, where decision must replace the luxury of time in evolution. Goodness and evil have served many ends; and our emotions cannot induce behaviour which our emotions can adequately judge. That is why I described an understanding of instincts in notes 15 and 16. We are creations of our understanding of our situation. The space between the individual and society is the invisible lever by which each creates the other. Because our emotions are defined (and learn their story) in childhood they cannot be solely rational – such would be the emotions of god. If there were a god he would be the last to judge us on whether we had been good or bad because he would know the irrelevance of such considerations to human welfare.

71.   People in uniforms and civilian clothes will go on murdering each other. They will do it for justice, which in the end is the legitimation of their needs. But in the post-modern world no one has needs. That is the paradox of our time of dearth, wastelands, dereliction, destitution, debt, drugs and crime. We have only wants because technology has placed the boundary under our feet. And so we cannot continue to be human without political justice. Religion serves only reaction and if our situation deteriorates religion will become openly fascistic, and in the United States it has already started to be that: it will treat crime as heresy and punish it as such.

72.   Post-modernity is the result of the exponentially increasing productivity of technology in goods and in the passing of information. This has given new spasms of vitality to capitalism. Socialism has not failed but many of the things which socialism was intended to struggle for (and in the struggle the threefold relations would have changed so that products could become humanizing) have been produced as it were out of the hat by technology, as if science had played a trick on history. But technology confounded with capitalism will produce terror, partly simply as the result of the performance of machines but more profoundly because it has destroyed the boundary.

73.   Why can't wants function as needs and so humanize the threefold relationship? Money can be a need only for those who do not wish to spend it; otherwise it is a want. When there are no needs the economy cannot integrate money into a humanizing threefold relationship. Money serves as a want, as a means to other wants. Perhaps the economy – which in capitalism depends on an invisible hand – could do the work once done by the mysteries of

good and evil, and perhaps even be less demanding of sacrifice? The economy cannot serve as the boundary. We are integrated into the economy by behaviour which the economy changes and for this reason no economy of wants can be well run and no safe predictions can be made about it. In capitalism everyone sees the economy as the enemy to be subverted – this is called competition. The consumer is the fifth column in the economy. The invisible hand becomes a strangler's hand. The consumer manipulates the economy to his or her advantage and so it is no more mysterious than roulette or the stock exchange – an inwardly-facing mystery with a starting line instead of a boundary and rules of procedure instead of morals. Imperialism tried to give the laws (not rules) of cricket ethical value, but that was trying to impose the objectivity of a game onto the *Realpolitik* of trade; the stock exchange is not a game but deadly earnest; you might as well ask criminals to make laws. The economy assumes a predetermined human nature, but economic loss and gain, expectations, solidarity etc change that nature.

The economist is like someone who tries to build bricks out of seawater because he's heard that the sea's currents are strong. Eventually government must intervene, with force or fraud, in the economy. But institutional defences against the economy's inherent self-enmity merely ramify manipulations. Just as the need to raise capital creates new ways of extending and managing debt, so institutions become the enemy of markets they are meant to defend. That is why we have an economy in the first place – it is the prison to be free in. If it were not so we could abolish the economy and our natural grace would see us through. The present surgence between technology and capitalism is a mirage with real consequences. It destroyed utopian vision and put consumption in its place. Almost anything is better than a Utopia, but our humanness has depended on two things: the structural discipline brought into politics and administration by our needs, and being able to use the boundary as the site of Utopia. What we have now are wants and markets. Utopia would be more wants. They cannot humanize the mind because they are outside it. We seem to have stepped out of history back into evolution but without the limitless time of evolution: instead we need to make decisions.

74. If we survive we will have a technology without an economy. We can have that only when we have lived through our lack of need and Utopia. The devil and charity are the only Utopias available to capitalism; and charity is the devil's only virtue. The

devil will not work for capitalism as he did for puritanism. Capitalism must end in fascism because that is the end of its mechanisms; we cannot ethically bank on the past.

75.   A just society would not need democracy because democracy would be implicit in the working of its technology. We did not need democracy to tell us we had needs but to legitimize them in the face of the technology with which we met them – and to use our needs as a way of being human. And we will not need democracy to tell us we need justice. These paradoxes belong to the world that post-modernism will create.

76.   Each radical change in the threefold relationship records how people got rid of the existing form of humanness and created a new form, a new meaning in the infinity of mind which runs like a river between the bank of civil corruption and the bank of private madness to an open sea. We cannot sustain our humanness without justice and we can no longer create justice by murder, either the calculated murder of politics or the blind murder of crime. Communities threatened by fascist regimes or fascist banditti must defend their young by arms. But all murder is now either the last dance before morning or the first slouchings of a beast. A just world would not arm fascists or take them into the commercial community.

77.   In the nineteenth century the old royal and republican arsenals were replaced by the armaments industries. In the twentieth century we produced weapons that will remain a scandal in any human memory; our ambition was not to torture individuals but whole nations at a time. Nuclear weapons provoked surrogate wars around the world; but even if it were true that they kept the peace it does not follow that peace could not have been kept without them; and they leave for others a legacy of enormity, a politics based on violence that could have destroyed the world. We would not have much regard for a man mounting the scaffold who boasted that he had survived the walk there. By any judgement the half century of peace will be regarded as a time of unprecedented barbarity. As each child was born we held a pistol to its head – what else is nuclear deterrence? Technology will be able to make weapons more destructive than H bombs. If we go on making weapons they will be taken into the threefold relation as a fourth factor; the devil will not be a medieval apparition invoked at need, but an autonomous robot-satan with a permanent seat in our councils. Weapons will become the emblem

of fascism – it is what we must choose to make them. And in a just world a sawn-off shotgun would be as scandalous as a nuclear rocket.

78.   The administration of things seems a utopian wish but becomes possible to people who live on the boundary. It is difficult to believe this because our culture has not yet built its own foundations. Its said that post-modern politics are aestheticised and ordinary life has become theatre. In many ways our situation is comparable to that of the christians and puritans when they closed theatres and created a church-god and a factory-devil. But capitalism theatricalizes life *and* uses theatres. Its aesthetics are iconoclastic, the ad-man's detritus. It manufactures (sometimes unintentionally) problems and solves them by medication and entertainment. This makes the problems static. The greeks used problems to humanize the mind; capitalism uses problems to belittle us. Spectacle becomes vicious excitement that appeals to biological resonances which capitalism wrongly supposes to be free of cognition; with the best intentions it trivializes spectators.

79.   Theatre need not formalise questions and consume audiences by empty entertainment. It could be iconoclastic but not static; not the dream world of performance art, the autistic world of minimalism or a return to the young Brecht. It has to be both iconoclastic and iconographic because that is the function imposed on it by the mind's need to humanize itself. It could create a new method of graphism. Texts would still have sub-texts (because they cannot be written wholly objectively) but they would now have a meta-text. A meta-text is designed to be broken down into smaller 'theatre events', either incidents in scenes or whole scenes. The production is a structured series of 'theatre events' (TEs). The actor does not leave his character to play the meta-text but creates his character in playing it. In this way the individual is generalised. Text, sub-text and meta-text form a unity. Unlike happenings, TEs are a means of analytical understanding. They make clear the cause and consequence of events, collecting the diffuseness of real life into illustration and demonstration – not dogmatically or symbolically but still in units of conflict: in this way the future would be chosen, not determined by the past. The deconstructivist problem of closure would disappear: *that* after all is how people live – they rewrite the story of their childhood in the precision of the new, so that the past becomes clues of what will happen. Theatre creates in the same way, but it can take things apart so that they subvert the past we know. This sort of theatre would free

us from the illusions of Ibsen's determinism, the nihilism of absurdity, and the enervating sensitivity of Beckett; it would use the theatre pioneered by Brecht but not reify his techniques – TEs make alienation narrative. The theatre would have the objectivity appropriate to post-modernism.

80. The difference between fiction and reality would disappear, as it did for the greeks, because it would have no use. Hyper-technology makes convention and tradition obsolete and much of their ways destructive; that means that living humanely means living a meta-text. But hasn't interrogation always made it that? The difference is that now it is a meta-text without a boundary. The mind's need to interrogate lost its earlier function when want swamped need (not as a psychological trait but as a technological, social imperative). The interrogator is now a prisoner in rags shuffling on a stage between the site of the old boundary and a barrier. That is the inner-icon of our affluence. For such a prisoner everything becomes a tool and an image. His theatre does not disinter the cause or meaning of things but creates them by his own actions. One day people will be amazed that their forebears thought ghosts had power over the living. Theatre will not be scripture, but there will be discipline in it, just as there was in the stages of the threefold relationship: but truths will harden not into dogma but into ambiguity – and then the clues will be oracles. We will not need Utopia because we will have real political responsibility. The difference between fiction and reality will disappear because for the first time we will know which is which.

81. First there was the theatre of people and animals, then of people and gods, then of people and the devil. Now we need the theatre of people and people. It is made possible by the use of interrogation in post-modernity. If we don't realise it, it is because we are as greedy as the man who wanted two graves.

82. All revolutions are written on the back of the calendar.

Edward Bond
from Notebooks
written in November 1989